Genetic Genesis

DNA Manipulation of Our Ancient Ancestors
FROM the Original Biblical Text

Translated from the
Original Hebrew

by

Albert E. Potts

Genetic Genesis: DNA Manipulation of Our Ancient Ancestors
FROM the Original Biblical Text

Table of Contents

Acknowledgements

The completion of this work would not have been possible without the help and assistance of my wife, Ruth. Her own outside-the-home employment over the course of decades has made it possible for years of research and reams of writing to have happened at all.

My late father taught me a fundamental principle behind the accurate translation of this first chapter of Genesis. His words to me were, "Words can be used to reveal *or* to conceal." My late mother left a legacy of unconditional love and the resources for all the preliminary research that went into this project.

Giving credit where credit is due, it was someone else who brought to my attention, early in 2015, the then-startling idea that the central actor in the Bible was an alien. Mr. H. Michael Holder, of Winnipeg, Canada, introduced me to that idea. It was in his own explorations in the book of Daniel that he correctly observed that the Hebrew word for "God" in that book (and only in that book) was *alaheen* [אלהין]. He applied the pronunciation principles of the *anatomic alphabet*, which I had fully developed in 2009, to anglicize the word *alaheen* into the more commonly known English word *alien.* It is he whom I credit for having clearly seen *aliens* in the Hebrew Bible. It took me some two years to warm up to the idea. It was he who told me again, in June 2018, that there were aliens in Genesis—on the basis that the word there for "God" is *alaheem* [אלהים]—so there *had* to be aliens there. It was Mr. Holder who also developed the idea that the first word of the Hebrew Bible (*bereshit*) should not be treated as a word with a prefix, a suffix, and a root word (namely, "in the beginning"), but rather as two separate root words—which when translated together as a phrase, convey the central reality of the Genesis story. His perfectly viable literal translation of the two root words that can be made of that first word is "to cut to set a limit." His influence has gone into fashioning a fuller understanding of Genesis chapter 1.

It must also be acknowledged that many unknown and forgotten ancient Jewish rabbis so diligently preserved the ancient Hebrew scriptural texts such that someone with obsessive interest and unremitting perseverance would have been able to decipher them for the purpose of extracting the information provided herein.

Introduction

What I Have Gotten Myself Into

I've studied the original ancient Hebrew. It's a very old language. It's not used today. It's a dead language. I took it on for the project I was working on that I'll share shortly. Written ancient Hebrew[1] is not the same as written "Biblical Hebrew," though the two are closely related.

The Genesis text that we have today began as ancient Hebrew, transcribed into the style of writing known today as Biblical Hebrew—itself based on Babylonian Aramean alphabetic characters[2]. From that transcription of the ancient text, it was then rendered into ancient Greek as the Septuagint[3] by ancient Jewish interpreters some 2,100 years ago.

The original ancient texts were written in the writing of *ancient* Hebrew. We know it because biblical text fragments written in ancient Hebrew (also called Paleo Hebrew) were discovered in 1947[4] in Cave 11 at a place called Qumran overlooking the Dead Sea in modern-day Israel.

Imagine my excitement when I took the time to read the first chapter of Genesis transcribed back into the ancient Hebrew writing! I read the opening chapters, which has not been done, not even by the Vatican, because there they don't read or write ancient Hebrew.

These moments feel historic, in that I am one of the few people who has taken the time to learn this dead language *and* then took the time to read the Genesis story as it was originally written. Due to the age of the language and natural slow pace of understanding what the ancient text is trying to communicate, half of the translation process is reading and the other half is decoding its words. To find the meanings of the ancient words and how its words create meaning in sentences is a slow process. I will explain how it all works so you can experience this unique language.

I have worked for two years making sure each word of this translation is right. The sentences I read made sense, but they didn't say what I expected they would say. It was like drawing a map by waking around a city. Measure and map; measure and map. When stepping back from all the additions to view the composite image, there's a map of the city. The further I went into the ancient Hebrew Genesis story, the more sense it made—even though the text did not say what I expect it to say.

When I read it as a whole, the text told me the story of the beginning of mankind and specific details about *how* that beginning began. Red lights started flashing: the ancient Hebrew text didn't tell the stories that we have been told are there. In the original scriptural writing was a whole new cast of characters—even some of the answers for which science has been searching. There's a radically different past; with every word an entirely new direction of understanding for the future.

I was elated—at the same time wanted to throw up. These are the biggest and scariest moments of my life.

Chapter 1

What Does Dad's God Look Like?

What sends a man on a boy's search for God? In one of my earliest memories, I was make-believe chanting at an altar constructed of building blocks, with round blocks as candles. Was I trying to talk to God, or was it just a case of toddler imitating what he saw his father do? I had watched my father many times at the altar of a small, rural mainstream Protestant church. Yes, I was a "PK," a preacher's kid.

Even if that practice might explain just almost everything about the *why* of a PK's *God Quest,* such explanation would be too pat, too trite, and too sanitary. The truths of any such God Quest contain elements from the *dark side*; and the dark side of a preacher's kid is as close or as far away as the preacher from whom the kid came in the first place.

Usually it was close by. Years ago, the title of a book I should have already written popped into mind: *God of Our Fathers—Our Father's God.* I imagined myself signing books for lines of buyers at bookstores across the country. In my mind, the book practically wrote itself—as I had two younger brothers who also would have tales to tell about growing up under the watchful and wrathful eye of our father and his strange, love-talking, anger-breathing, fault-finding, punishment-issuing God.

The eight-year-old I was in 1957 had just walked into the kitchen of our new home in a freshly constructed suburb of a medium-size city in eastern

Tennessee just in time to witness my youngest brother in the process of experiencing *his* earliest memory. He had laid out long-playing records (the kind old folks listened to) on the floor and had turned on the faucet. Water was still running out onto the wood floor of an adjacent dining area. Within seeming moments our father had the two-year-old miscreant upside down and was paddling the living daylights out of him. If he learned to fear his father, he came by it honestly.

In that same year, I had my first—*and last*—encounter with a lost glasses situation. Just as with the ruined records and overflowing waters, that deed infuriated father, too. The physical reminder to never lose a pair of glasses was of sufficient quality to last a literal lifetime.

Some three decades after my little brother's upside-down paddling, our mother—that preacher's wife—shared with me our father's final private commentary to her on the matter: "He's the turd you shit from your vagina."

My father's repulsive words reverberate more than a half-century later. They represent the vilest words I had ever heard before or since and ought to provide ample reason for a man to be on fire to find the hiding place of father's *God.*

That hiding place was usually well out of the public's view. In 1957, my father had been given free reign to design the medium-sized church of his dreams. When it was completed, he went about the business of filling the pews with what he then called the well-heeled, well-to-do, do-good Episcopalians of our medium-size city in the American South. He was a priest of impeccable tastes in the cathedral-style interior design of his church, of the conduct of the liturgy, and of the music that seemed to lift souls to wherever it is they are lifted. He delivered silver-tongued oratory of the first rate from the high pulpit.

More than once the irony struck me, almost literally, of a man who preached the love of God from the pulpit and then came home to beat his wife and sons.

Public spectacles weren't off limits, however. Father's church hosted a men-and-boys breakfast, common in those days—at least once-a-year common—and on an early spring morning in the 12th year of my young life, the preparations leading up to the serving of pancakes, eggs, and sausage were progressing at a snail's pace. In boyish fashion, I took up an imaginary fork and knife and began cutting an imaginary sausage link. *Blackest pain. Acute pain* . . . in a moment became my immediate, dreadful, and dreaded companion. One square centimeter on the left side of the back of my young head was throbbing. *Pure pounding pain* heating my interior with humiliation and embarrassment from an encounter with an unseen projectile in the form of an incoming closed third-finger knuckle of a dominant hand as behavior modification. Father had a term for that style of discipline—a *head-knocker*.

Pain does not prevent clear-thinking prudence of the prudent *PK* in such a moment, though. Father's unwritten rules of behavior were as potent and particular as the written commandments of his *God*—accompanied by swift recognition and retribution if not obediently followed when they occasion to be observed *and* unquestioningly followed—which I did. *Do not cry out. Do not cry. Do not show any emotion. Do not betray father*. The consequence of any of these actions, although deferred, would be imaginably more severe. I never spoke of that incident to my father at any further point in his long life.

Within the same year, I awoke from a sound sleep on a top bed of the bunk bed in the boys' bedroom adjacent to the parental bedroom. It was the sound of father's voice. He was shouting. Shouting expletives punctuated with my name. While beginning to feel sad and sorry for myself, I was sufficiently mature by that time to do my own brand of severe self-talk—*you always said you wanted to know the truth of things. Now you know.* I asked myself an ageless question, "Happy now?"

In the following week, I was contemplating my father's words—still stinging—on the stairs to the lower level of a newer house in the same suburb. My mother asked what was wrong. I related what I had heard. She listened, but then told me that he had not been talking about me at all, but about another priest with the same given name who had annoyed him beyond his endurance earlier that same day. The 12-year-old in me was not comforted. It was just a matter of time before I was in the crosshairs—again.

Before my 12th year was completed, I found myself one Saturday afternoon (when father was home) wrestling with my brother on our carpeted living room floor. Brothers wrestle and roughhouse. That's natural enough. Middle brother had his left arm across my throat, and his right arm over my mouth. It didn't take long for me to realize that I couldn't draw in a breath. Even though I was aware of the consequences to a PK brother who bit another, I bit him as lightly as I could, knowing that father would have a fit. Predictably, brother screamed out that big brother had bitten him.

Also predictably, feared father rushed onto the scene. Grabbing the offender by the arm, he moralistically intoned, "We don't bite." His leather belt was off in a second. So frightened I was that I couldn't speak a word. The dreadful summary discipline commenced as he forced voiceless son over a convenient chair. What I took from that outcome was that one's own survival is less important than obedience to a fearsome father.

PK No Longer, but Lessons Continue

One morning in early spring, a lifetime ago, in 1963, father and mother sat their three boys down at the kitchen table to talk—the first and last instance of such "togetherness." Children cry when their parents tell them that they are getting a divorce—even children who fear their father (or mother). I cried.

Within a period of several weeks, the reverend father whom we revered out of fear was divorced, remarried, and excommunicated. He had renounced his priestly vows and was summarily defrocked by the bishop of the Episcopal Diocese of Tennessee. He had, in those brief weeks, achieved what he later exhorted his sons, *If you're not smart enough to be born rich—marry rich.*

Life went on, but the change was superficial. In my fifth decade of life, father provided a belated, though not final, lesson that would give further reason to fear father. He himself set the stage of the tragic drama: the living room of his quite well-to-do new sister-in-law in the early 1970s.

As he related it, he was in the process of insulting my middle brother's new wife in front of them both. With an accompanying hand motion, he described his middle son raising his own right fist level to his own eyes in a gesture of warning, having just received the verbal deprecations from his father about his wife. Our father, highly animated, quoted himself with overtones of moral indignation, "You put that fist down or I'll pick up that poker over there and beat you to death. I'd rather spend the rest of my life in Brushy Mountain State Prison than have a son of mine raise a fist to me."

Even at that age, the lesson was not lost on me. To the day he died, I don't think I ever stood closer to him than the length of an extended arm. Late in his own 78th year, I stood that far from him, silently and self-consciously asking myself why I still had fear of an old man dying of cancer. In that moment, I had not yet begun to think about my PK's God Quest as it related to the dark side of fear of father.

Shouldn't any self-respecting God Quest begin, and perhaps end, with what the prudent PK student of the Bible is able to learn about God in what are supposed to be *His*—as some put it, *God-breathed*—words? That's why I put myself into a year-long study of introductory Biblical Hebrew some dozen years ago. If the Hebrew Bible was where God was hiding out, I wanted to be able to encounter, confront, or converse with its author in the language in which I was told "He" wrote—*or caused to be written*: His own words.

Chapter 2

Me, a Translator? After 2,000 Years, Why Me?

It all started with seeing seemingly indecipherable words on a page—words in the English language—and having a burning and unquenchable desire to know what those letters-in-patterns meant. I vividly recall, as a very young boy, wanting to know how it was that people could know how to make sense of them by just seeing them laid out on pages of print.

Sitting beside my mother during services in my father's newly built Episcopal church in 1958 at the age of nine, I first began to pay attention to the words printed in the *Book of Common Prayer*—the "old" prayer book of 1928. It was as if the words called out, *What are we saying—and how are we saying what we say?* At the beginning of some paragraphs the first letter was much larger than those that followed. I knew letters. I just couldn't figure out how to decipher what they said when they were strung together in long sentences in long paragraphs in page after page after page. I wanted, above anything else, to be able to decipher those words, those sentences, and those paragraphs. I learned to read those words by conscientiously following along in that prayer book. Through following each word week after week, I became immersed in the language of the Episcopal liturgy through the sounds and the cadence of its elevated language.

It was absorbing and led to other absorbing matters. Having had no sisters caused me to think deeply about the nature of reality as I endlessly thought about the female of the species. *Dad* preferred girls over boys. Some days I wanted *to be* a girl—not as a sexual thing, but as an insatiable want to understand the existence of being such a creature.

Such a creature was second grader Margaret Payne. In grade school in those days, pupils were always seated in alphabetical order. Her desk was in front of mine. Every day her name was called out as attendance was taken and then mine. By the time I arrived in that classroom, I had already taught myself how to write the cursive letters, one at a time, by having endlessly practiced writing them from a workbook my mother had supplied. It was by watching very pretty Margaret write out her exercises in perfect handwriting right in front of me that I learned how to string the cursive letters together.

Other captivating lessons followed. The Boy Scout troop to which I belonged was located in the Roman Catholic Church of the Immaculate Conception, which was across the street from my father's Episcopal Church and about a mile's walk from Bearden Elementary School. All of the boys of that troop, except my best friend and I, were Roman Catholic. On occasion, the troop would be in attendance as parishioners were saying the Rosary—over and over. I paid close attention to the words and the wording. I thought deeply about the mechanics of the language—the familiar English words and the theologically foreign narrative that the words, repetitively spoken, wove. *What does all this mean?* Like the story of Mary, the mother of Jesus, I pondered all these things in my heart.

As a high school freshman, I elected to take a first-year course in Latin. In 1964, high schools still had rigorous academic courses. I would love to say that I was fully invested in learning Latin, but the less glamorous truth is that I was more fully invested in gazing at the back of Sandy Perkins' head.

Mrs. Luton, who lorded over her Latin class with humorless discipline, seated her students in alphabetical order. As the roll was called, I would answer "here" just after Sandy Perkins' name was called. Not wanting to have the opportunity to learn Latin, but to study the color and arrangement of the sandy-brown hairs of her head, I never missed a day of school. I suffered silent disappointment when she was absent from that class for any reason.

Paying rapt attention to the part of her to which I had the most visual access didn't mean that I wasn't also paying attention—*okay*, partial attention—to the translation exercises and the Latin phrases. I did pay attention to how translation is done. I experienced how it is done. I was well aware of being seeped into a world of declensions, declining verbs, ablatives, nominatives, fifth declentions, moods of verbs, verb stems, verb endings, verb tenses, cases of nouns, the rules of Latin, gender rules, i-stem rules for third-declention nouns, past-perfect and future-perfect conjugations, parts of speech, first- and second-declention nouns, imperative and subjunctive moods, and word order. The best view of her sandy-brown hair was not all I managed to get out of the best first-year Latin class in Bearden High School in the early 1960s.

The first day of Algebra II at that same school in 1965, the teacher walked to the blackboard and wrote with white chalk these words—which constituted the first examination (and last) in which I received the highest mark. She wrote, "The null set equals the void set. True or false?" She then called on each student, row by row. Each would call out, "True." Student after student. When my name was called out, seated as I was in what I thought was the safety of the fifth row over—I boldly called out, "False."

Each successive student, after I had the temerity to do that, called out "True." After each had given a reply, she announced, "Everyone fails—except Mr. Potts." The value of that lesson was, *stick by your guts and your convictions even though you might be quite alone*.

I didn't know what either the *null set* or the *void set* was, but I obviously had a greater appreciation than others for how words conveyed meaning—and I knew that the word *null* didn't necessarily mean the same as the word *void*. That's why I answered as I did. I was a student of words. A student of algebra? Not so much. And there was no girl in that algebra class to stimulate even a peripheral interest in learning its arcane rules. But I acquired enough to take and understand differential and integral calculus during my college career at The University of Tennessee in Knoxville. And some years later, to take probability and statistics—with the highest marks.

It was that same school year that I encountered the world of Harry Kroll's Chemistry class. His chemistry experiments forced students to think. The first exercise in his class was to list 100 observations about a burning candle. In those days, prior to the hand-held calculator, students were expected to learn how to use a slide rule—which I still have today, along with its crumbling, faded instruction manual. Using it was an exercise in learning about how things are put together mathematically. With it could be found ratios and proportions, squares and square roots, cubes and cube roots, and logarithms, as well as allowing you to do multiplication and division. The lasting value of that education was to learn exactly how multiplication and division are inversely proportional—a concept that would pay handsome benefits in my Genesis translation. His chemistry class was yet another place to think deeply about how the world around us is actually put together.

Wendy Myers taught English grammar and literature to high school seniors. Her students were required to memorize one story from *The Canterbury Tales*[5] by the Middle English poet Geoffrey Chaucer. I seldom would complete my boring grammar lessons. She warned me at the end of the school year that I would fail her English class. I was bold enough to retort to her that even though I would, that I would still remember in my old age the lines of Chaucer that I memorized while her *A* students would have long forgotten everything except the name Geoffrey Chaucer. I still have my collection of his tales in my personal library. I still remember the first line of the tale I committed to memory.

By the time of the early 1970s, I had acquired a bachelor's—if not education, then exposure—to the liberal arts of western culture. Such an auspicious beginning fully prepared me to take on a three-year army enlistment. With thanks to what we called *the big green mean machine,* I was trained to be a journalist and photographer. A perfect place to further learn the craft of army journalism (cynics might call it "propaganda") and acquire a photographer's eye for composition and detail. Though I excelled at wordsmithing and photography, an enlisted career just didn't feel like it was right for me. Within five years, though, I was back in an army uniform—as a surgical technician in the army reserves. More close attention to detail.

It was during that training, in 1983, that I developed a medical problem for which a surgical operation was the cure. A brief hospitalization followed. On an open surgical ward with 40 other enlisted soldiers at Brooke Army

Medical Center, one registered nurse oversaw the postoperative medical care for all of us.

In those days it was expected that the men in later stages of recovery aid and assist men in earlier stages—such as helping them in the shower, feeding them, and in the cases of illegal immigrants caught up in the knife-and-gun-club scene, to translate from and into Spanish for them. It was from closely studying the young twentysomething registered nurse on that open ward that I came to see that she had no particular qualities of intellect to do what she was doing. I thought to myself, *If she can do that, I can do that.*

It was in that sick bay that I resolved to put myself into nursing school—knowing that upon coming out a registered nurse that I would get a direct commission from the army, become an officer, and as we enlisted men used to say, *sit at the table with the adults.* It was through nursing school at the University of Texas Health Science Center that I acquired a journeyman's knowledge of human anatomy and physiology, chemistry and microbiology, the science (and the art) of nursing, the biology of human sexuality, and how to do detailed medical research at the medical school library.

That education was what prepared me for the high-tech narrative hidden behind the Hebrew words of the first chapter of the Bible's book of Genesis. As it turned out, three decades of nursing practice were wrung out of me before I would turn my total attention to that chapter's Hebrew text—and to what that text was trying to say from behind the words, written as they have been for two millennia, in the alphabetic letters of "Biblical Hebrew.

Overcome Illiteracy—Learn to Read

You know, we've been kept, as a species, totally illiterate regarding the ancient biblical writings. Once a full retrospective translation of all the existing biblical text has been accomplished, an entirely different mix of biblical stories will emerge. Some will apparently be true, some near-true, and—let's be frank—some will be *just stories.* Unfortunately for traditionalists, the Genesis creation story is . . . *just a story*. Additionally, the unfortunate truth is that the account that *is* there is absolutely true. It is the truth of the ancient Hebrew scripture *as written*.

What I want to share is some of what I was feeling while figuring out what the Hebrew words actually said; how they are constructed to say what they say. The exercise is going to be just like telling a story—*that* story. There were obstacles to figuring it all out. There were consequences—not to not getting it done, for it was done some two years ago—but to getting it done at all.

When I began the work I thought I'd just see biblical terms we're familiar with, but as I worked through the text I knew that the Hebrew language works differently than is officially taught. You cannot just read and translate. You *must* do some research. Almost each word we encounter in the Hebrew text is different than as traditionally put out for more than 2,000 years. The intrepid translator has to look at such a basic element as, *What is the definition of the actual "root word," which informs us as to how the ancient text is to be read—or translated?*

I'm very knowledgeable about Hebrew. I first delved into Biblical Hebrew about a dozen years ago. To do this work, one has to have a working knowledge of the Hebrew alphabets—modern and ancient. One has to have a working knowledge of the grammar of each. My work with Biblical Hebrew provided me with knowledge about its own brand of grammar. At the conclusion of my study of the Biblical Hebrew scripture, I was able to sight-read from a Hebrew Torah scroll.

It was while studying Hebrew that my own life took a radical transformation: I believed that I had received a calling—from *God*—to turn myself into a prophet of old. That is, to take on the vow of a Nazarite and not cut any hair on my head and to follow the Levitical laws. That I did for about a decade. It was during that time that I received another calling—to produce, from scratch, an exact replica[6] of the Ten Commandment tablets that Moses would have brought down off Mt. Sinai. That calling provided the need to become proficient in writing the ancient Hebrew letters—as it is my conviction that what was carried off Sinai was written in the ancient writing. Taking a page from my second-grade experience, I tirelessly practiced writing the 22 letters of the Hebrew alphabet. I created a word-processing font for its ancient letters.

So deeply did that language seep into me that I spent two years reading directly from the Biblical Hebrew scriptural text[7] and developed about a hundred pages of lists of Hebrew words that had similar characteristics. By having made that list, I was able to deduce the actual grammatic functions that Hebrew prefixes, suffixes, and inserted letters have within words in which they may appear. To have gained that knowledge is to have knowledge of the *actual* grammar of a language—which is what has to happen in order to be able to decipher the Hebrew text written on the pages. I found different words than traditional translations tell us are there. In taking on an actual translation, I planned to just translate—and to then let the pieces the ancient story tells fall where they may.

What *is* the truth of it all? The truth is that Genesis chapter 1 is *someone's* executive summary of a full-blown hybridization program—complete with detailed descriptions of in vitro fertilization (IVF) and interspecies sexual experimentation.

Only someone with modern-day familiarity of ancient Hebrew, Biblical Hebrew,[8] and ancient Greek[9] would have been able to defeat the translational flimflam perpetrated on ancient Hebrew from ancient times. The exercise of translating—or being the first to translate Genesis' chapter 1—is principally an exercise in tireless research of Hebrew word definitions and of high-tech genetic engineering and artificial fertilization . . . silhouetted against a backdrop of scientific education and years of self-disciplined study of (ancient) Hebrew as a viable means of human communication. This translation work has required a willingness and ability to think outside the box of the 2,100 years of traditional translation—no matter how far out of the box and no matter where thoughtful and studied translation led.

In taking up a word-for-word translation, in early June 2018, I originally thought that there might possibly be an alien there, but that it would end up being a case of *maybe there is and maybe there isn't*. What I found wasn't just a damn alien—it was the *executive summary* of their own hybridization program.

Of course, I struggled with a word here and a word there. One particular word is defined in standard Hebrew dictionaries as a "coulter."[11] I had to research to find out what a coulter was. It's an agricultural tool—a thin hollow tube that drops seeds into a furrow for plantation. I then had to research what an ultramodern high-tech version of a coulter might possibly be. Some nights I could not sleep. I would mull a word over and over in my mind even during the sleep that I did get.

It was very early on in the re-translation of Genesis' chapter 1 that I realized I was getting a whole new document—a whole different creation account. This account had the ring of truth to it—the truth as to what the Hebrew words were actually saying; and the truth of the radical narrative spun out the newly translated words when strung together as sentences. What grounds this translation is that it all can be proven.

CHAPTER 3

Inside the Translator: How Does Translation Happen?

I've shared that the Genesis creation story (as it has been known for the past 2,100 years) doesn't say what we have been taught that it says. I want to share my own journey through the process of coming to know exactly what it says in translation—and how that translation didn't come from out of nowhere.

It came from coming to see the story from a point of view unhitched from the idea that the scripture was "God-breathed" and that it just couldn't be come up against or challenged in any way—because "God said it and that settles it." It came from coming to be able to decipher what it actually said, rather than reading into the Hebrew what we have been told it said.

Clearly, challenges exist in translating a work, any work, comprised of words that, up to now, have really not been defined accurately. The first word you probably have in mind that has to be somehow overcome is the word God. Does it have to be translationally tortured to confess *aliens*?

From the get-go of this original translation, the translated word "God" was never even in the running. Why not? Because the ancient word in the text is plural in meaning; so, every traditional translation should have read, "In the beginning, Gods . . . . " But they do not. As a preliminary working hypothesis, the word aliens, or strange biological entities, or extraterrestrials, or simply the words, beings or entities, had to be used.

It doesn't take long in the first verse of the first chapter of Genesis to validate the preliminary use of *extraterrestrials* (a.k.a., aliens). As it turns out, they are not creating any heaven or any earth at all. How not? That's one of the challenges—less of translation than of research.

The Hebrew word for heaven is from the definition "to be lofty".[12] That word is derived from the word for to ruin,[13] which is derived from the word *shimem*, which means "to stun, to devastate, or to be astonished."[14] The word choice here for me was amazements, since the Hebrew word is plural. But the word in translation could just as well be astonishments.

So, from the beginning we are not dealing with any created heavens but of some kind of created (or fabricated) astonishments *or* amazements. More verses would have to come into full view before heads or tails could be made of what these amazements were.

Midway through the first verse of Genesis, one word presented a challenge as to what meaning it was trying to convey. That challenging two-letter word is pronounced "*ăht*". The resources of the Library of Congress were not needed—a simple reference like the Hebrew Dictionary[15] of any *Strong's Concordance* will provide the raw information for accurate translation. That translated word has to make sense on its own; and it has to exactly fit the context of the surrounding words. The surrounding context has to do with aliens or strange biological entities and something that represents an amazement.

The most unhelpful and useless definitions in that Hebrew Dictionary—or, as that goes, in any Hebrew reference—was that the word pronounced "ăht" is a "direct object indicator".[16] The most helpful was that the word refers to a "coulter."[17] Anyone can find in any English dictionary—or online—that a coulter is the part of a seed drill that cuts a furrow for the seed. I'm no farmer. I don't even like to garden. But that visual image was pretty clear. But how, exactly, is a seed drill cutting a furrow going to shed light on aliens and amazements?

What, I asked myself, could be some kind of high-tech kind of coulter that aliens might use? Consulting any available thesaurus will get anyone

one step closer to a solution to this word puzzle. The one I looked in gave the word microtome. That's an instrument for cutting extremely thin sections of material for microscopic examination. As I pondered the word microtome, I thought, *That might lead somewhere. High-tech aliens sure might be using a microtome if they had anything at all to do with the creation story.* Another thought was, *Why was that word left untranslated in all versions of the Genesis story?* Since that word *did* make sense in translation and it was *in context*, that word, microtome, would do for the present time. There was the rest of the chapter to be translated, where that word is used more than two dozen times. More light would have to be shed on its meaning and function as instances of "ăht" are examined wherever the word was to appear.

What's the big challenge of taking a simple concept like the earth as expressed in Hebrew since dirt was being made? If there were aliens, amazements, and a microtome, wouldn't it be expected to find them on earth doing whatever it is they, according to this never-seen-before translation, have done? Exactly. To take on this word challenge it was critical and necessary to have spent years reading in the original Hebrew scriptural texts, compiling long lists of words that conveyed the way in which what I'll call the "actual grammar" of the ways in which the ancient Hebrew language works to convey meaning.

One of the long lists that I have available to me contains words where letters of "root words" are dropped—that is, not included in the spelling of the word in the text but are assumed to be there because the use of the word in relationship to the words around it. In other words, because the meaning of the word with a letter (or letters) dropped is known *in context*.

An example would be a simple word in English, such as the word god if the context of the word were "a god time." We may assume from the context that the word is good, as in "a good time"; and that one of its letters (the letter *o*)—had been dropped or omitted.

That concept is useful for considering the Hebrew word for the earth.[18] The Hebrew word for earth may be seen, or treated, as having had its last letter dropped or omitted from the text. When we add back the most likely letter dropped from the word, we end up with the word for accomplish.[19]

When we have that word, we just look at the first two letters of the word in the text, which are both prefixes with commonly known meanings, and put their meanings in front of accomplish. The first of the two letters means *the*; and the second of the two means *I*.

The word, in actual translation, turns out to be "the I-Accomplish." Now we are left with the beginning, *no pun intended.* The greater challenge is about how all the rest of the words of the Genesis story shed light on the alien-sounding concept of aliens creating or fabricating amazements and the I-Accomplish.

In considering the simple words "and void,"[20] in the account's second verse, the person (your translator) who took on the challenge of that word would also have needed to have studied how Hebrew is actually structured so that the Hebrew word could be pulled apart to see what really lies behind the sleight-of-hand translation. By pulling apart the word it can be seen how "and void" is the real translation or not.

The Hebrew word has a prefix. That's for certain. The first prefix is "and". Then there is the word for "void". In the traditional translation the word void is used as a noun, as in "the void". In this translation it is being used as a verb—"and voids". Someone might wonder how a noun, such as in "the void", may be made into a verb, such as "and voids". The answer is that the Hebrew word behind void is *bo-hoo*[21] (not a joke) and that many words may be nouns *or* verbs. It depends on the context in which the word appears. The definition of bo-hoo [בהו] is "to be empty".[22]

So, the challenge of the concept of "and voids" in the fake context of the void of space is solved by the accumulated knowledge of how the language actually works—so that it may more readily be seen that the Hebrew word in the biblical text actually means "and voids"—in the context of the aliens' actions in the first verse *voiding* the former existence of the bipedal hominids they encountered on this planet. Why do I care so much about how words are put together? In my childhood and adolescence, both of my parents were sticklers for the way words were put together to make meaning, as well as for the sounds that distinguish one similar-sounding word from another. I was 12 years old when my father impressed upon me, then and forevermore, the difference between the word *duty* and the word *dooty*.

The difference is crucial. In the actual Hebrew biblical text, much of it so unashamedly points to the presence of aliens as the principal actors of the Genesis story. As it turns out, the story is not a story. It is historical documentation.

Another word from the second verse is a two-letter word that, in context, might mean "upon"[23]—as in darkness being upon the face of the earth. It didn't require my inner rocket scientist to step up to the drafting table to be able simply look at the other definitions of that particular two-letter word. One of its definitions[24] is yoke—the fastening framework on the shoulders of two oxen or two horses. That kind of yoke. My third-of-a-century nursing career helped inform me as to the kind of yoke—as a fastening framework—the aliens might be writing about. I supposed that they would be referring to the fastening framework of the phosphate-deoxyribose yoke[25] that holds together the other nucleotides of the DNA double helix molecular structure. Why would that be supposed? If, as I began to suspect, aliens were involved in fabrication or creation of our species, then we should expect to encounter the DNA molecular structure.

It's easy to be misled by words you think you know. Everyone familiar with Genesis can recall the part where the spirit of God moved upon the face of the waters.[26] Who would want to mess with such an idyllic scene? Only the person who has spent years of studying the ancient Hebrew texts to find that there can be a vast distance between what we are told the text says and what it really does say. The word "moved" provides another such example.

The main value that a person would get from spending several years compiling lists of Hebrew words placed into categories of similar words is that to accurately translate words, it is essential to know how specific categories of letters give meaning inside of a word. Such a word is the one for "moved".

When I began to research the word in the Hebrew Bible for "moved" [מרחפת], the first thing I noticed—by using a software system[27] that will locate any word in Hebrew, Greek, or English in a variety of Bibles—is that this second verse of Genesis 1 is the *only* place in the Hebrew Bible that the word appears. Slight variations of the word appear in two other places in the biblical text. At one place, it appears as "flutters"—as an eagle fluttering over her young.[28] In the other place, the variation appears as "shake"—as in "all my bones shake".[29, 30] What I was able to know at that point is that this word definitely conveyed fluttery, shaky *movement*.

The word for "moved" has on it a particular prefix letter. The prefix letter, in conventional Hebrew grammar, generally means "from". But as I had compiled multiple word lists that included the "from" prefix, it became very apparent that for some words the prefixed "from" just didn't convey the meaning of "from." Turning to my own studies about the structure of Egyptian hieroglyphics, I knew that certain glyphs belonged to a category called "determinatives".[31] In other words, a glyph—or character— identified as a determinative is there to help the reader determine the meaning that the writing intended to convey.

The word for "moved" has a prefix that can be fairly and accurately called a "utility determinative". I coined that term after multiple observations as to how the presence of the letter prefix (*měm*) at the beginning of a word determines how the word conveys utility or *usefulness*.

So, we have the concepts of movement, flutter, and shake. Through my extensive nursing experience, I knew that if the text was talking about any kind of creation—and that tied to that creation (or fabrication) was information about DNA—that the place to get movement, flutter, and shaking was a centrifuge machine. The presence of a centrifuge early in the Genesis story meant that it was definitely trying to convey something high tech; it fit right in context with the presence of a microtome.

Where was the fake concept of *moved* moving? It was on the face of the waters. To look up the word for water in any *Strong's Dictionary of Hebrew* is something that anyone can do from the comfort of home. As the definition is read, given what the translated text has said is there—aliens, a microtome, and a centrifuge—the last entry of what Dr. James Strong wrote about water ought to jump right out of the water. He wrote that, "by euphemism", the word water can mean "urine" or "semen".[32] At the end of the second verse I knew (because that's the meaning of what the definitions of words are saying), that it was semen that was going to be centrifuged. By the end of the actual translation of just the second verse of the Genesis story, I knew. And now *we* know beyond doubt, that the Genesis account is about extraterrestrials doing some kind of DNA machinations with semen—or sperm—*with their own* and *with that of our ancient hominid ancestors*.

Genesis, the Story; Genesis, the Account

It takes a sense of fearlessness for a translator to translate what the ancient scripture actually conveys—*as well as* for the reader who is willing to read what is actually conveyed. Both translator and reader must have come to realize that the traditional scriptural narrative is simply a *constructed narrative*—a falsely constructed narrative. Once I saw, through the definitions of the Hebrew words themselves, that the traditional Genesis account was simply a false narrative, I was hooked. I was able to translate at the rate of about one verse a day. The entire first chapter of Genesis took about six weeks to translate.

In the third and fourth verses of the traditional story, we encounter the concept of "light"—as in, let there be light.[33] But going into the third verse I knew that what was actually going on was that there were extraterrestrials and that there was high-tech centrifuge of semen. And since there was semen being centrifuged, IVF would be right around the conceptual corner.

Starting with the ancient Hebrew word that we're told by the experts means "light" is the need to see the word in a way that it has never been seen before. To see it as if it had never been seen before was only possible because of the years I had spent in solitary study pulling Hebrew words apart in order to learn how each letter functioned inside of any given word.

That Hebrew word falsely relayed as light is a three-letter word. When looked up by its spelling or by its Strong's Number, its definition—not surprisingly—*is* light.[34] But the concept of light isn't in context here. How else to see the word? Here's how: I had a long list of words that began with the first Hebrew letter (our letter *a*) which acted as the common prefix for our word "I." I knew that we were dealing with "I" followed by a verb of some sort, as in "I *do something.*" But what something was being done?

Just as with words seen in the first verse where the word's last letter had been dropped, either by its author or by a later editor, I knew that if a common final letter were tacked onto the second and third letters of the Hebrew word, there would be a different root word altogether. That is the case with the Hebrew word for light in the ancient text here.

The other thing I knew was that the original author substituted one common letter for another in the word in the text. That change had the effect of modifying the meaning of the word. The definition of the actual root word in the text was "to cast"[35]; the modified word could be translated as "to place". The modifier letter could also make the word an "-ing" word. The word for light ceased to be the word for "light" and became the word for "I placing".

In the translated narrative, that's the place where the aliens refer to how they placed the tiny sharp hollow needle used in IVF,[36] when the placement was happening right at that moment. When I understood that the aliens were writing about the placement of an instrument, I knew that the instrument had to be an injecting pipette.[37] Here is the actual high-tech equivelant of a low-tech agricultural coulter. Once all the words of the third and fourth verses were translated, I knew that what they were writing about was *artificial fertilization* and about how they could manipulate our ancestors' genetics to do any type of genetic engineering or DNA manipulation they desired.

Here was the place where this radical, but reality-based, translation became real—became alive—for me. It became alive as I thought deeply about the concept of light as bioluminescence. That kind of light is revealed in the fifth verse of *this* Genesis translation. It is in the two Hebrew words behind the traditional translation, "the light Day"[38] that I could see bioluminescence—because the Hebrew word for day did not necessarily have to be *the day*—it could be *the foundation*.

Well, that's what I thought—because I had just done a search of how the Strong's Number for day [3117] was translated in the 2,287 places[39] where it appears in the King James Version of the Bible. That number is translated as "the foundation" in Exodus 9:18 of the KJV Bible. *There it is*, I thought. The concept that the alien entities were trying to express was of foundational light—that is, light as bioluminescence. That certainly made high-tech sense.

I basked so long in the light of that discovery that bioluminescent blindness was beginning to settle in when it came to me that it would be prudent to check that translation against the wording of that verse in the Hebrew

Bible. There, the words almost jumped off the page. The Hebrew word for "the day" was there; but so was the Hebrew word for "the foundation."[40]

That discovery put a huge monkey wrench into foundational light. It appears, in retrospect, that the KJV team simply combined the literal concepts of "the day" and "the foundation" into their wording "the foundation thereof". The upshot for *this* translation was that the word day is not in context; and the definition of "foundation" for day no longer had any foundation whatsoever.

Any up-close examination of the Hebrew word quickly reveals that it is not "the day". There's no "the" prefix on the word. It's just "day." It's only a three-letter word in Hebrew. The concept of "day" just isn't in context in the verse. What to do? I couldn't squeeze anything out of the Hebrew word that fit the verse's actual context. I slept on the matter.

It was in the blackness of dreamless sleep that I saw the three letters of that ancient Hebrew word—each letter appeared to be several inches tall—and appeared slowly, one by one. The first, the letter *yăd* [Z], I saw in its role as a common prefix for the first person singular subject pronoun "it." The second, the letter *ōōă* [Y] (or *văv*), I saw in its role as a common prefix meaning "and." The third, the letter *mĕm* [M], *I* saw in its role as a common suffix meaning "them." There it was—"it-and-them"—mistranslated as "day." Now I had "bioluminescent it-and-them" on my hands. As it turns out, the ancient text was to eventually reveal, in verse 18, that living organisms are bioluminescent—but not if no longer living. There was no mystery as to what "it" and as to what "them" were. The "it" was a solitary egg cell. The "them" referred to a mass of sperm cells around a solitary egg cell.

It's also in the fifth verse that the traditionally translated word night appears—as in "the darkness he called night". By the fifth verse I knew that night probably wasn't in context with what was going on inside the aliens' brand of disclosure. To find out what is going on inside the Hebrew word [לַיְלָה] in the ancient text all I had to do was to look it up. The Hebrew dictionary in any *Strong's Concordance* is quite sufficient to provide the full scoop about what *night* is all about. I encountered the standard definition, "a twist away from the light."[41] There's our night. Right. Sure. I thought, *That's twisted.*

In that dictionary, the reader—that is, I, myself—was then directed to another explanatory definition, which was "to fold back; a spiral step—winding stair."[42] What I was supposed to see here was the concept of day folding back upon itself to be night. But what I saw instead was a visual description of what we call the DNA molecular structure. That dictionary then refers its reader to yet another explanatory definition, which was "a loop".[43] I wasn't seeing an endless loop of day twisting away from the light folding back upon itself in a continuous cyclical loop of day and night. What I saw was "a loop", "a twist", "folding back", and a "winding stair". What I translated from these explanatory definitions was a "twisting spiral"—as that's what the verses' authors called what we call the DNA molecule. These definitions reinforced to me that to accurately translate the ancient creation narrative all I had to do was to let the definitions of words simply speak for themselves. At that point I knew, if I hadn't before, that *this is not interpretation—this is translation.*

Is there is a translational relationship between the actual ancient document early in the chapter and the fake-out translation of the Genesis account of creation? In the sixth verse, I found that there *can* be—on occasion. Three particular words provide good evidence.

I tied my exact translations to the words, in order, in the King James Version but noticed that the word "firmament" in KJV is translated in another useful Bible as "expanse".[44] When I looked up that Hebrew word in the ancient text, the definition is "spread out"[45]; and the proof citation[46] is from Job 37:18, "spread out the sky". As it turns out, that meaning is all the translational firepower that is needed for the ancient word. So, what's going on here?

The real-life consideration for the E.T. scientists (as well as for our today's fertility doctors) is that of assessing a sperm specimen for fertility.[47] If the aliens had a high semen volume in proportion to their sperm cells, that would dilute, or spread out, the concentration of spermatozoa in a given volume of semen. That dilution would be a real-life problem. The real-life technical solution? IVF.[48]

The KJV word "divide"—as in "let it divide the waters"[49]—provides another example that there is a relationship between the fake-out word concept and the actual concept in an actual translation. When I looked up the Hebrew word I could see, as easily as you would be able, that the word means "divide"—that is, *in various senses, literally and figuratively*[50]. The synonyms "separate" and "distinguish" are given.

Using my utility determinative, I took the word *separate* to mean to "sort out." I could have just left it as "to separate"—as a research article I found made that translation pretty clear. The article? You can find it as easily. It's "Sperm separation to improve IVF success rate."[51] Again, each word in actual translation builds upon the previous word—presenting a seamless and compelling narrative based on the actual science of the challenges that the alien beings had as they progressed with their program of DNA manipulation of the primate hominid species they encountered on our planet in the remote past.

In that same sixth verse, I couldn't help but notice that the translated word "waters" appears three times.[52] I've looked up that word dozens of times, and each time the same definition is there staring me in the face. Dr. James Strong, author of his own Hebrew dictionary, tells, with a straight face, that the Hebrew word means "water."[53] With an equally straight face he tells that it can also mean "juice." Okay. I can only guess that his face is straight when he tells that, "by extension," water can also be urine . . . or semen.[54] Well, semen is *mostly* water.

For a translation, though, I knew that semen would turn the 2,100-year-old traditional (fake) translation on its head. I wanted more than just Dr. James Strong's say-so that the Hebrew word for water could also mean "semen". I wanted proof. So, I set out to retranslate some verses from Song of Solomon[55] that I suspected had references to semen, or some type of body fluids, within them.

It's the Hebrew word *mem* (or *mah·yim*)[56] that gives the meaning of either "water, urine, or semen"—depending on the context; and that word appears in Song of Solomon 4:15, 5:12, and 8:7 as waters. In 4:15, I read (as you can, too) about "a fountain of gardens", about "a well of living waters", and about "streams from Lebanon".[57]

All I had to do to retranslate was to simply look up each Hebrew word, in succession, and write down their meanings. "A fountain of gardens" is actually a "fountain of satisfaction".[58] Note: the word fountain is double-meaning word play. "A well of living waters" isn't far from the straight-up translational truth. It is actually "raw life water"[59]—which I took, *and take*, to refer to semen because of the phrase that follows. "Streams from Lebanon" is actually "gushes out whatness white one"[60]—or, more clinically, gushes out a mass of whiteness. In any physician's clinic *that's* semen. How do I—how do we—know that? Because the definitions of the words, in succession, are: "drip, drop," "gush out,"[61] plus "out of, from whatness"[62] plus "to be or become white".[63]

When I read Song of Solomon 5:12, I wanted to scratch my head as to what it actually said. That verse has the word waters in it. From the KJV, "His eyes are as the eyes of doves by the rivers of waters, washed with milk and fitly setting."[64] That his eyes are fitly set is nice to know but not relevant to the word explorations here. All that was needed for this verse was, as in the case of the previous verse, simply to look up the definitions of the Hebrew words, in succession, and simply write down the definitions.

When I did that, *his eyes* all of a sudden becomes, "his fountain as an effervescent intoxicant."[65] I could clearly see that King Solomon wasn't playing fast and loose with his word play—it was actually soft porn. "The rivers of waters" suddenly became "a stream of seminal fluid."[66] And "washed with milk and fitly setting" suddenly became "washes me with overflowing milky-fat."[67]

Do you doubt that? Then just look up the definitions of the Hebrew words, one by one, and you'll see what I saw. It's not that I wanted to doubt or not to doubt. As far as I was concerned the exercise was all about finding *translational truth*.

When I read Song of Solomon 8:7, my natural curiosity had reached fever pitch. Knowing, as I did, that waters was semen (or seminal fluid), the prospect of "many waters cannot quench love, neither can the floods drown it"[68] was intriguing—to state it mildly—or to sate it mildly. As I looked up the Hebrew word definitions, one by one in succession, even I was flabbergasted by what emerged.

Exactly what does "many waters cannot quench love" mean? The definitions of each of the Hebrew words in succession told me that those words don't mean that at all. What it told me was that ole Solomon had a penchant for descriptive prose. This is what that fake phrase actually says, "Many projectile semen is not its prevailing in respect to his hardness at the sex act."[69] That's what the words' definitions[70] tell us. Frankly, I wasn't sufficiently interested or intrigued to put that into poetic English prose. I was content to know that waters was semen—not something else.

The phrase, "neither can the floods drown it", became, in quick succession, "and his stream!—it overflows him."[71] It didn't take a great deal of fertile imagination to understand what *that* meant. I suspected, also, that the extraterrestrials might have been similarly affected by the physiology of orgasm.

Knowing that in (actual) translation the Hebrew word for water is semen (or spermatozoa) allowed me to know exactly what was going on inside of this sixth verse. The verse wasn't talking about sex, it was talking about a physiological phenomenon that would necessitate the E.T. beings' perfecting IVF to deal with their own low sperm cell count in relationship to their own volume of semen. In addition to the aliens' sperm cells being too spread out in their own semen, they had to sort out their viable sperm cells among ones that were or were not rejected by the hominid female's egg cells.

Each successfully translated verse, in succession, had the effect of producing a most powerful pounding headache. I called it a "neuron-ache"—as if the very neuronal networks in my brain were in a state of expansion due to the need to create additional neuronal networks and pathways to handle the additional neuronal traffic and raw information having to do with expanding human knowledge about our true collective beginnings. Sometimes, I would be driven to take a headache remedy. Sometimes I would just endure the pounding ache.

The seventh verse of the actual Genesis documentation repeats the concepts related in its preceding verse. The real twist I found in that verse was hidden behind the Hebrew word translated as "which"—as in "which were under the firmament". The second was hidden behind "were under".[72]

The Hebrew word for "which" at this place in the Genesis story is used over a hundred times in the biblical text. The Hebrew dictionary resources will tell that the word is a "relative pronoun", and that it can mean "which, whose, wheresoever, where, and whereas."[73] My years of making lists of common Hebrew prefixes and then deriving their meanings from their uses in context, alerted me that the Hebrew word there had a prefix commonly translated as "I". From that I knew that the two remaining letters had a dropped third letter to complete it as a viable "root word". When I looked up the definition of the resulting root word, I found the definition "to free" or "to unravel".[74] The real breakthrough came when I examined where in the Hebrew Bible that word appeared and how it was translated in The Interlinear Bible.[75] As it turns out, what I'll call the target root word appears at Daniel 5:12 in the context of "solving". With that find, I translated that word "which" as "I solve".

Additionally, I also knew that when something is solved that it is some problem that has been solved. So, my translation had to include the answer to what problem had been solved. Hidden behind the two words "were under" was to answer the question of what kind of problem was solved.

To solve the translation of "were under" was a problem in itself. I could easily see (as could you) that the Hebrew word traditionally given as "were under" had only four letters.[76] Taking off the word's prefix leaves a three-letter root word[77]; and looking up that word only gives the definitions of "bottom," "below," and "under."[78] But again, those definitions aren't in context.

To translate what has never been translated, one must be a dedicated, intrepid word detective. From my childhood I was taught, instructed, urged, and sometimes humiliated, to use the *right* word in the *correct* context and to pronounce it properly. To translate, I *became* the intrepid word detective. So, if the Hebrew dictionary references aren't yielding up the word's definitional secret (or secrets) where else might it (or they) be yielded up?

There's a relatively simple, but extremely thorough, software[79] that anyone may download. I had it available and at the ready. All I did was to ask the software to locate every verse in the Hebrew Bible where the target three-letter root word was located. I got six hits—as the name of a place identified by a Strong's Number spelled exactly the same as the word for "under".[80] Each one of those verses had the name of a place called "Tahath".[81]

What does *that* mean? One reference[82] informed me that was a "place" in the desert. I just asked myself some very elementary questions. What is a "place" in the desert? That's an *oasis*. What's an oasis? I thought the most elementary definition that I could come up with was that an oasis is a place of fertility inside of a larger place that is not fertile. With that elemental and critical definition—"fertility"—the root word portion of the ancient Hebrew word in the text was solved. All that remained to be solved was the word's prefix—a common prefix I came to term a utility *determinative*.

The next set of elementary questions began with, *What is the usefulness of fertility?* Well, fertility in and of itself is useful. So, what purpose would a utility determinative have when tacked onto the front of a word like fertility?

What is the definition of utility? That would be "useful". That, I thought then, was a first-class translation of this word's utility determinative—as useful. Put together, the translation of the Hebrew word (formerly translated as "were under") in the Genesis story becomes, by way of research and reason, "useful fertility". And that translation just happened to be exactly in context with what was going on in the rest of the verse. And what was going on in the surrounding verse was that some E.T. solved the problem of useful fertility in regard to their problem of low sperm concentration.

There was an added translational bonus. When I translated the famous phrase "And it was so"[83] it turns out that the grammar of the word "was" wasn't past tense but present tense.[84, 85] The Hebrew word for "so" may also be a word that means "true."[86]

So, the alien beings were writing, by way of this ancient *thought-to-be-sacred* text, that what they were writing . . . was true. I thought of all the Bible believers of the world. What was I to say to them? *Hey, you believed the Bible yesterday when you didn't actually know what it said. And today, now that you know what it actually says and how it says it, you don't want to believe it? What's up with that?*

Humanity's knowledge of Genesis is only what we have been told for eons. A sea of ink has been used by theologians and their theological brothers and sisters to write, over the past 2,100 years, about the famous seven days of creation. Inquiring minds want to know: *What's up with those days*? What seems to make a biblical day? Evening and morning.[87] How do I translate "evening"?

Sure, when I looked it up I found (just as you would) the definition "evening".[88] But I was intimately familiar with how words are spelled in both the Hebrew alphabets, *modern* and *ancient*, so it didn't take long to see that there are about a dozen entries for the Hebrew word in the *Strong's Dictionary of Hebrew and Chaldee*. One other[89] of the entries with the same spelling furnishes a definition that just happens to fit the context of the now-proven narrative.

The in-context concepts that were there for anyone to see were intermix, mixture, and mongrel race.[90] From the definition for intermix, I simply used a synonym for my translation—"*interbreed*"—since that's what is going on in the context of the updated and modernized Genesis story.

The matter of the morning[91] was treated in the same way. I looked up the word given in the Hebrew text. I see that it can be morning; but Dr. James Strong tells his readers that the Hebrew word is derived from a word—conveniently enough with the same spelling—which can mean to "search" or to "seek out".[92] I asked myself what word, in translation, means "to search", which is also in context with what the aliens were doing. The word I easily came up with is "research". So, the evening and the morning didn't have anything to do with any day. The concepts were never there from the fabled beginning. What was always there and what *is* there is the extraterrestrials' own *mission statement*—to interbreed and to research. Research what? Since the Hebrew word "day" follows the word for "to research", what they are researching is "it-and-them". What is "*it*" and what is "*them*"? The "it" is the solitary egg cell. The "them" is the mass of roiling sperm cells. *Case closed.*

The Prime Directive and the "Shame-Cause"

To put such a header on translation research that has not yet been explained might be to put the proverbial cart before the horse. I translated each word in succession, one after the other. Sometimes the newly (and properly) translated words, when strung together as sentences, made sense.

Some of the sentences required that I use brackets to supply their *contextual* meaning. In the ninth verse of my translation (among many others), I made use of brackets to explain that the translated words, "the semen", is to be "useful" in IVF. That concept is completely in context with what was going on inside the freshly translated verse. The words of the fake-out sentence that followed were "and let the dry land appear."[93]

As I examined the Hebrew word given for "and let appear"[94] I noticed (which you can, too) that the word had two prefixes attached to it. The first prefix meant "and".[95] That translated prefix meant that the traditional translation sometimes told the truth about what elements of words (and some entire words) said. The second prefix was a letter that, from having compiled my lists and lists of words demonstrating prefixes, suffixes, and what we could call, *inserted letters*, I knew that the word's second prefix could be translated as "you," as "your," or as what I came to call, *an* exclamatory emphatic—our exclamation point. The most apt choice depended on the context of the word *in translation*.

The word's root word was common enough. The most common definition of the word is "to see",[96] but another legitimate definition is "to discern".[97] *That* was the word, in translation, that I settled upon. In Hebrew, there is no strictness about the time something happens. It could be in the present, in the past, or in the future. The tense of the translated words "and discern" could be determined as a judgment call, when the actual definition of the ancient words behind the next phrase "the dry land" was fully explored.

There is a particular Hebrew word for the words traditionally held out as "the dry land".[98] That word has slightly different spelling than its root word.[99] The simple but effective software informed me that the Hebrew root word was used 78 times[100] throughout the KJV.

The same software could also inform me how the Hebrew word was used in each instance in the King James Bible. Just by looking at the words in traditional translation, I could see that the word "dry" only appears three times. *Three times*. The words wither and "up" appeared most often. But the curious word, "ashamed" also appeared three times—so, it was a clear contender as an apt translation of the Hebrew word. The word "shame" appeared two times. I reasoned that if there is something to be ashamed about, there must be a cause for the shame; and since the word "shame" is a legitimate contender for "dry" it provided the basis of the word in translation "the cause of shame". When that concept is tacked onto the concept of "discern", it might easily have been already discerned—that is, in the past. So, the completed concept in original ancient text would have been *and discerned the cause of shame!*

At this point several other nagging questions come up. The extraterrestrials themselves discerned that what they were doing was a cause for shame? What was the cause for shame? Would the verse that follows, which contained another reference to "dry land", shed enough light on these questions as to answer them? Or would whatever light was shed only pose additional questions?

At this point I couldn't help but think about the Prime Directive of the late 1960's television series *Star Trek.* All its fans, and many others, know about the Prime Directive. In the series it was General Order Number 1 of Starfleet Command. It was a guiding principle that prohibited interference with the natural development of (alien) civilizations they might encounter on their five-year mission of space exploration. Since this ancient E.T. text itself brought up the matter of a cause for shame, I wondered if the alien beings might be aware that they, themselves, might be—or were—violating some kind of similar prohibition that even they knew about. I also wondered what the verse that follows would bring. Admitting guilt? Grand excuse-making?

Going into the 10th verse, the phrase "the dry land" is repeated in the (fake) context of God calling the dry land "Earth".[101] I knew that the matter would again be addressed by the text itself. And the text *does* address the matter. But before addressing the matter, the now-disproven traditional translation refers to a "gathering together of the waters called he Seas."[102] Since there was "water" and "seas", I pretty much knew that there was some kind of semen[103] or sperm that would be present in actual translation. What an honest translation of "and the gathering together" gives us is, "and in regard to binding".[104]

The immediate question becomes, *What was being bound?* The translation of "waters called seas" supplies that answer. To determine exactly what type or kind of semen or sperm would be the tricky part. So, I thought, the text is talking about binding. What's the context? The context is of the process of IVF binding something. The instrument that would be doing the binding is what we today call an injecting pipette. So, where does the binding take place? It takes place inside the hominid egg cell. So, if the same word for "waters" (as "seas"[105]) being sperm of some kind, appears again after the word for *called,* what would the text have to be referring to? My best educated (and researched) answer was that the text was talking about, in the first instance, *spermatozoa* in general—since that's where the E.T.'s sperm specimen for IVF would come from. But the injecting pipette only binds *one* sperm cell into the egg; and one sperm cell is called a *spermatozoon.*[106] I saw that the aliens were describing the process in which one sperm cell is bound inside of one egg cell. I suspected that the punch line of their reference to a cause for shame would probably be hidden behind the words, "and God saw that it was good."[107]

I knew that if I simply substituted the word "extraterrestrial entities" or "aliens" for the word "God" that I'd pretty much have their own reply to their own bringing up the matter of any cause for shame. The translation literally says, "and it saw that good."[108]

Yes, knowing that I had to supply some sort of additional explanation—which would need to be inside brackets (to indicate that wasn't in translation). It would simply be my explanation of the word good. I added the two words "technical solution" as that is exactly what the aliens were looking for—and researching: good technical solutions. So, the punch line was that they were not worried about any cause of shame at all—because they had good technical solutions to their technical problems that had necessitated IVF in the first place. All I thought was, *That's coldly technocratic.* All I felt was revulsion.

Going into the 11th verse of the traditional Genesis fable is the command, "Let the earth bring forth grass (and) the herb yielding seed."[109] Earlier in my *actual* translation I explained how "the earth" is actually "the

I-Accomplish". So, the first challenge of this verse became a reexamination of how we get the word "let".

There is no Hebrew word at this point in the ancient document for "let". That word was simply added, in *faux* translation, to the now-familiar phrase. I could easily see (as you can) that the actual Hebrew word[110] is the same word as given for "bring forth".[111] Except in the first instance, the Hebrew word has on it a prefix—the one I call an exclamatory emphatic—our exclamation point. Literally, the word means "to sprout".[112] That's conceptually pretty close to "bring forth."

But, I thought, the ancient narrative isn't talking about plants, it's talking about *beings*—so, the synonym "to germinate" is a better fit, in terms of translating the concept that the narrative has been pointing toward. So, in translation, I ended up with "to germinate [!] is the I-Accomplish". What does that mean?

I spent many sleepless nights thinking about what the text was saying—turning it over and over in my restless mind. The meaning to the E.T.s is that to have germinated a hominid egg cell with one of their sperm cells represented a real accomplishment. The lead alien scientist who perfected the technique wanted the credit—thus the prefix "I" on "accomplish". He (or it) wanted all future generations to know that.

The next phrase begins with the same translated word "germinate". The word that follows is the Hebrew word given for "the herb"[113]—except that I could see that there is no "the" prefix on the ancient word. It was easy for me (and would be for you, too) to simply look up the word's definition. It means "to glisten" or "to be green".[114] So, I translated the word after germinate as "green".

The traditional word that follows is "yielding". It wasn't difficult at all to see that the Hebrew word[115] required a bit more than simply looking up its definition—which, by the way, is "to sow *or* to disseminate."[116] The Hebrew word has a prefix—the one I call a utility determinative—which means that the concept the aliens were going for was *the utility of dissemination*. It didn't take very long to realize that the utility of dissemination in the case of hominids, or the extraterrestrial "visitors" for that matter, was *to ejaculate*. As scandalous as that might be, that concept exactly fits the narrative of the

E.T.s' own genesis document. The Hebrew word also had an inserted letter—one associated with modifying the meaning of the word. In this instance, the modification is to make the word *past tense*—as *ejaculated.*

The traditional word that follows is "seed".[117] As I looked up the ancient word's meaning, I was not surprised to see that it meant "seed".[118] I asked myself, *What do we call the seed of homonids?*

"You have an amazing grasp of the obvious" was a favorite phrase of my late father. It might be time for me to trot it out since it may apply here. We call the seed of hominids (like us) spermatozoa—or sperm for short. So, now, a completely different concept was emerging from the soothingly familiar words about letting the earth bring forth grass and such. What emerged in translation was "To germinate (is) the I-Accomplish. Germinate green spermatozoa."

So, what did they do with their green sperm? It, I found, was simply used in IVF because of their low concentration of sperm cells in relationship to their own volume of semen. The alien scientist who figured out the technical problem and solved it with a good technical solution also claimed the credit for himself (or itself). The effective solution was referred to as "the I-Accomplish". As an added bonus for us readers today, he (or it) added that what was being written down was . . . true.[119]

Lights in Firmament—Neither Lights nor Firmament

As I began to approach the 14th verse of the Genesis tale-turned-translation, it was certain that the ancient word for "lights" might be something other than light. It could, however, be some other kind of light—such as bioluminescence. How, exactly, could the Hebrew word in the text be tackled so as to make sense of it?

One of the workhorse tools of translation is an inch-and-a-half thick book, originally published in 1848 as *The Analytical Hebrew and Chaldee Lexicon*[120] and compiled by Benjamin Davidson. The invaluable work of Professor Davidson was to put into one volume every Hebrew word in the Hebrew Bible, to define the word, give its exact grammar (as he understood it), to offer scriptural citations (where appropriate), and to list the word's "root word"—or where appropriate—the several root words from which the word under study could be derived.

As I dutifully looked up the Hebrew word for "light"[121] in his lexicon, it listed two possible root words. One was the Hebrew word for "light".[122] The other was the Hebrew word for "to bitterly curse".[123] How does that happen? The word in the text is a four-letter word. The first letter is a prefix—that utility determinative. The middle two letters are two letters from the word's root word (which could be either *light* or to *bitterly curse*). The word's fourth letter is a suffix—an exclamatory emphatic—in other words, our exclamation point. I could easily see that the word for light could be "assumed" into a translation, as the root word is *ăōōr.* But I could just as easily see that the word in the text could be "to bitterly curse" as that root word is "*ărĕr*".

The actual translation of the phrase following the fake phrase "in the firmament" would determine the proper context for either "light" or "bitterly curse". I knew that the Hebrew word was a reference to something being spread out[124]; and that it was a reference to the E.T.s' own low sperm concentration, which necessitated their having to resort to IVF. The proper context for "light" versus "to bitterly curse" was now known. There was no light here . . . but there *was* some bitter cursing. All that the Hebrew word with the root "to bitterly curse" needed was the translation of its first letter—that utility determinative.

What is the "utility" of a bitter curse? Its utility is in the expression of extreme and intense frustration. The concept seemed to be that what the alien beings were trying to accomplish was technically difficult. This exact Hebrew word in this verse appears one other place[125] in the Bible—as *curse.* I took the two concepts, "curse" and "frustration", and simply put them together as "cursedly frustrating". The word's suffix, our exclamation point, was in context—and exactly *on point.*

That verse, the 14th, has the words "the night" in it—as in "to divide the day from the night."[126] I had already translated the Hebrew word behind the fake night and knew it was actually "the twisting spiral".[127]

That twisting spiral is what we call the DNA molecule. In my mind, the text itself would explain what its authors were doing with our ancestor's DNA molecular structure. The fake words "and for seasons"[128] provides a really good example of how the Hebrew in that place in the traditional genesis narrative conveys pertinent information in keeping with the actual context of the DNA molecular structure the E.T.s were working with.

To take on the challenge behind the ancient word "and for seasons" it will have been necessary to have spent years studying how words appeared in the ancient text and how each letter in any given word contributes to the meaning the word is trying to convey. During the years I spent doing just that I could not fully appreciate the value that the self-imposed training would contribute to being able to take apart the ancient word here. I know that accounting for the meaning of each root word, each prefix, each suffix, and for any inserted letter, is essential to being able to know, with complete confidence, what the Hebrew text is *trying* to tell us. And it *does* tell us—in spite of what traditional translations have said on the matter for over 2,100 years.

I could see, as that's what's there on the page of the Hebrew text, the word (with syllables separated) *ōōă·lă·mĕ·ōō·ōd·ēm.*[129] Years of word-listing helps identify the word's prefixes—three of them. I already knew that the first prefix means "and". The second prefix means "in regard to". The third prefix was that utility determinative—so, I knew that it would address the matter of the *usefulness* of whatever was the meaning of the root word.

Since the word's final syllable was a common suffix that makes words plural, the matter of translation would fall right into place. The root word that was revealed when each of the prefixes and the suffix was accounted for was a three-letter *variant* of a common root word that meant, "to fix upon by agreement, to meet, to summon" *or* "to direct in a certain position."[130]

Ah, I thought, *the direction of certain positions.* Some basic research about how DNA molecules reproduce themselves teaches the interested reader about the behavior of enzymes such as DNA gyrase and DNA polymerase.[131] *That,* I thought, is exactly what the text is trying to convey.

Looking again at the utility determinative, it seemed clear that its proper translation should be simply the word "useful". The first letter of the word's three-letter *variant* of the word's root word acts to modify, in some way, the meaning of the root word—or *basic concept.* Given what the text was trying to express, it seemed also clear that the proper *modification* of the basic concept was to re-name *the direction of certain positions* to "positional directions", which would be in context with the positional directions of the enzymes involved in DNA replication of itself.

The completed translation of the somewhat complex word became, then, "and in regard to useful positional directions." Each of the word's letters (as syllables) and the word's root word had been accounted for—and the accountable translation was completely *in context* with what was going on—both in the verse itself as well as with all of the text leading up to that verse.

The pulling apart of the Hebrew word behind the verse's last two fake words "and years" was to provide the verse's next essential information about the alien beings' experience with the *cursedly frustrating twisting spiral* molecular structure. Some references, such as my four-volume *The Interlinear Bible* (J.P. Green, Sr., editor),[132] will just hand you the Hebrew word's Strong's Number—then it can handily be looked up. When I looked up the number for the Hebrew word in the text,[133] there was the definition: "a year".[134] A *slam dunk* you'd think. I knew, though, to look at the word's *other definition entries*. There are five of them. The definition "year" isn't in context. That's out. The definition "sleep"[135] isn't in context. That's out. But the definition "to duplicate (literally or figuratively)"[136] was exactly in context.

Knowing the context of the preceding translated phrase, I knew that the word, in translation, had to be naming something and that the word had to be plural. It did not take word-smithing rocket science to come up with the translation "and duplicates". With that wording, the entire 14th verse makes itself known to its 21st-century readers.

The E.T.s' decreased concentration of sperm cells necessitated IVF. They figured out the functions of the DNA molecule and the functions of the enzymes involved in its various functions—including the function of DNA self-replication. They related that they, themselves, were amazed at what they found in the course of their research.

Lights to Rule? Really? How?

In the 16th verse of traditional Genesis 1, we encounter God making two great lights. In the actual first chapter, though, the alien beings are informing us that someone (or *someones*) prepared the Clustered Regularly Interspaced Short Palindromic Repeats (CRISPR) technology[137] that they prefer. How did they do that? The third word in the ancient text, *one of those traditionally untranslated words,* is the word *ăht* [את].[138] The thing about this word is that it *does* have definitions—it *can* be translated. One of the definitions is the word "coulter".[139] We could call that word *ăht*, a *concept placeholder*—because, as it turns out, the E.T.s employed several different concepts for the word *ăht.* One of the concepts is that of the injecting pipette used for IVF. The other is the high-tech concept of CRISPR.

Knowledge of CRISPR came through the back door of research as to exactly how high-tech E.T.s would be doing genetic editing. How they did that would come out of wanting to know what tools our modern scientists use to cut snippets of DNA wherever they intend.

The answer, as close to you as a simple search via your preferred internet search application, is that CRISPR technique is standard high-tech tool of genetic engineers. Something that they call a CAS-9 "cleaver" breaks the double helix DNA like a pair of scissors at preprogramed places in order to make precision changes. The acronym "CAS" comes from the modified acronym "**C**RISPR **AS**sociated." With that technology, it does not take a genetic scientist to see exactly how a species of advanced extraterrestrial biological entities could modify and engineer DNA as well as genetically edit the hominids they encountered in our remote past. *That* is what is going on in this verse.

Sure, the traditional story tells us that there are two "great lights". Not every Hebrew word has to be freshly researched every time it appears in the ancient text. In the case of the first instance of "lights" in this verse, the same word had already appeared in the 14th verse (previously explained) as "cursedly frustrating"! What is going to be cursedly frustrating? The Hebrew word that follows will have the answer to *that* question. The traditional word there is "great".

Something very obvious pops out when looking at the Hebrew word[140] traditionally translated as "great", as in "two great lights". The word is a plural word. It has a prefix on it that makes it "the"-somethings. That's not great for the home-team traditionalists; but it is for the truth-telling ancient narrative.

When the definition of that word is tracked down in a standard reference (such as *Strong's Hebrew Dictionary*), it means "to twist".[141] The word here is a synonym for a word seen in the fifth verse. When I simply put the definition "twist" with its prefix "the" and its suffix (which makes a word plural)—what we get is "the twists".

That's the beings' descriptor word for what we call the DNA molecular structure.[142] Its complexity is what they found "cursedly frustrating". Another important *and* interesting thing that I could see was that the same physical phenomenon—the DNA molecule—was being described in the same way by two different words.[143] And the translation of both of these words fits exactly into a cohesive and internally consistent narrative.

The exact same root word that means "twist" is used by the ancient text in the next fake phrase "the greater light".[144] The ancient word there for the fake "the" is a word already seen—the word *ăht*. That word refers to how the aliens' scientists snipped the cursedly frustrating twisted spiral molecule where they wanted to—with the "CAS-9" cleaver at the CRISPR they identified.

I could easily see that the ancient text itself puts the light, *as bioluminosity*, before the word for "twist". And I could easily see that the word for "twist" was not pluralized and that it had the prefix that meant "the" on it[145]—as "the twist". Putting the phrase together gave "CRISPR manipulated the bioluminosity (of) The-Twist" [at a site on the DNA molecular structure]." What the E.T.s were saying was that they used the CRISPR technique or something equivalent (such as their own analog) using the bioluminosity of the DNA molecular structure itself as a guide to make their exact DNA edits.

As I looked at the phrase "and the lesser light to rule the night".[146] I suspected that it wouldn't take a rocket scientist to work out what the Hebrew behind *those* words[147] was saying. "And the" was, in contextual translation, *and CRISPR manipulated*. In their word order, *light* was *the bioluminosity*. The Hebrew word behind "lesser"[148] presented a bit of a challenge—even if a *lesser* one.

Of course I wanted to know how many times the *Strong's Hebrew Dictionary* number associated with the word "lesser"[149] appears in the King

James Version. It appears about a hundred times—as "little", "least", "small", "smallest", "younger", and "youngest".[150] But those words (in translatation) are derived from some other, though related, Hebrew root word[151]; and *that* root word is defined as "to cut off".[152] How's that, I thought, for translational sleight-of-hand? The word in the ancient text has the prefix for "the"—so, a more apt translation for the concept of "cut" coupled with "the" becomes "the cutting off". Although I didn't have a completed concept, I knew that the translation was on the right track—because the actual definitions of words are *in context* with the beings' own narrative.

The fake-out words "to rule" required some word-sleuthing to figure out what is really being communicated by the Hebrew word there.[153] Something that struck me as I religiously looked up the definitions for the ancient word behind "to rule" was the amount of creativity that had to have gone into changing what the ancient Genesis document actually read and transforming it into the "let there be light" story—still with us after some two millennia.

As I looked up the Strong's Number associated with the Hebrew word for "to rule",[154] it seemed that Dr. Strong had to create a number *just* for this word, as his definition of the word is "rule".[155] But since the eminent Dr. Strong was a very talented word compiler who, uh, didn't actually *read* Hebrew, we are to overlook the inconvenient fact that the actual word in the ancient text has two prefixes that change the meaning of whatever is the definition of its root word among several candidates.[156] The word also has one suffix that adds meaning—meaning that Dr. Strong, along with everyone else, has overlooked or blown-off. The upshot is that Dr. Strong is not even handing over the definition of the word's actual root word. To have done that would have thrown a giant translational monkey wrench into the traditional Genesis story.

The actual three-letter root word of the Hebrew word behind "to rule" has a very different Strong's Number; and *its* definition is "to resemble".[157] Once I had that as a root word concept—that is, the concept of *something that resembles something*—I could see that concept was exactly in context.

How is it in context? Well, the preceding concepts were CRISPR (DNA editing going on there); bioluminosity (some kind of marker for DNA-manipulation going on there); and the cutting off (DNA-editing going on there). What is the exact context of *something that resembles something*? It is a reference to the self-replicating ability of the DNA molecule. With the correct root word "resemble"[158] in the bag, all that had to be done to translate the ancient word that appears in the text was to translate the word's two prefixes and its suffix.

The first prefix means "in regard to". The second prefix is my utility determinative. So, I ask myself, *What's the utility of resemble?* Well, the utility of resemble is "resemblance"; and what's a common word in English that could be used as a synonym? That word is "replicate". The word's suffix, from my extensive private collection of common Hebrew suffixes, is an exclamatory emphatic—our exclamation point. So, the translation of the Hebrew word behind the fake "to rule" is "in regard to a replication!"

The context is given additional reinforcement in the Hebrew word that follows—the actual word behind the fake word "night". And the actual translation of that Hebrew word is "twisting spiral". There's the DNA molecular structure once again.

The Hebrew word that follows[159] is simply left untouched by the traditional [non]translation. The word is a real workhorse word in the E.T.s' narrative document about their activities in our ancient past. The word there is *ăht*[160] with an "and" prefix. So, the word, in translation, means "and CRISPR manipulated".

The last phrase of the traditional 16th verse is "he made the stars also."[161] The actual Hebrew there is one word—*one word.*[162] It's a seven-letter word. It has one prefix—the prefix for our word "the". It has an apparent three-letter root word[163]—which, strangely enough, never appears by itself in the Hebrew Bible. It has one of two commonly inserted modifier letters[164] (again—from my private collection of such letters and *how* those inserted letters modify words). The word has a two-letter suffix that is commonly used to make a word plural.

The special software[165] quickly revealed that the root word of the seven-letter word in the text never appears in the Hebrew Bible at all. But the root word with its *modifier letter* appears *twice*.[166] That's two times! Both times it appears in the King James Version of the Bible as the word "star".[167]

But "star" is *our* relatively modern word. *What*, I wondered, *is the definition of the word according to Dr. James Strong*. His definition is right on target: "in the sense of blazing".[168] The presence of the *modifier letter*[169] inserted into the three-letter root word is our clue that the word—in the sense of "blazing"—was being modified by the ancient writer to describe something that they (the beings) were seeing under their own microscopes. And what *would* they be seeing? *Tiny blazings*. And isn't *that* how "stars" actually appear to us when just looking up at the night sky? So, as it turned out, there is a *kinda-sorta* relationship between the fake *stars also* and what actually comes out in translation—as *tiny blazings*.

After translating each word of the verse, what emerges is that the E.T.s found the structure of the DNA molecule was not just frustrating, but *cursedly* frustrating. They used the DNA molecule's own bioluminosity as bio-markers to determine exactly where to cut our ancient ancestor's DNA to make the DNA-edits they purposed to make. They figured out how DNA replicates—or copies—itself.

A Word About Word Variety

Hebrew root words can appear in a variety of different forms—just as words can in English. We don't call our "root words" by that name—we just call them "words". Rather than offer up a list of unrecognizable Hebrew words to illustrate a variety of different word forms, consider our English word *exist*. Here are a variety of different ways in which the word *exist* can appear: Exists, existed, existing, existence, existences, existential, will exist, had existed, would have existed, will have existed, preexist, preexisted, *and* preexisting. This list is an example of how I compiled lists as well as lists of how Hebrew words could be grouped together to understand their meanings—in the various contexts in which they appeared in the ancient text. All that personal research about how Hebrew words convey meaning is a major part of how we today know what narrative, and what information, the ancient biblical text is transmitting.

The Case of Misshapen Sperm Cells and Low Sperm Counts

I'm being serious. I've already shown how the biblical text itself explains that the alien beings had a high semen volume in proportion to their sperm cells, which diluted the concentration of sperm cells. They called that problem the "spread out," which was a real-life problem for them. The off-planet beings had another technical problem. The beings themselves will let us know what that problem is; and how they will solve that other problem.

Where is even the hint of a technical problem facing the E.T.s in regard to what they were trying to accomplish? Certainly it's not in the traditional opening phrase of the 17th verse of the Genesis story. In the King James Bible, we read "And God set them in the firmament of the heaven."[170] There is no hint because we in the Western world have been kept quite illiterate as regards our being able to read our foundational sacred texts. When we learn to read the text on the page, we see that the first word in that verse (the one held out as being "and set") is a four-letter word that has two prefixes and a two-letter root word.[171] The first prefix is "and"; the second is "it".

I could easily see in what has passed for the traditional translation that the presumed root word is *naw-thań,*[172] which *can* mean "to set".[173] The kicker, though, is that word *naw-thań* isn't in the ancient text. But the two-letter root word *tăn* is.[174] As I read the definition of *that* word I was puzzled as to exactly what was going on. When you read the word's definition, here's what you'll see: "From an unused root probably meaning to elongate; a monster (as preternaturally formed)."[175] Now that you see it, what do *you* make of it?

The first thing that I wanted to do was to find out what in the heck *preternaturally* means. Even though I had taken Latin (okay—*first year Latin*) in high school (okay—over half a century ago) I had forgotten that the Latin prefix "præter" means "beside" or "contrary to".[176] Beside of what? Contrary to what? Beside or contrary to the natural order of how we think things happen in the universe. In other words: things that we would call *supernatural*. I blew that off—I wasn't looking for the supernatural, just the unexplained natural. I got my own quick answer when, on a hunch, I typed into my internet search tool the words *elongated sperm in IVF,* which provided all the information necessary to connect the word *elongated* with the word *monster*.

A simple bit of internet research brings up the word "teratospermia".[177] More Latin here. That word's prefix *terato* means "monster"[178]—as in *monster sperm cells*. The alien beings' green sperm cells were elongated. They suffered from what today's doctors call *teratospermia.* Today's doctors deal with that fertility issue by using IVF through a procedure known as intracytoplasmic sperm injection (ICSI).[179] Fertility doctors use an instrument called an injecting pipette to insert the most normal-looking sperm cell available into a readied female ovum (egg). Supplied with that information, the ancient Hebrew word is *actually* translated as "and it (is) elongated". I supplied the "is" (in parentheses) as we English speakers need the word "is" to complete the concept the ancient writer wanted to get to us from across the eons.

The phenomenon of *bioluminescence* is again written about in this verse. How do, or how *would*, I know that it's *that* kind of light and not, say, sunlight? Fair question. First, *sun*light isn't in context here. The ancient text isn't about the yellow dwarf star around which our planet revolves. It's about DNA-editing and manipulation. Second, the spelling of the word in the ancient text provides its own major clues as to why it's not about what is generally thought of as *light*.

It's about context, as my father had often lectured me. At the top of his lecture lists were ones about intricacies of theology *and* semantics—a fitting combination—as *semantics* could be said to be *the science of meanings*. At about 12, I was trying to pay close attention in church to the words of the plainsong chant *Agnus Dei*—Lamb of God. What I heard took my breath away: "Oh Lamb of God that takest away the sense of the word, have mercy upon us." Dumbstruck, I thought, *If God takes away the sense of the word then God must give the sense of the word. Dad is right—it IS all about semantics.*

I thought I had come into full realization of the relationship between God and what words mean—or don't mean. The following week as I was again paying close attention to the chanted words of the *Agnus Dei,* I felt a sinking feeling in the pit of my stomach when I heard, "O Lamb of God that takest away the sins of the world, have mercy upon us." I thought, *Well—so it's about taking away the sins of the world. But still—it* IS *all about semantics.* That revelation, even if personal, made it possible for me to approach a sacred text many thousands of years old where its meaning had been settled for at least 2,100 years and look at it from the aspect of "What *is* the science of the meanings of its words?"

The words at this place in traditional Bibles are "to give light (upon the earth)."[180] So, *what is* derived from the science of the meaning of the ancient Hebrew word[181] behind "to give light"? Again: it's not *rocket science.* The equivalent Biblical Hebrew word[182] is five letters long. It has two one-letter prefixes. The first letter can be translated as "in regard to". In all fairness, it can also be translated as "to" *or* "toward". The second letter is generally always translated as "the". The root word in the word in the text here is supposed to be the word for light—*ăōōr.*[183] But in the text it appears as *ăēr.*[184] What I first noticed is that the middle letter of the three-letter root word had been swapped for another letter.[185]

With my extensive list of Hebrew words where those same letters are swapped in words throughout the biblical text, I was able to observe that such a letter swap *signaled* to the reader that the usual meaning of the word is being changed. Its change, *in context*, is from *light* to *bioluminescence.* The *re*translated word then became *in regard to bioluminescence.*

The next traditional word after "to give light" is "upon"—as in "upon the earth".[186] The ancient Hebrew word from which "upon" is wretched is a two-letter word.[187] There is a Strong's Number that reveals its meaning.[188] (Does it matter that it's Strong's H5923?) It has a two-word definition—"a yoke". Even though this word has been previously explained, in dealing with such a radical translation of the Hebrew text it is worth going over again. The "yoke" refers to the fastening framework of the phosphate-deoxyribose *yoke* holding together the other nucleotides of the DNA double helix molecular structure.[189]

Here, the word "yoke" requires a slight change in the translation of the previous words "in regard to the bioluminescence" to "in regard to the bioluminescent *yoke*". Of course, in translation, in order to make that word understandable, an explanation would have to be added in brackets—*as a phosphate-deoxyribose fastening framework yoking the double helix structure together.* Yes, the added explanation is my own; but that's an explanation *in context. Giving light upon* is not in context.

As I approached the 18th verse I could see that it wouldn't take a quantum mechanic to figure out what was going on behind the two-millennially parroted narrative of "light" ruling over the day and over the night. Those phrases had already been solved for what is actually going on inside the verse.

In that verse I again encountered "the light"—as per the traditional story, "to divide the light from the darkness".[193] To my surprise, in this instance, the Hebrew word behind "the light" *was* the word for "light"; and it had the proper prefix for "the". The context for that light, however, is light *as* bioluminescence.

The Hebrew word behind "and to divide"[194] turns out to be "and in regard to the differentiation".[195] The traditional word "from"[196] may be defined (just by looking it up in a standard Hebrew dictionary) as "to distinguish".[197] The traditional words "the darkness"[198] are actually (again—just by looking up the Hebrew word) "withholding light".[199] The context of *absence of light* is that the literal absence of bioluminescence is associated with an organism that is no longer living. What these examples show is that sometimes there is a relationship between the falsified narrative we are all familiar with and the actual narrative that we all must become familiar with.

The Beings Turn Their Attention to Raw Sex

Earlier I explained how I dealt with the aliens' "mission statement" of *interbreeding* and *research.* That exact concept is how the one-sentence 19th verse begins. Here's the idyllic passage—"And the evening and the morning were the fourth day."[200]

My own research into the Hebrew word behind "the fourth"[201] informed me as to the part of *interbreeding* the alien beings were writing about. I already had the word "day" as "it-and-them"; but did not immediately suspect *sex*—at least not until I simply read the definitions of the Hebrew word behind "fourth".[202]

Does it matter what the Hebrew word in the text is? Probably not—but in transliterated *ancient* Hebrew it's *rĕb·ē·ō·ē.* (In Biblical Hebrew it's *rĕb·ēē·ēē.*[203]) I looked up the Strong's Number associated with the Hebrew word (H7243). What's there is "fourth"; but what's also there is a reference to the word's root word. I looked at the *Strong's Hebrew Dictionary* definition of the given root word. It says that it's a root identified with H7251 through the idea of sprawling "at all fours". *So, that's,* I ask myself, *actually what's supposed to convey the numeric idea of "fourth"?* All I had to do to gain enlightenment on the matter was to look back one Strong's Number entry (to H7250) to be able to read, "to squat or lie out flat, that is, in copulation."[204] *Now,* I thought, *we're getting somewhere.*

The ancient Hebrew root word is *rĕbō.*[205] That word is used three times in the Bible's book of Leviticus[206]—and each time in the context of copulation. Again, the *semantics* wordsmith in me couldn't help but notice that the ancient word in the text has a common "inserted" letter placed into the root word.[207] That's where *rĕb·ē·ō* fits into the word *rĕb·ē·ō·ē.* As I already knew, an inserted letter (like the one in the word in the text) can change the meaning of a word—sometimes to an adjective, sometimes to past tense, sometimes to an "-ing" word. Sometimes, it changes it to a closely related concept—as from a noun, "copulation", to a verb, "copulate".

The word *rĕb·ē·ō·ē* has a suffix. Its common suffix denotes our words "me" or "my".[208] In translation we wouldn't say "copulate my" or "my copulate"; we would use our word "I"—as "I copulate". When the translated words "it-and-them" are tacked on the full "mission statement" about *interbreeding* and *research* in *this part of the narrative*, it is: *to interbreed; and it is to research it-and-them.* The word *rĕb·ē·ō·ē* follows. I translated it as "I will copulate."

As I approached the 20th verse, I read (as easily as you can, too), "Let the waters bring forth abundantly."[209] Already knowing that "waters" was going to be "semen"[210] in some form, I was almost giddy with excitement about what the one Hebrew word behind the English "let bring forth abundantly"[211] would reveal.

The memory of my father's often recited naughty limericks helped me get in touch with my *inner adolescent.* They were invariably crude and sexist; but the ability to handle really off-the-wall crude sexuality is a critical ability for taking on the out-of-the-box research into the science of word meanings in this ancient Hebrew text. So critical was that ability that without it, we might not today have the benefit of what the ancient biblical text *actually* says.

As I read this verse's opening phrases (in Hebrew), I could see that one Hebrew word was behind the (fake) English phrase "let bring forth abundantly"[212], and another one behind "the waters". [213] Behind that first phrase is a five-letter Hebrew word. It has a prefix, the pronoun "it".[214] It has a suffix, the pronoun "him".[215] The root word has nothing at all to do with abundance. The basic definition is two words: "to wriggle".[216]

The only thing that came to mind was that this was the ancient text's way of referring to the spasmodic muscular contractions associated with ejaculatory orgasm. The translation of the Hebrew word simply fell into place: "it wriggles him". That out of the way, the next word to take on was the word behind "the waters".

The question then becomes, *What is it that wriggles him*? There's also the question, *Who is it that wriggles*? My answer to that question was the text's own answer—an alien being referred to by the handle (or assumed name) "I-Copulate". So, what wriggles him? From previous work here the immediate answer is *the semen*[217]—but more particularly, or should we say, more correctly—the release of *the semen*. To translate that meaning is only as tricky as knowing that to release semen is to ejaculate; and that the noun form of "ejaculate" is simply the same word, but with the accent on the word's second syllable, as ē·jac′·ū·lăt. Thus, the *re*translation of "the waters" is "the ejaculate"; and thus, *in actual context*, the answer to what it is that wriggles him.

The KJV English word that follows is "the moving"—as in "the moving creature that hath life."[218] I could hardly contain my inner teens' sense of male adolescent humor when I realized that the Hebrew word behind "the moving"[219] was the same root word behind "let bring forth abundantly". That would be just the one word, "wriggle".

The King James Bible English word that follows "the moving" is "creature". The dictionary definition of the Hebrew word is "to breathe, to breathe upon," *and* "to be refreshed".[220] To translate I simply used the present tense of "to be refreshed"—as "refresh".

The King James Bible English words that follow are "that hath life."[221] The Hebrew word behind it is a three-letter root word[222]; and it means "to live, to revive", *or* "to be vigorous".[223] To translate, I simply used the word "revive".

The English words that follow are "and fowl that may fly."[224] I wondered, *What could fowl that may be flying be about?* I was on the lookout for definitions that would have, *or could have*, a sexual context. The first thing that struck me was that the Hebrew word generally used for the concept of *birds* is a different word altogether.[225] The word in the text is a four-letter word.[226] It has the common prefix "and". Looking at its Strong's Number definition, I saw the words "a bird".[227] *Ah*, but this word *fowl* is a homonym—that is, a word that is spelled the same or pronounced the same, but has a different meaning (in context, of course). Another meaning, one Strong's Number entry away, is "to faint".[228] I could have left it at that. But I was not after the *art* of word meanings but the *science* of word meanings—*semantics in its truest sense*.

There's a standard reference[229] that gives the root word (or root words) for any Hebrew word in the Hebrew Bible. The three-letter Hebrew root word in the ancient text[230, 231] is one letter off (by observation) from the actual root word.[232] That word has a more descriptive definition when looked up by its own Strong's Number. Its meaning is "languid, faint" *and* "weary".[233] Well, "faint" and "weary" are synonyms. And to be languid is to be "exhausted." I had my translation: "and exhausted".

It didn't take long to realize the sexual connection. Don't we all know that in the aftermath of sexual relations there is, or can be, a sense of feeling faint, or weary, or exhausted, or simply spent? The E.T.s were simply making some *real-life* observations. The thing that most struck me at this point was the vast distance between the high-sounding words of the traditional (false) rendition and the raw, earthy narration of the actual Hebrew words when allowed to say what they have been waiting patiently to say for millennia.

Onto the rest of the ancient story. The Genesis story's traditional words bring us God creating *great whales*[234] in its 21st verse. By the time I got to *that* verse I highly suspected that no such creating was going on. The Genesis story's actual first phrase revealed the meaning of *create* as "cut". The context is *cutting* off or adding snippets of DNA at the places where the alien beings deemed most expedient for their project. So, what did the aliens cut? To find out, I just wrote out the Hebrew words in the order in which they appear in the Hebrew Bible. The word behind "whales" appears first, and then the word behind "great".

The Hebrew word behind "whales " is a six-letter word.[235] After writing it down in the letters of ancient Hebrew, I could clearly see that the word had a prefix "the "; a never-used three-letter root word[236] with a commonly inserted *meaning-changing* letter[237]; and a common suffix "them".[238] The Strong's Number definition associated with the Hebrew word here means "a marine or land monster."[239] But Dr. Strong provides a strong clue of another, and more accurate, meaning. His definition includes the information that word is from the same root as one other of his famous numbers.[240] The meaning of that other (though same) root word is "to elongate".[241] When Professor Benjamin Davidson was consulted to weigh in on the matter, he wrote that the root word meant "stretching out or extending".[242] That seemed to settle things. I had my translation—"the elongated them". What was referred to as *them* would be revealed by the translation of the word that followed in the text.

The Hebrew word[243] that follows is traditionally taken for the late King James' English word "great"[244]—as in "great whales". But to translate accurately, each Hebrew word in succession must be scrupulously and scientifically examined. The Hebrew word here has the common prefix "the "; a three-letter root word (not "great" at all) as a concept seen before here as "to twist."[245, 246] It had a common two-letter suffix that pluralizes a word.[247]

The most apt translation, then, is "the twists". When put together with the previous translated word "the elongated them", I could readily see that the "them" referred to "the twists "—so, the word "them " didn't really have to be translated; neither did the word "the". The translated concept that came to mind was "the Elongated Twists". That's the alien beings' accurate description of an elongated DNA molecular structure.

The 21st verse is a long one. What did the beings do with, or *to*, the Elongated Twists (a.k.a., *DNA*)? Their two-letter variable descriptor word *ăht* informs that they cut it, presumably using their version (or analog) of the DNA-editing technique that today's scientists use—CRISPR. They also used IVF, by way of their use of the same two-letter variable descriptor word (*ăht*). What were they attempting to do using both scientific techniques? Most likely, I thought, doing what was about to be revealed by the Hebrew words behind the English words "every living creature"[248]—or rather, the words placed in the order in which the Hebrew words appear as "every creature living".

When I found the definition of the two-letter Hebrew word[249] supposedly translated as "every" or "all",[250] I found that it is derived from a similarly spelled root word that means "to complete" or "to make perfect".[251] *That's* the translation I settled upon—"to make perfect". The next and obvious question is "To make perfect *what*?"

Whenever the word "obvious" comes up, I am almost always reminded, simply by the word itself, of one of my father's workhorse quips whenever I grasped something that to him seemed perfectly obvious. His words still ring in my ears today: "You have an amazing grasp of the obvious." What was yesterday's *put-down* is today's translational practical necessity.

It was also quite apparent that the word "creature" in this verse was the same fake English front-word for "creature" in the previous verse. The Hebrew word, in translation here, is "refresh". The not-so-obvious answer, then, to the obvious question, is to make perfect "refresh". It's fair to ask, "What is *refresh*?"

"Refresh" must have been employed here as a metaphor for the act of copulation in the target species—the genetically engineered bipedal hominids. The hybrids are being engineered to replicate themselves through the observed act of what the aliens termed "refresh". We call that "sexual intercourse"—or just *having sex*.

Our English word "living" is from the same Hebrew root word as the word behind "that hath life" in the previous verse. The only difference is that the word here has the common prefix "the" on it—giving us "the revive".[252] The revive? Well, in context, that too is one of the alien beings' euphemisms for *copulative relations*—or *having sex.* We all can understand that.

So, what's going on here? The beings had figured out how to *jury-rig* (manipulate) our hominid ancestors' DNA so that a male hominid hybrid and a female hominid hybrid could reproduce themselves through sexual intercourse—which the aliens call "refresh" and "the revive". Perhaps so that we today do not miss the point, it is made by two different words in succession.

In the fake translation, what do "the living creatures" do? By simply reading the next word we see what they are able to do: "that moveth".[253] I wrote down, in the ancient Hebrew letters, the word associated with "that moveth".[254] It is the root word *rĕmĕsh.*[255] That word, in its context here, is not a verb. It is a noun.[256] It has the common prefix "the" and a common suffix (what I term an exclamatory emphatic)—our exclamation point.

As I referred to the Strong's dictionary definition associated with the Hebrew word, I could readily grasp where the fake word "moveth" came from, as the word's meaning is given as "to glide swiftly". I could *also* obviously grasp that the following entry[257] (with the same spelling) is given as "a reptile".

I knew enough from reading and researching about other people's ideas about *what kind* of aliens are "out there" to know that there was a type (or species) known as "Reptilians". Talk about a sinking feeling in one's stomach. I said to myself, *People are going to flip out. They're going to pull their hair out by the roots.* I cannot say that I didn't think, for at least seconds, about destroying my work and abandoning the retranslation project altogether. To me, the thing was, I knew *too* much. And, I thought, if such creatures *are* behind our becoming wise humans (*homo sapiens*) then the damn truth had to get out one way or the other—*as it is said*, though the heavens may fall.

The English word that follows the translated "the reptile" is our word "which"—as in "which the waters brought forth *abundantly.*"[258] Before tackling "which" there wasn't any difficulty recalling that when the phrase "brought forth abundantly" previously appeared, the actual translation was "it wriggles him". In the word that appears at this place there is no prefix. There is only the root word "wriggles" and the common pronoun suffix for "it". That translation was easily nailed. The word "which", however, appeared to be a more difficult nut to crack.

In traditional translation, "which" from the Hebrew word *ăshĭr*[259] is a very versatile pronoun. When looked up there is a long laundry list of English words used to convey its meaning.[260] I wrote down the word using the ancient letters.[261] If using our English letters, the word would appear as *AShR*. I stared at the ancient Hebrew letters waiting for some flash of insight—which was supposed to come out of my years of compiling lists of Hebrew words into something that we would today call *grammar*.

In the course of minutes I could visualize the word *AShR* morph into *A ShRaH*—which was *AShR* with the common pronoun prefix for our word "I". There was a three-letter root word (*ShRaH—shĭn-rĕsh-hāy*), but with its third letter dropped from the text—a very common thing to see in the written Hebrew biblical text. Looking up the root word *shirah* (by its Biblical Hebrew spelling) in *The Analytical Hebrew and Chaldee Lexicon,*[262] I read the wide range of meanings offered there. Such as "contend, wrestle, to be a prince with, to prevail, to loose, *and* to set free."[263] There was another offered—"dwell".[264] Professor Davidson even gave a scriptural citation for that definition.[265, 266] That word[267] seemed to be more in context than the other ones listed. What's more, I could see the outlines of a double meaning in a translated assumed name, "I Dwell". Why be coy about it? I could see the double pun of some alien being—and now, per the biblical text itself—a reptilian (presumably a bipedal reptilian hominid as opposed to a bipedal mammalian hominid like our ancestors) *dwelling* inside a female hominid through *copulation* and dwelling inside manipulated DNA that contained snippets of its own DNA.

It wasn't a great feat of translation to put the previous two translated words together as "I Dwell wriggles it." Nor did it take great speculative power to imagine what *it* referred to—especially since the Hebrew word that followed had been very recently seen as "the waters" and retranslated as "the ejaculate". That sealed it. Of course, there's a bit more to the verse; but

I'm certain that the more-like-this doesn't need to be any more spelled-out than it is already.

What I was able to take away from that verse was that the alien Reptilians had perfected the ability of their hybrid to pass along their modified DNA through their own copulation. Another takeaway was that the reptile, *or Reptilian*, going by the handle "I Dwell" became a sperm donor for their IVF project—which they regarded as a form of successful copulation. The final takeaway from the verse was that they saw their technical solutions to their technical problems as being "good". *That* should ring some bells.[268]

The central visual concept conveyed by the traditional reading of the 22nd verse is that of multiplying and filling the earth. So, it is in this *re*translation. But in the actual translation it is the hybrid hominids who are doing the multiplying and filling *after* the Reptilian beings perfect their DNA-modifications and their IVF technique *so that* the hybrid hominids will *self-reproduce* through *copulation*. The punch line is delivered behind the fake words "in the earth".[269] How? The Hebrew word given for "earth" is *AReTz*.[270] I revisualized it as *A ReTzaH*.[271] That reading gave a different root word (not "earth"). The actual root word means "accomplish".[272] The *punch line* of the detailed description of the aliens' hybridization project becomes "in I-Accomplish". In other words, Reptilian alien Dr. "I Dwell" is taking credit for the completed and perfected accomplishment.

In the 24th verse, the central visual concept of the traditional reading is of "bringing forth the living creature after his kind."[273] Specified are "cattle", "the creeping thing", and "beast of the earth".[274] I suspected that something similar to the translation of previous verses might be happening in *re*translation of this verse. A close inspection of the Hebrew word behind "Let bring forth"[275] begins to confirm that suspicion.

It didn't take long to ponder on Dr. Strong's meaning of the Hebrew word in the text—"to go out" or "to bring out".[276] It didn't take long to observe that the Hebrew word had on it the prefix associated (in this present work) with our exclamation point. *This* Hebrew word did not have to be retranslated. Under scrutiny it could translate into English as "bring forth"—practically the same as in the traditional story.

Then there's the already solved matter of "the earth". In retranslation, that's "the I Accomplish". Putting the Hebrew words together for this translation gave "Bring forth the . . . ." Context being everything, it was necessary to tweak the words "I-Accomplish" to a noun form, "the Accomplisher." And what does "the I Accomplisher" accomplish? Well, since the Reptilians are talking *sexuality*, they're talking about "refresh" and "revive." And how are we to know when refresh and revive happen? The Hebrew word behind the fake word "cattle"[277] answers that question.

Sure, I looked up the meaning of the Hebrew word given by tradition as being behind "cattle". Not surprisingly, it's "a dumb beast—cattle."[278] But this is a scientific treatment—a treatment never attempted before with an ancient text considered by some as "God breathed". Who's going to mess with *that*?

I'll tell you who: a *preacher's kid* sufficiently self-taught in these ancient languages to observe that the Hebrew word given for "cattle" had on it a common prefix meaning "in".[279] Once that prefix is admitted into evidence we see a completely different root word. The "new" root word, *hāmĕăh,* means "to make a loud sound."[280] Dr. Strong lists some appropriate synonyms: "tumult", "rage", "clamor", and "moan".[281] That's the word choice here: "moan"—as in "in loud moaning". My memory of hot passionate sex is not so impaired as to have forgotten the relationship between in loud moaning and what goes on in passionate, uh, *copulation*. That descriptor, "in loud moaning", is but another of the beings' prescient observations about what is associated with the act of copulation—and another of their euphemisms for it.

In the middle of the 25th verse there is yet another reference to ICSI via an injecting pipette by way of the often used word *ăht.*[282] The word that follows is one already seen—the translation of which is "to make perfect".[283] The word that follows is the Hebrew word *remesh*[284]—which could have been left as "remesh"—or translated as "reptile". *So, here they are again.*

The wording that follows, in the familiar English, is *"upon the earth"*.[285] But the spelling of the Hebrew word easily shows that there is no "earth" there, but there is a familiar name inside the word—*ADAM.*[286] The traditional “translators” going back 2,100 years took great liberties with that word—just as they had with practically every word in the entire Genesis document. Be that as it may, another spoiler alert is that we will not be encountering anyone named “Adam”.

As I approached the scientific dissection of the Hebrew word I could see, at a glance, that it was a five-letter word with one obvious common prefix—”the”.[287] It had an *apparent* root word, *ă·dăm* (not *Adam*). It had an obvious suffix—one that could feminize the word[288] *or* denote that the word is in what I have come to refer to, as adapted from Professor Benjamin Davidson’s Lexicon[289] its “absolute state”.

That *absolute state* is less about science than it is about license—a judgment call regarding exactly how the word should be translated. I wrote the word *ă·dăm* out in the ancient alphabet [𐤌𐤃𐤀] and stared at it. What I saw was the syllable “*ă*” [𐤀] as another common prefix on the word in the text,[290] making the word’s second prefix our pronoun *I*.[291] What was left was a two-letter root word [𐤌𐤃] *dăm*. It has one meaning: “blood”.[292] The only thing left to puzzle out was *“What’s the absolute state of ‘the I-Blood’?”*

After staring at the word some minutes more, it came to me that its *absolute state* is in having been *genetically engineered*. I put the translated elements of the word together: “the genetically engineered I-Blood”. I capitalized the word “blood” as *that’s* the first name designation that the beings, *the Reptilian aliens*, give to their hominid-alien hybrid—because it contained *their* blood. . .in the form of their DNA. That’s not the complete picture of the 25th verse; but I think you get *enough* of the picture. I got more than enough of the picture—even after having translated the rest of the verse.

At this point in retranslating the Genesis story in the way the story’s actual authors wrote it, I was wracked with two conflicting thoughts. The first was to apologize for what the text was saying. The second was to take the attitude, “*Hey—you believed the Bible yesterday when you agreed with what it said, and now that you know what it says, you don’t want to believe it anymore? What’s up with that?*”

Bombshell Alert: Here's Where Man Was "Made"

From the get-go of the 26th verse I knew, as if I didn't already, that this was going to be a *bombshell* of a translation. Even though you may know it *by heart*, for the convenience of those who do not, in King James English that verse begins "And God said, Let us make man in our image, after our likeness."[293] From the translation get-go I knew that the word "God" was not a reference to any *uber-deity*, but to what should be called either "aliens", "strange biological beings", "Extra-Terrestrials", or, to use our government's own designation, "Extra-Terrestrial Biological Entities"—in their lingo, "E-BEn's." (Don't believe me? Do your own internet search on that acronym. You'll get *a bunch* of hits.)

As I plodded along, I translated the Hebrew behind the traditional "said" to our word "declared". Next up was "Let us make". The Hebrew word there is four letters[294]—the first of which is a common prefix that can make the word "reflexive"—or something that one does to one's self. (As in, *We did it to ourselves.* Or, *Sometimes I crack myself up.*) The word's three-letter root word is a common workhorse word *ōshăh.* A Hebrew dictionary will tell us that it is used "in the broadest sense and widest application". I used the software that I had so I could locate every instance where the word had been used in the Hebrew Bible. I found *one* instance where it had been traditionally translated as "accomplish".[295] Since the text's author (or authors) themselves had already put the word "accomplish" into use, I thought that its use, in place of the word "made" was a fitting and judicious translation—as "ourselves accomplish".

Accomplish what? "Man" of course. I'd seen the Hebrew word here before—as "earth"[296] in the previous verse—as *ă·dăm·ăh.* The translation fell right into place as "I-Blood".[297] The Reptilian beings declared that they, themselves, would accomplish the "I-Blood"—a hybrid being with their blood (as DNA) in it.

The traditional words that follow are "in our image".[298] The plural "our" in the traditional scripture must have given more than one theologian indigestion. But right off the bat I could see that's what is there—the proper (and common) pronoun suffix for "our".[299] I could have left the traditional words "in our image" as they were—for the definition of the Hebrew root word here is "phantom, illusion, resemblance, idol", or "image".[300] But I wanted to know more about that English word "image".

My preferred English dictionary was published in 1946.[301] No politically correct definitions there. From it I learned that the word "image"[302] is from the Latin word *imitari*—referring to "an imitation or a likeness". That word "likeness" is the word I chose to translate the Hebrew root word here. The word in the text[303] had a common prefix meaning "in". Fair enough, as that is reflected in the traditional translation. Put together, the Hebrew word means "in our likeness". I assumed that wasn't too much of a stretch—as I assumed that the E.T. beings were *bipedal reptilian hominids* in a similar way that we are *bipedal mammalian hominids*.

The traditional English words that follow are "after our likeness".[304] After having just used the word "likeness", I was anxious to get to the bottom of the Hebrew word.[305] To dive into the word, I began with the word's prefix—another common prefix that means "*like, as, or in respect to*".[306] The seven-letter Hebrew word then had a two-letter root word—"blood".[307] It sported two two-letter suffixes. The first suffix I recognized from my hundred-page searchable database in which I had long lists of Hebrew words that illustrated quite plainly (and sometimes exhaustively) the actual grammar of this ancient language. The first suffix[308] meant "as-related-to". The second quite-common suffix means "us".[309] Putting the elements of the word together I wrote down "in respect to blood as related to us". That's sufficiently plain and stark. But there you have it: from the Bible itself.

The phrase that follows in the verse has been the bane, and literally, "the living end", of multiples of the earth's animal and plant species—as we human beings are supposedly to have been given dominion—over "fish of the sea, fowl of the air, and over the cattle, and over the earth."[310] Here, I'll simply share the actual translation of "and let them have dominion" because it represents yet another deliberate mistranslation of biblical proportion.

The Hebrew word[311] there is but five letters. It has the common prefix "and"; and a common pronoun suffix "him".[312] At first sight I could see that the word "did not" have the common pronoun suffix for "them".[313] Its three-letter root word means "to subjugate".[314] Putting the elements together gives "and subjugate him". Again—I had that sinking feeling in my stomach: The "him" in that word refers to "*him*"—the hybrid being. That "him" refers to "us"—the living hybrid's progeny and descendants.

That picture was all I needed to have, even though I went on to translate the rest of the verse—and indeed, the rest of the first Genesis chapter. It's also probably all you need to have.

As I reflected on the verse, as well as all that came before it in this heavens-falling translation, I couldn't help but think about the practical necessities that the ancient interpreters who put the ancient Hebrew document, their Torah, into the Greek of that day—some 22 centuries ago. They had to transcribe the ancient Hebrew writing (which had existed for at least a thousand years by the time they started working on their "translation") into a completely different alphabet—known then as the alphabet of the Aramaen dialect of the Babylonian Empire.[315] Today, we know that alphabet as *modern Hebrew*. They had to have spent months or years on this first section of "Genesis"—coming up with creative ways to shoehorn the actual narrative into the narrative that we know so well today. They used the Greek language and the Greek alphabet to, in effect, launder the actual narrative of the text into their contrived narrative in Greek.

The total effect was that their handiwork could not be detected by anyone anywhere unless some "someone" had specific and intimate knowledge of the alphabet and structure of all three languages—ancient Hebrew; its usurper language, "Biblical" Hebrew; and ancient Greek. I'm forgetting some other practical necessities that *the someone* somewhere would have needed—*or needs*—to detect *and* decipher the ancient translational fraud. That would be a *fourth* language, like, say, English with which to sort out the elements and meanings of those three ancient languages, standard references that define words, some rapid-fast software with which to do searches of any word in the English or Hebrew Bibles, a scientific background with which to be able to see and describe the science behind the ancient words, and tempered-steel motivation to take on the Bible's Genesis story.

Within 200 years of rendering the ancient Hebrew biblical text into Greek, ancient rabbis devised a complex system of tiny markings to be put under their recently minted Hebrew alphabet. The net effect was that no one, other than rabbis trained in their system, could even read the plain scriptural text. From the time of the publication of their finished product (the Greek Septuagint[316]) virtually every translation into any other language is a translation—not of the actual Hebrew—but of the actual Greek-language-laundered narrative text. As I reflected on all of those things I could hear the voice of an old high school friend taunting me, "*Don't sugar-coat it. Tell us how you really feel.*" I could also hear in my mind's ear the famous dictum—paraphrased as "Tell the truth though the heavens may fall."

Caution—Heavens Falling

As I approached the 30th verse I was struck by the seeming repetition of phrases and words. This will sound (or read) familiar: "And to every beast of the earth, and to every fowl of the air, to every thing that creepeth upon the earth, wherein there is life, I have given every green herb for meat; and it was so."[317] Behind each of these English words is a Hebrew word that has been creatively altered to be the very words so familiar to us. They were initially altered to be those familiar words—first through the medium of the Greek language and then diligently and dutifully translated—that is, *actually* translated—into other languages from there. First, into Latin—for the ancient Latin Vulgate[318] tells the same Genesis story as the ancient Greek *rendition*. Every Bible translated into English tells the same Genesis story as is told in the Greek *rendition* and in its translation into Latin.

By the time I arrived at that verse, I had a searchable database in my word-processing program with which I could easily and quickly find, and translate, the Hebrew words in the ancient text. The English words "and to every" are the fractured front-words for a four-letter Hebrew word[319] with two common prefixes: "and" plus "in regard to". It has a two-letter abbreviated root word.[320] It can mean "whole". That's how the word "every" is supposed to have been derived. But the two-letter abbreviation may also be read as the three-letter root word from which it is derived. That word means "complete" (or "to make perfect").[321] That phrase appears three times in short order in the verse. It actually says, "and in regard to complete".

Complete what? Exactly. The *complete what* is provided by the Hebrew word [*khēt*[322]] from which the front-word "beast" is supposed to have been identified. That word had appeared in the 25th verse. I looked up the word again. Here's what I read: "alive, life, raw (flesh)".[323] It's only "beast" because the ancient original crew who laundered the language into Greek needed a beast to complete their false narrative.

This is a great place to illustrate how the language flimflam was pulled off. The Hebrew word *khē*[324] (alive) was carried over into Greek as the word *theriois* (θηρίοις[325]). That means "wild beasts".[326] There's your beast.

Complete what? "In regard to complete Alive." In other words: "In regard to (the DNA-manipulated hybrid) being completely alive." I thought, *That's what the phrase is actually trying to say*. The next appearance of that same phrase offers (as the E.T.-beings' answer to "*complete what?*") in the Hebrew word behind the English (fraudently translated) word "fowl."

My word-processing database easily brought up "fowl" in the 20th verse. There, my translation of the Hebrew word behind "fowl" was "exhausted". I recalled that is one of the Reptilian beings' euphemisms for copulation. When putting the phrase "And in regard to complete" with "exhausted", I knew that the word had to be altered slightly—to *exhaustion*—to make the concept work in English. We could just as easily say that they said "In regard to complete copulation." In other words, not to put too fine a point on it, the "in regard to the DNA-manipulated hybrid being completely alive was because of complete copulation, after which the being who had been copulating was completely exhausted."

The third time the same phrase appeared in that verse I could see that the familiar "that creepeth" followed. The actual Hebrew word[327] there looked very similar to "reptile".[328] Except in this instance the word for reptile (*rĕmĕsh*) had a commonly *inserted letter* that would modify its pronunciation (to *rōōmĕsh*) and also its meaning. A short examination of the context led me to conclude that the modification was to make the word a collective noun in its possessive form—as "*reptilian*". *There it is,* I thought; *they are telling us exactly what, and who, they are*. As for wanting to know the truth—no, I was not happy now.

The English word that followed is "upon". The Hebrew word behind that word is a two-letter word meaning "yoke". It is the ancient writer's word for the fastening framework of the phosphate-deoxyribose "yoke" of the nucleotides of the DNA molecule.

The English word that followed is "wherein". The Hebrew word there is *ăshĭr*, a contraction of *ă•shĭrăh,* which means "I dwell"—which I changed to "I Dwell"—as that is the handle (or name) adapted by the lead Reptilian scientist in charge of their hybridization project. The punchline (to follow) of his handle (or name) being there was obscured behind the falsely translated words, "there is"—as in "wherein there is life".

The real significance and practical value of having studied a language (like all this Hebrew stuff) is in learning, over time, to recognize basic elements critical to understanding even its basic concepts. The two-letter Hebrew word[332] behind "there is" is *bōō*. I knew that the first letter gives the sound of the letter *B* and the second letter gives the sound of "oo" as in "boo" or "moon". I couldn't find that word in Strong's dictionary. That's because the word consists of two different elements of basic Hebrew grammar. The first letter is a common prefix for "in." The second letter is a common suffix for the pronoun him or it—and rarely, her.

Putting together their references to *copulation* didn't take an Einstein to see that the Reptilian genetic scientist "I Dwell" was using his adopted name as a play on words to convey to all future readers that he was *inside* a her—a female bipedal hominid—one of our own ancient ancestors.

How do we know that he was *copulating* with her? His story tells us so. The English word that follows is "life." That word had already presented itself earlier as "refresh"—another of the Reptilian's euphemisms for. . .*copulation*.

So that we *do not* again miss the point, the properly translated word that follows is "revive"—yet another euphemism for *copulation*. It is now not hidden behind any English word. The Hebrew word (*khēăh*) was simply ignored by King James' faux-translators.

But that word was *not* ignored by the ancient interpreters when they did their Greek-language laundering thing. I wanted to be as thorough as possible, so I read in the Greek Septuagint—that is supposedly the Hebrew Bible in Greek. There, the Greek phrase (in translation) is "which has in itself breath of life."[333] The Hebrew word *nōōpfāsh*[334] (refresh) was taken into

Greek as "breath"[335] [(φυχην) *psuchen*]. The Hebrew word *khēăh*[336] (revive) was taken into Greek as "of life"[337,338] [(ζωης) *zoes*]. What I was thinking was, *People are going to pull their hair out by the roots*. I also thought, *But this is what the biblical text says—what it actually says. Either we want to know the truth of things—or we don't.*

As I read into the second chapter of the Genesis story—even in English—it seems apparent that the first chapter's story goes on for three additional verses. The third verse of the second chapter is actually the last verse of the first chapter's original story. The final words of that verse are . . . "*God created and made*".[339] I was fully stoked for this last phrase.

Of course, the word "God" couldn't be "God". My scientific inquiry into each Hebrew word had proven that. What we are dealing with are "strange biological entities" who identify themselves as *Reptilians*.

As I took note that the Hebrew word fronted as "created" came before the word for "aliens/strange biological entities". Looking up the Hebrew word there (*bĕră*)[340] gives the meanings "create, form, fashion, cut", or "cut down".[341, 342] The word, in context there in the biblical text, is "cut"—as they were cutting our ancient ancestors' DNA to suit the necessities of their hybridization program. Since the word "cut" came before "aliens," to bring the concept they wanted to convey into English it would need to be "cutting aliens"—that is, a specialized group of them.

I read the English words "and made".[343] I took note of the Hebrew word[344] there. It's a five-letter word with a common prefix that means "in regard to".[345] Within that word is a two-letter abbreviated root word[346] with its third letter dropped by its writer or by a later editor. The root word here is *ōshăh.*[347] It is a word used "*in the broadest sense and widest application.*" Following the spirit of *broadest sense* and *widest application*—and knowing that the context of the phrase was about "cutting", I translated that Hebrew word as "cutting". The last two letters of that five-letter word I recognized as the suffix that denotes what we would call "matters". I deduced that from my own list of multiple words with that suffix; and the concept of "as related to" was what all the various words with that suffix had in common. I reduced that concept to the one word—"matters".

With that concept, the translation fell into place: "*Cutting aliens in regard to cutting matters.*" Their cold statement of fact seemed a fitting and apt (even if as cold as a metal examination table) summation for the executive summary of alien beings' (who now we know self-identified as "Reptilians") own ancient hybridization project. I struggled then—as now—to wrap my own neurons around the enormity of it all, the horror of it all; and the effect this new knowledge will have on the world.

Let me share why, though, I have loved translating this foundational Genesis document. It is to have experienced discovering the "absolute truth" of something (the absolute truth of the genesis of our species) in this world of the absolute lie about virtually everything. The brand of translation that I have described here is something that can be done to find "truth" —however radical—inside these ancient Hebrew documents called "scripture".

This translation may seem complex. The actual true story of their hybridization program is full of detail; but is not all that complex. In the next chapter I will share what could be called a simplified version. It's what the ancient text says in English—as plainly and as simply as I am able to write it. It will relate the entirety of the beings' executive summary. This version will be particularly helpful if you do any exploration through the *researched explanations* in Chapter 7. Admittedly, my straight translation of how these beings express themselves is kind of hard to follow—even when put into what seems like plain English.

Chapter 4

What Genesis 1 Really Says— The Simplified Version

~retold to make the actual account as understandable as possible~

A very long time ago, but not as long ago as the beginning of the world itself, there was a small group of intelligent beings. Today we would call them *extraterrestrial visitors* or *aliens*. They knew all about the ways of genetic engineering that our modern scientists today have only recently discovered.

This group left a written record of what they did way back in our remote past. They didn't give us any kind of ancient time frame for when they did their genetic engineering projects. In their written record they wrote that their projects were amazing—even to them. They wrote that what they did was quite an accomplishment. They delighted in crediting themselves for what their genetic engineering project accomplished.

The intelligent beings weren't gods. They were just beings that kind of resembled us. But they were very technologically advanced while our own ancient ancestors were quite primitive. To the beings, the genetic engineering that they did on our ancestors was so amazing that they thought that who our ancestors were before their amazing DNA manipulations was no longer of any consequence whatsoever.

The DNA manipulations had the effect of putting some unspecificed restraints on the abilities of our ancient hominid ancestors. The beings thought that their DNA manipulations represented their own actual presence inside of our hybridized ancestors. The beings also figured out how to put their own DNA into the sperm of our ancient forefathers and into the eggs of our ancient foremothers.

These ancient intelligent aliens had what today is modern technology. They could place a microscopic hominid sperm cell inside of a hominid egg cell. Today we call that process in-vitro fertilization (IVF). That's done using a tiny hollow needle that has the sperm cell just inside of the needle's sharp, beveled tip. The tiny sharp needle is pushed inside of the egg cell to fertilize it. The aliens had two ways of referring to when they injected the tiny needle for fertilization. The first way was when the placement was happening right at that moment. The other way was when the placement had already happened.

The extraterrestrials thought that their idea of artificial fertilization was an especially good technical solution. They also knew the difference between artificial fertilization and their program to manipulate the way that seeds and eggs join together through a complex microscopic genetic process. They knew how to manipulate basic genetic processes so that they could accomplish whatever genetic engineering they intended.

The ancient E.T.s knew about the biochemistry of light that can be seen inside cells when using a special kind of microscope. They had that kind of high-level technology. That light inside cells is called "bioluminesce". They saw that kind of light in the molecular structure of the hominid egg and sperm cells. The beings wrote that bioluminescent light played a role in placing the kind of restraints that they wanted to place.

They also had their own name for the famous double helix molecule that we know today as "DNA". Not surprisingly, they called it the "twisting spiral". They wrote down what they intended to do with our very ancient ancestors. They intended to do all kinds of high-tech research about how they could interbreed with our ancestors. After their research was finished, they intended to use the knowledge to interbreed with our ancient ancestors.

The ancient E.T.s even wrote about some of their own high-tech problems that they discovered during their research about their breeding with our ancient ancestors. One huge problem was that they discovered that they could not get our female ancient ancestors pregnant. A second problem was that they found that our female ancient ancestors' egg cells rejected the beings' own sperm cells because they were, well—alien.

Some of the beings made up names for themselves for their ancient written records. One E.T. being whose "real" name wasn't mentioned wrote that he came up with high-tech solutions to the problems discovered through their research. One high-tech solution was IVF to help the beings with their own problem of low sperm concentration. The other high-tech solution had to do with manipulating our ancestors' DNA.

It might be surprising to know that the beings themselves were surprised and amazed that they couldn't get our female ancient ancestors pregnant. They were so amazed that they doubled down on their research efforts. They again wrote that they intended to do all kinds of high-tech research about the hominid egg and sperm cells. They still intended, after their research was finished, to use the knowledge to interbreed with those ancient ancestors of ours. The ancient beings wrote down that they were eventually able to place one of their own sperm cells inside the tiny hollow needle and then inside the egg cell of an ancient female ancestor. They were quite proud of themselves. They were very self-congratulatory.

The ancient E.T.s must have had some kind of Prime Directive like the one on our own *Star Trek* television series—because they knew they were violating the Prime Directive against interfering with the beings on less-developed planets. After admitting that they knew what they were doing might be shameful, they wrote down that their written account of their program of genetic engineering on our ancient forefathers (and foremothers) was true.

They knew that they had violated some kind of Prime Directive, but their attitude was, *So what?* It didn't matter to them because they had great success with their high-tech methods. They even went on to brag about what they had successfully done.

They were able to manufacture a genetically manipulated sperm cell made with their own alien genetic information and the genetic information from one of our ancient male ancestors. Then they successfully placed that altered combination sperm cell inside of a genetically altered egg cell of an ancient ancestral female.

They wrote down another catchy name for their big accomplishment. The ancient E.T. scientist who had the largest role in their ancient genetic manipulations wanted everyone who read their executive summary to know that *he* was their *go-to guy*. He called their (or *his*) accomplishment the "I Accomplish."

The prideful beings are so extremely proud of their own sperm that they write what color it is: green. (That's the color of crocodile sperm. Surprise. Surprise.) They again write that they solved the problem of low sperm concentration. They again write that what they're writing is true.

Did you get the part about the beings being proud of their own green sperm? They're so proud that they call their own sperm the "I Accomplish." They're so proud that they again write that they solved the technical problem of having low sperm concentration. They're so proud that they can't help but to brag, in writing, that their high-tech technical solutions were pretty doggone good.

So proud are they that they again crow about all research on the hominid egg and sperm cells, and how to interbreed with our ancient ancestors. They are so intensely focused on this work that the alien genetic scientist describes it as—*intense.*

These E.T.s seem to live on pride—so much so that they wanted everyone who reads what they wrote an unbelievably long time ago that their problem of having low sperm counts frustrated the everlovin' green out of 'em. They came up with a super solution: IVF. These aliens were so into the whole microscopic research thing that they even knew that there are specialized enzymes that have specific roles to play when living DNA reproduces itself.

They are so into the whole research thing that they knew that microscopic bioluminescence in living cells played a role in their low sperm concentration. They were so into it that they knew that bioluminescence was present in the structure of DNA molecules themselves. They were so into it that they couldn't help but again write that what they were writing down was true.

The ancient beings knew all about super high-tech DNA slicing and dicing technology that our brainiac genetic scientists know about today. They knew how complex the structure of DNA was. They knew exactly what it looked like under high-power microscopes that they must have had, because what our scientists call the "double helix," they called *the twists*. They had a name for the DNA molecule that even our own modern-day genetic scientists could have used: The Twisting Spiral. That's pretty close to the observations that our scientists made when they first figured out what DNA looked like. The E.T. beings really were very sophisticated genetic scientists. They knew that they could copy DNA itself; and they knew how to cut out single segments of DNA so that they could accomplish their super accomplishments that they wrote were true.

The beings' microscopic techniques were so good that they could document that their own sperm cells looked somewhat abnormal. The way that they described the way they looked is exactly the same way that genetic scientists today describe sperm cells that are too long to be effective at fertilizing an egg cell. The ancient beings knew what our scientists today know—and that is that if sperm cells are too long, they have to put a bunch of them under intense magnification to choose the most normal-looking one in the bunch.

The normal-looking one got its big chance to be mechanically inserted by the E.T.'s scientist inside an ancient hominid female egg cell. So sharp are the beings' scientists that they can see that the molecular "backbone" of the DNA molecule is bioluminescent. So sharply proud are they that they can't help but to again crow about the success of their genetic engineering and interbreeding project. That's right: they called it the "I Accomplish".

You would have to get up earlier in the morning than these E.T.s did some half-billion years ago to notice that under their ultra-high-tech microscopes they could see that DNA and RNA were bioluminescent when cells were alive; but that DNA and RNA didn't have any bioluminescence when cells weren't alive.

The beings didn't want the hybrid's decendants who read their writing way far in the future to miss anything, so they again repeated that one of their own prime directives was all about their being able to interbreed with our primitive primate ancient ancestors. So that we, in their future, didn't miss or overlook that their mission was about interbreeding, even by, well—you know, *sex*; their lead genetic scientist wrote straight-out that he *will* copulate with the subjects of their research and interbreeding. "Copulate", by the way, is a coldly technical 25-cent word for *having sex with.*

Now, I don't know what your mom or dad told you about what it's like to have sex—but when sexually active people have sex together it doesn't last *forever*. Eventually they get so hot and bothered that one of them or both of them experiences a sexual climax. That climax, in a male or a female, is characterized by mild involuntary spasms that are intensely pleasurable. Those mild involuntary spasms are called "orgasms". The beings had orgasms when they had sex with our ancient ancestral females. Those aliens also experienced that they were just plain physically spent after an intense orgasm. They knew they were totally wiped out—exhausted.

They weren't, however, totally exhausted. They had enough energy to document that the DNA structure of our ancient ancestors was genetically engineered through their *I Accomplish* project of which they were so immensely proud.

They also knew that they intended to mass produce hybrid babies in a project they called "Amazements". The project was called Amazements because they themselves were amazed with the results of the project. And the result of the project were intelligent biological beings whom we today call *human beings.* Not surprisingly, the scientific name by which we call our own species is *homo sapiens*—wise humans. Well, we *are* intelligent. Wise? That might be debatable.

If things weren't dicey enough already, here's where things get even diceier—or more interesting. The beings' genetic engineers slice and dice molecular DNA in just the right way, based on their innumerable years of research, to be able to get the male hybrid DNA to be able to reproduce itself with the female hybrid DNA. In that way two hybrids of the opposite sex could have sex and produce a baby hybrid with the same hybrid DNA that the hybrid dad and the hybrid mom had.

As an added bonus in the beings' own story of how they produced a new hybrid species, they identify the lead E.T. genetic scientist by a name that he, himself, came up with to commemorate his having had sex with ancient female primates. The commemoration extended to the fact that his own DNA dwelled inside the DNA of the hybrids. He called himself "I Dwell". That was on account of when he was having sex with any of our female ancestors, he would physically dwell inside of her for a little while; and because he would permanently dwell inside the DNA of all future hybrids in all of their generations forever.

Before going onto the next accolade bestowed on the E.T. guy, I Dwell, their own writing ever so casually lets us know that he is what we call a—*don't flip out now*—a reptile.

This E.T. reptile-guy, I Dwell, is fingered as the sperm donor for the beings' whole IVF project. So aware are the aliens that their DNA lives inside of all future hybrids (that is, us—*homo sapiens*) they consider that doing IVF to perfect their hybrid species is just the same as accomplishing that result through sex with them. Did you get the part about their pride in their genetic engineering of our ancestors' DNA with theirs? Good—because they repeat that their technical solutions to the low sperm count problem and the egg rejection of their sperm cells were good solutions.

There's nothing like giving credit where credit is due—so, the reptile aliens properly credited the expertise of their scientist, *I Dwell*, as being the brains behind their technical success. So well credited is I Dwell that he gets to have the "I" in the name for their technical success—"I Complete." Because of him, the hybrid project was successful *and* complete—a complete success.

Just in case we missed it, the reptile aliens repeat their mission statement as being all their research about interbreeding with our ancient hominid ancestors, today called *homo erectus*, because they walked upright like we do instead of slouched over like our primate cousins, chimpanzees and gorillas.

At this point in their own "executive summary" they write that their research into the hominid egg and sperm cells will include harnessing some of the Reptilian scientists' own biomechanical powers. You also won't be surprised that the reptile aliens associate their famous *I Accomplish* project with hot sex between the male and female hybrids. So aware, and proud, are these beings that they write that their main man—er, main Reptilian—lives in the sperm of each of the self-reproducing hybrids—supposedly from that time on. Forever. So proud they are that they again call the successful hybridization project the *I Accomplish.* So meticulous are they that they again write that what they are writing is true.

The alien beings, who refer to themselves as *reptiles*, again write that it was because of low sperm counts that they were driven to achieve success through their IVF project. They again give credit to *I Dwell* in yet another reference to his *I Accomplish.* So that no future reader of their ancient story misses the point, they again write that putting a sperm cell into an egg cell in IVF is just the same as if they had done that through successful hot sex with the hominid females while on their road to biologically perfecting their hybrid species. So desirous of wanting us in their future to know that what they did is factual, they again write that their technical solutions were good.

The Reptilian aliens write that it was they, themselves, who fabricated their hybrid beings (our ancestor *human beings*) in their own likeness. Where have you heard something like that before? They coin a new term for the hybrid—in recognition that their own blood, *as DNA,* is inside the hybrid. The newly coined term is the "I Blood". They could just as well have written "My Blood"; but they wrote "I Blood". The way they say "I Blood" in their language is *ădămăh*. They shortened it to *ădăm*. (Not "Adam".)

Now here comes part of their, what you might call, *evil genius*. They openly write that they are going to subjugate the hybridized *I Blood* species through its genetically engineered hyped-up sex drive—through its own sexual procreation. Ingenius, huh? They perfectly genetically engineered the DNA molecular "backbone" structure they call a "yoke"—just like you'd yoke two oxen or two horses together to do whatever work you had in mind. Proud to their extraterrestrial reptile bones, they again call what they just documented, *the I Accomplish.*

The Reptilian aliens are perfectly aware that their hybrid (that is, us—or rather, our ancient *homo sapiens* ancestors) have been DNA-manipulated. They write that the hybrid, now called *I Blood*, was fashioned in their own likeness—as the hybrids were (are) related by blood—via DNA.

Not to be misunderstood, they again repeat that they used specialized high technology to genetically engineer the hybrids in their own likeness. So that no future reader misses the point, they write that they were accurately able to mark and puncture the eggs of the female hominid at just the right point so that they could accurately place the thin, hollow IVF needle into the egg.

So that no one misses the point, they again write that their IVF project was expertly accomplished. So important is it to the reptilian beings that they write that when they heard their hybrid intelligent beings speak, it sounded like "animal sounds".

But even in writing that observation they still referred to their hybrids by one of the terms that they used to refer to themselves: "biological entities". Talk about full disclosure but without informed consent, they write that they intend to greatly increase the number of hybrids by having genetically engineered the male hybrid (yes, that's male humans) to obsess about having sex often—and with any female on whom hands can be laid.

In case you missed the point earlier, they again write that their successful IVF project is called *I Accomplish.* We could say that isn't called *I Accomplish* for nothing. They write, perhaps in the interest of full disclosure—not that there's anything you can do about it—that they intend to subjugate the hybrid species.

So—fasten your seat belt, because they write that they will subjugate the hybrid species from inside their *under-seas spacecraft* that also fly through the air. Their subjugation project is also called—perhaps appropriately enough, from their perspective—The Amazements. Full of full disclosure, they write that their successful manipulative genetic engineering is what they, themselves, refer to as a reptile yoke. So, it looks like the *yoke* is on us. You will not be surprised that they call the successes just written about as *the I Accomplish.*

Nor will you be surprised that the aliens again brag about the fact that they have given the hybrids their IVF success—which they again write is just the same as having achieved success through successful copulation with the targeted species (our ancient hominid ancestors). They write that whether through IVF or through successful sex with the hominids, the same result is achieved: that their perfect reptilian DNA-information is passed on through the genetics of all future generations of hybrids (us). So cocksure are they of their demonstrated and proven success that they regard their own sperm as being physically present in the DNA of the hybrids.

That proven success again honors *I Dwell*, as the success is called the *I Accomplish.* So that their complete success is not missed, they repeat that it is through IVF that the DNA-manipulated sperm cell and the DNA-manipulated egg cell of the hominids have been specially fabricated to be able to produce offspring (baby *homo sapiens* as human beings), which can then grow into sexual maturity and then reproduce themselves through their own sexual activity. They again describe that wonderful success as *I Complete*—in recognition that their main Reptilian scientist, *I Dwell*, was responsible for the success being complete.

It is here in their *executive summary*, which is the actual ancient Hebrew account renamed by ancient human editors as "Genesis", that they make some—what we might call—startling revelations. They coin a new term for the ability of their hybrids to reproduce through their own sexual activity. The term is "complete alive". And so that future readers don't miss the point, the complete alive also comes under the heading of The Amazements.

It is at this point in their own brand of full disclosure that they identify, in their own language (which we call ancient Hebrew), what they call themselves: *Reptilian.*

They use that term for their DNA modifications: *Reptilian DNA-modifications*. That isn't all. The successful *Reptilian DNA-modifications* are referred to as *I Accomplish.* The lead Reptilian E.T. genetic scientist wants us to know one of the reasons why he calls himself (or calls itself) *I Dwell.* He (or it) makes a play on words. The play on words is in a reference to having sex with a female hominid. His (or its) play on words is, "*I dwell in her.*"

No one said that these aliens were models of discretion. Not to be outdone in the word-play department, they refer to IVF as "*spitting green sperm*" as it relates to the famous *I Complete* of the Reptilian scientist, *I Dwell.* So that you do not misunderstand or doubt in any way, they again write that what they write is true.

There's nothing like giving credit where credit is due. Here, in the Reptilian aliens' own narrative, they recognize that their scientist, *I Dwell*, is the one who successfully prepared the tiny hollow needles for successful injection into the hominid female's DNA-altered egg used in their IVF research project. As masters of the obvious, they call their success *good interbreeding*. Never seeming to tire about bragging about their successes, they repeat that their mission was about research toward interbreeding. Again, not to be outdone in the word-play department—while at the same time giving color credit where color credit is due—they recognize how the sperm cells of their self-reproducing hybrid male are packaged as *the white stuff*.

As the first chapter of the E.T. Reptilians comes toward a close, their lead genetic wizard of ooze, *I Dwell*, again refers to his successful projects as *The Amazements* and *the I Accomplish*. Their cold executive summary calls the hybrids *a mass of slaves*.

The lead Reptilian scientist, *I Dwell*, is the one who completed the Reptilian's hybridization project—now called *The Completions*. No time is lost to recognize that it is he, *I Dwell*, who unraveled the hominid's DNA molecular structure—again referred to *The Completions*. Once again, not to be misunderstood, the Reptilian, or human scribe, writing the ancient narrative text repeats that *The Completion* is the result of having unraveled the hominid's DNA.

To wrap it all up, the Reptilians' written introductory executive summary credits their own expertise with IVF for having achieved success with uniting the genetically manipulated egg and sperm cells—which they again call *The Completions*. They write that their scientific lab staff prepared the tiny hollow needle with the successfully DNA-manipulated hominid sperm cell for their own lead genetic scientist, named again as *I Dwell*. The successful DNA manipulations are referred to—*no surprise here*—as "*Completion*". The Reptilian beings' final sentence of their own executive summary accurately, even if coldly, sums up their entire hybridization project: that they are biological entities in the pursuit of DNA *slicing, dicing, manipulating,* and *fabricating*.

Chapter 5

A Speculative *un*Natural History of Our World

By the reckoning to our solar calendar it was some 445,000 years ago that a contingent of off-planet extra-terrestrial beings, the "Anunnaki", came to our planet.[348] The author, the late Zechariah Stichin, has a well-known series of books that describe what they wanted here (gold); and how they intended to get all of it they could—by way of the labor of a hybrid slave species.[349] That hybrid species was a cross between segments of their own DNA and the DNA of our direct ancestor species. Stichin refers to those ancestors as "Apeman" and "Apewoman".[350] This speculative history identifies our ancestor species as *homo erectus*.

Here also this speculative history identifies the Reptilians of the ancient Hebrew Genesis document as the Anunnaki species of the "creation myth" of ancient Sumer (or "Shumer"[351]), the Enuma Elish.[352] The Enuma Elish has been regarded, by traditional scholars, to be the source material for the Genesis creation story.[353] Because this history is informed speculation, there may be a speculative connection between the transliterated name-place "Shumer" and the transliterated species-name "Remesh". Without the sounds of transliterated vowels, R-M-Sh is Sh-M-R when spelled in the customary Hebrew way. It should be noted that the word *Hebrew* can mean "other"[354] in Hebrew.

The Reptilians spent a long time, perhaps up to 20,000 generations of our ancestors, to perfect the outcome that we still know today as *homo sapiens*.

Not to put too fine a point on it—we, ourselves, are the hybrid species that they fashioned from their DNA and from our ancestors' DNA to fabricate what we would call *the human race*. At some point after that long period of time is when the ancient Hebrew account was written.

During that expanse of time there were other species of E.T.s coming to this planet.[355] There were Reptilian colonies throughout the world. We know that because there is ancient statuary all across the globe that depicts an ancient race of *reptilian hominid beings*[356]—as opposed, say, to ancient statuary of ancient *mammalian hominid beings* resembling our planetary ancestor, *homo erectus*.

We will find, as subsequent chapters of Genesis are opened up for the first time in over two millennia, there is an epic struggle going on among the Reptilians. The struggle is principally between the Reptilian lead genetic scientist going by the moniker I-Dwell, and the militaristic faction of the Reptile-beings. As we will learn in subsequent early chapters of Genesis, I-Dwell fell in love with the female hominid he had sexual relations with during the course of his research on how to hybridize the planetary hominids with his own species. He loved, and loves, that female, designated appropriately enough, "I-Fabricate", because she fabricates newborns in her own body. His love for her extended to those of her species: the hybrid species. He attempted to befriend and defend the early hybrids; but became persecuted by the militaristic Reptilians.

It is he who spoke to Moses on Mt. Sinai—not from any burning bush—but from inside solid rock where he had been sequestered by the militant militarists. It was he, and his voice, that became the voice of morality throughout the Hebrew scriptural text; and it was the voice of an unnamed Reptilian impersonating I-Dwell who was the voice of *kill them all, the cattle too, and steal all their stuff.* His voice of acquired morality opposing the cold, mechanistic, utilitarian, militaristic faction of Reptilians provides the moral tension throughout the Hebrew biblical text.

During the Babylonian captivity (about 570 BCE to about 500 BCE), a select group of captives of Judah were taught the language and customs of the Babylonians.[357] Their education doubtless included the historic ancient cuneiform writings of Sumeria and Akkadia and with their many writings about the ancient Annunuki-beings[358] who had lorded over that area of the planet.

Jewish interpreters[359] during the reign of Ptolemy Philadelphus (285 – 247 BCE) accomplished their rendition of the ancient Hebrew texts into a sacred scripture, in Greek.[360] Their rendition would give the Greek pharaoh moral cover behind an uber-being called "Theos."[361] From behind that façade the temporal overlord was afforded irrefutable and unopposable justification to his rule. The Jewish interpreters[362] took as their templates two main written works for their made-up Genesis story. (Read or review them for yourself; be your own judge.) The first was the Theogony of Hesiod,[363] written about 700 BCE—or some half-millennia earlier than the Greek Septuagint. The second was the Enuma Elish[364]—of much more ancient origin.

It was during the composition of the Septuagint (the Jewish Torah in Greek) that the Jewish interpreters changed the ancient Hebrew lettering[365] to the writing form of the Aramaen dialect of the former Babylonian Empire.[366] That type of writing is now variously called "Biblical Hebrew," "Hebrew," or "modern Hebrew." Sometimes it is referred to as the "Jewish script."[367]

It was during the composition of the Septuagint that the Jewish interpreters rendered a "sacred text" in Greek, but which, according to a contemporary commentator, ". . . differ not a little as to the things said in them."[368] What was produced was a scriptural narrative in keeping with the demands of their Greek overlords. The Torah in Greek was simply an adaptation of The Theogony of Hesiod and the Enuma Elish—adapted to fit a sacred scriptural narrative that would reinforce Greek overlordship of Hellenized Egypt and over the Greek-speaking Jews of Egypt.

The historical Christ Figure was the "Anointed One" of...not "God"... but of the alaheem—the Reptilian E.T.-beings. The Reptilian I-Dwell was probably cloned; and by way of ICSI and IVF, came back into the world of humans in order to introduce a higher morality—the morality of doing unto others as one would have done to one's self.[369]

I-Dwell was acutely aware of the tremendous karmic debt incurred by the Reptilian species due to the Reptilian intervention into the lives of the ancient *homo erectus* and the violation of an Inter-galactic Prime Directive of non-interference with life forms on other planets/dimensions without the full consent of its resident inhabitants. It was the willingness of I-Dwell to give up his reincarnated life for the expostulation of real morality (as opposed to the utilitarian amorality of the Reptilians) that was meant to go toward the repayment of Reptilian collective karmic debt.

The bloodline of ancient kings is from alien hybrids specifically selected by out-of-sight militaristic Reptilian earthly overlords to rule over the mass of a hybridized humanity. Those bloodlines extend into the current present of humanity.[370] There is an ongoing struggle, out of the sight of the mass of humanity, between our planet's *hidden* alien overlords and a group of out-of-sight aliens[371]. There is a group among the Reptilian species who have committed themselves to the repayment a cosmic karmic debt, and to assist in putting humanity *back* on the track of humane cooperative life between humane human beings as well as with all of the planet's other life forms.

Chapter 6

Several Necessary Explanations

Starting at the Very Beginning

The book's title *is* its own brief explanation. It informs, except for the reptiles in the details, what's going to shake out between the front and the back cover. In that sense the shocking revelation has already been made: that the genesis of humans derives from alien beings—specifically the type known as "Reptilians"—and not from any God or god-beings. It also reveals that what we call "Genesis" is a façade—a cloaking device manufactured out of words—Greek words and the words of "modern Hebrew". We, *homo sapiens,* are the "Amazements". The Reptilians of the ancient Hebrew documentary text are "in whose image". What you will read here is the actual information preserved in the ancient Hebrew language—and was written by the Reptilians themselves or by a hybridized scribe.

Because no one has previously published any sightings of any Reptilians in the Bible's book of Genesis, this work represents the first such. Owing to the amount of detail that is put onto these pages, this work will present to humanity the final full disclosure on the whole matter as to what the ancient Hebrew scriptural text actually says about our beginnings as a species. The account to be told is historical. It is not fiction. It is no longer a matter of speculative anything.

The plain words from the ancient Hebrew text will, for the first time in human history, be allowed to simply say what they say. These pages will also give an account of exactly how the words say what they say. That accounting is what separates this story of our ancient beginnings from every other genesis story spun over the past 2,100 years. The story itself is simple and straightforward. The complexity is in the detail that the Reptilians themselves provide throughout their own narrative—referred to as "Genesis" since it was spun from out the fabric of the actual ancient Hebrew text into Greek some two millennia ago.

How did that story become the accepted word? From the Fandom website (https://memory-alpha.fandom.com/wiki/Cloaking_device) we learn that in pop cultural *Star Trek* terminology, "a cloaking device (also known as a cloaking system, cloaking shield, or invisibility screen) was a form of stealth technology that used selective bending of light (and other forms of energy) to render a starship or other object completely invisible to the electromagnetic spectrum and most sensors."

That description could be adapted for how the ancient Greek Septuagint (the ancient Hebrew scriptures put in the Greek language) was linguistically engineered as a low-tech cloaking device. The low-tech cloaking device was in the form of the Greek-language Septuagint. It was a form of ancient stealth technology that used selective bending of ancient Hebrew words (and other linguistic tricks of translation) to render a narrative that had been in plain sight in the original ancient Hebrew to then become invisible to all future readers of the ancient text.

Each reader of the ancient text is owed a candid explaination as to how the ancient aliens, called "Remesh" in the original Hebrew scriptural text (and here called by the very definition of that word—"Reptilian"), were never originally cloaked. They disclosed themselves from the scriptural beginning.

It is not, however, until verse 21 (in the traditional way of numbering) that a Reptilian is first referenced. When looking at Genesis 1:21 in the Bible that you are used to reading, you definitely will not see the word "Reptilian"; but you may see the words "every living creature that moveth." The words "that moveth" are the traditionalists' translation façade (or cloak) over the Hebrew word *ha·remesh·*eet. That word's Hebrew root is associated with Strong's Number 7430, which means "to glide swiftly". But . . . the word is actually Strong's Number 7431, which means "a reptile".

This translation will not mince words. This "reptile" is a Reptilian. This work also will use the actual Hebrew word for "reptile," *rĕmĕsh*, as a word transliterated into English as "Remesh".

Where did we get the word "reptile"? It is supposed to have come into English from the French word *reptile*. We can easily find it in the online resource of the Centre National de Resources Textuelles et Lexicales. The French word is taken from the Latin word *reptile*. Indeed, we will find the word *reptile* in Genesis 1:25 and 1:26 of the Latin Vulgate—which was finished early in the fourth century.

We will also find that the Vulgate—the biblical text in Latin—reinforced and maintained the linguistic cloaking device over the in-plain-sight reptile beings of the ancient Hebrew text. For instance, in the Vulgate's Genesis 1:21, the Remesh (Reptilians) are cloaked behind the Latin words for "that moves" as *atque motabilem*. In Verse 26 we will again encounter the Remesh. They are again cloaked behind "that moves" as *quod movetur*. We will encounter the same Remesh in Verses 28 and 30. In the Latin they are again cloaked, in both instances, behind "that moves" as *quæ moventur*.

Transferring the analogy of the *cloaking device* to the situation of there actually being E.T. Reptilians clearly visible in the ancient Hebrew scriptural text (as will become all too apparent), the ancient interpreters in Alexandria, Egypt, used the low-tech device of the ancient Greek language as an "information screen" in order to make the objects (the Reptilians) and concepts (the Reptilians' hominid-Reptilian hybridization project) invisible to all future readers of the ancient text.

Here's the thing we have to wrap our minds around: that the ancient Hebrew scriptural text was originally about, and has always been all about, the ancient alien Reptilians themselves being fully visible from the beginning—as the ancient Hebrew text was their own written record of their hybridization project—left as perpetual and permanent documentation for the descendants of the original hybrids. We are those descendants.

In official circles of those who make a career studying "aliens," a very different term than "aliens" is used to identify off-planet aliens—typically those known as "grays". That term is an acronym: EBENs—or, "**E**xtraterresterial **B**iological **EN**tities."[372]

The Reptilians called the hominids *ălăhēm*—in other words, "aliens"—and when they heard the hominids speaking, they called what they heard "animal sounds". The Reptilians are strange to us; and we are strange to them. That is the concept that will be used here to define, in the context of this opening Genesis chapter, the ancient Hebrew word *ălăhēm* ("aliens"). The phrase "strange-biological-entities" will be the fresh translation of that ancient word as it is used throughout the foundational Genesis document.

It is in the manner described that the all-pervading presence of reptilian hominids as "strange-biological-entities" has been linguistically cloaked behind the ancient Greek words of the Genesis *cloaking device*. They are as uncloaked here as they were in the original ancient text.

What the Ancient Letters Do Inside Their Ancient Words

To be able to have cracked the code of Hebrew—or, as another way of thinking about it, *hack into* that language—as software, which could also be called "code"—a slow, methodical, and painstaking study of how the words convey meaning had to be undertaken. The study, as detailed observations, had to assume that nothing at all was known about this language. The study took place on and off over 10 years before taking on Genesis chapter 1.

The only way that the reality of what the ancient text of the Bible actually said was to learn how its letters and words are actually constructed and how they actually convey actual meaning. Once learned, the role of language-detective must be taken on so that it may be figured out what words mean in the context of the verse under study. The language-detective will want to also know how a given word is used other places in the Hebrew text.

The shape of each ancient Hebrew letter used here is actually a two-dimensional model of three-dimensional human anatomy of speech where the sound that the letter makes is produced and pronounced. The way that the letters convey meaning is straightforward. There are 22 letters in the actual (ancient) Hebrew alphabet. The principle here is that *form follows function*. In other words, the form of each of the letters—their shapes—comes from how our anatomy of speech functions to produce the sounds associated with each letter. Each letter has a name that was given to it far back in our ancient past.

The human anatomy of speech itself instructs as to the pronunciation of each letter. Because the letter shapes are modeled on our anatomy of speech, there is a one-to-one relationship between the writing *and* the pronunciation of each word. The language is purely phonetic. The way that words convey meaning—their grammar—is also straightforward. Certain few letters act as prefixes, some as suffixes, some are inserted into the middle of words to alter meaning; and some are routinely dropped from a word.

Armed with that conceptual framework, we are ready to take on the translation of this foundational book of the Hebrew Bible—and by extension, of the entirety of the genesis of human beings.

A Brief Explanation about Reapproaching Genesis 1

How can this ancient writing be tackled so that we can make sense of it? Our making sense of it must also be in a way that hasn't ever been done before.

𐤀 (A / a)	ălă*pf*	א
𐤁 (B / b)	bĕt	ב
𐤂 (G / g)	gĭmĕl	ג
𐤃 (D / d)	dălăt	ד
𐤄 (H / h)	*hāy*	ה
𐤅 (W / w)	*ōōă*	ו
𐤆 (Z / z)	zăēn	ז
𐤇 (*Kh*/*kh*)	*kh*ĕt	ח
𐤈 (Th / th)	thĕt	ט
𐤉 (Y / y)	ēăd	י
𐤊 (K / k)	kă*pf*	כ / ך
𐤋 (L / l)	lămĕd	ל
𐤌 (M / m)	mĕm	מ / ם
𐤍 (N / n)	nōōn	נ / ן

𐤎 (S / s)	sămĕk	ס
𐤏 (O / o)	ōyĕn	ע
𐤐 (*Pf / pf*)	*pf*āy	פ / ף
𐤑 (Tz / tz)	tzădē	צ / ץ
𐤒 (Qw/qw)	qwōō*pf*	ק
𐤓 (R / r)	rĕsh	ר
𐤔 (Sh/sh)	shĭn	ש
𐤕 (T / t)	tōō	ת

The first thing to be done is to get hold of, either as a physical book or as online resource, the *Hebrew and Chaldee Dictionary of the Old Testament* by Dr. James Strong. That dictionary can be found as a free online resource or at the end of any edition of *Strong's Concordance*. (Note: Interested Jewish readers need not be put off by the term "Old Testament." By and large, the definitions of the words we'll be looking at are from the same words as are in Torah.)

The next thing we'll need to do is to develop a handy chart matching the letters of the ancient Hebrew alphabet with those of the more familiar Jewish letters.

The next thing to be done is to secure a resource that contains the "modern Hebrew" text of Genesis (*Bĕrĕshēt* in Judaism), as well as the convenience of an English translation of each word, and a "Strong's Number" associated with each word.[373]

The Bare-Bones Need-to-Know

There are 22 letters in this ancient alphabet. Half of its letters are ones that all of us already know.

There are nine ancient Hebrew letters that look very similar to our letters. They are: 𐤀, 𐤃, 𐤊, 𐤋, 𐤌, 𐤍, 𐤏, 𐤒, and 𐤓.

Letter	Name	Sound the letter makes	Associated English letter
𐤀	ălă*pf*	***a pure vowel, short-***ă	A
𐤃	dălĕt	the /d/ sound	D
𐤊	kă*pf*	the /k/ sound	K
𐤋	lămĕd	the /l/ sound	L
𐤌	mĕm	the /m/ sound	M
𐤍	nōōn	the /n/ sound	N
𐤏	ōyēn	***a pure vowel, long-***ō	O
𐤒	qwōō*pf*	the /qw/ sound	Q
𐤓	resh	the /r/ sound	R

The other 13 letters are introduced similarly, below.

Letter	Name	Sound the letter makes	Associated English letters
𐤁	bĕt	the /b/ sound	B
𐤂	gĭmĕl	the /g/ sound	G
𐤄	*hāy*	the /h/ sound	H
𐤅	*ōōă* [“waw”]	**the vowel diphthong sound, ōō**, (as in “boo”)	OO
𐤆	zăēn	the /z/ sound	Z
𐤇	*kh*ĕt	the /kh/ sound (the “ch” of in German —as in “Bach”)	Kh
𐤈	thĕt	the /th/ sound	Th
𐤉	*yăd* [as “ēăd”]	**a pure vowel sound, long-ē**	E
𐤎	sămĕk	the /s/ sound	S
𐤑	tzădē	the /tz/ sound	Tz
𐤐	*pfāy*	the */pf/* sound [a cross between /p/ and /f/]	Pf
𐤔	shĭn	the /sh/ sound	Sh
𐤕	tōō	the /t/ sound	T

The Ancient Hebrew Scriptural Text—A Perfect Time Capsule

What will be seen in the ancient writing that follows is the complete text[374] of "Genesis 1" in anatomic alphabetic ancient Hebrew.[375] These letters, as formed into words, are represented to be what the original writer of the ancient text actually wrote. The text as presented here has been exactly transcribed from writing referred to as "Biblical Hebrew"[376] into the anatomically stylized ancient writing.[377] The text to follow is what is under intense inspection here. Such scrutiny, as you will see, has never taken place over the course of the past three-and-a-half millennia. (Note: If such scrutiny has taken place, it has not been universally offered as it is here.)

It is believed in Judaism that the ancient writing known as the Torah was given to Moses at Mount Sinai—as long as 3,500 years ago. It is also believed in Judaism that not one letter has been altered since that time. What shall be encountered on the pages that follow will now prove—as well as for all time—that this ancient text is most certainly a perfect time capsule. The ancient text, as translated here, certainly reinforces the idea that there has been no substantial alteration of the text since it was written.

How do we know what the original ancient biblical text looked like? Humanity does have an excellent example from a portion of the text of the book of Leviticus as preserved in the ancient cave system at Qumran—in the form of what's called the "11Q Paleo Lev"—that's the Leviticus scroll in Paleo-Hebrew (ancient Hebrew) in Cave 11 at Qumran, Israel.[378]

The account revealed within this translation of the ancient text has been preserved not simply for believers—but for all humanity. This story spells out not our "creation"—but our "fabrication"—by a type of beings specifically stated in Hebrew as strange biological entities. As radical as the translation might appear at first, second, or third reading—it accurately puts into modern English what the text plainly conveys in ancient Hebrew.

The ancient writing is right-to-left.

(Traditional verse numbers are added to the way the original text was written. The following text has been adapted from the *Biblia Hebraica*[379] and transliterated into an ancient Hebrew manner of writing.[380])

𐤁𐤓𐤀𐤔𐤉𐤕 𐤁𐤓𐤀 𐤀𐤋𐤄𐤉𐤌 𐤀𐤕 𐤄𐤔𐤌𐤉𐤌 𐤅𐤀𐤕 𐤄𐤀𐤓𐤑 1:1

𐤅𐤄𐤀𐤓𐤑 𐤄𐤉𐤕𐤄 𐤕𐤄𐤅 𐤅𐤁𐤄𐤅 𐤅𐤇𐤔𐤊 𐤏𐤋 𐤐𐤍𐤉 1:2

𐤕𐤄𐤅𐤌 𐤅𐤓𐤅𐤇 𐤀𐤋𐤄𐤉𐤌 𐤌𐤓𐤇𐤐𐤕 𐤏𐤋 𐤐𐤍𐤉 𐤄𐤌𐤉𐤌

𐤅𐤉𐤀𐤌𐤓 𐤀𐤋𐤄𐤉𐤌 𐤉𐤄𐤉 𐤀𐤅𐤓 𐤅𐤉𐤄𐤉 𐤀𐤅𐤓 1:3

𐤅𐤉𐤓𐤀 𐤀𐤋𐤄𐤉𐤌 𐤀𐤕 𐤄𐤀𐤅𐤓 𐤊𐤉 𐤈𐤅𐤁 𐤅𐤉𐤁𐤃𐤋 1:4

𐤀𐤋𐤄𐤉𐤌 𐤁𐤉𐤍 𐤄𐤀𐤅𐤓 𐤅𐤁𐤉𐤍 𐤄𐤇𐤔𐤊

𐤅𐤉𐤒𐤓𐤀 𐤀𐤋𐤄𐤉𐤌 𐤋𐤀𐤅𐤓 𐤉𐤅𐤌 𐤅𐤋𐤇𐤔𐤊 𐤒𐤓𐤀 𐤋𐤉𐤋𐤄 1:5

𐤅𐤉𐤄𐤉 𐤏𐤓𐤁 𐤅𐤉𐤄𐤉 𐤁𐤒𐤓 𐤉𐤅𐤌 𐤀𐤇𐤃

𐤅𐤉𐤀𐤌𐤓 𐤀𐤋𐤄𐤉𐤌 𐤉𐤄𐤉 𐤓𐤒𐤉𐤏 𐤁𐤕𐤅𐤊 𐤄𐤌𐤉𐤌 1:6

𐤅𐤉𐤄𐤉 𐤌𐤁𐤃𐤉𐤋 𐤁𐤉𐤍 𐤌𐤉𐤌 𐤋𐤌𐤉𐤌

𐤅𐤉𐤏𐤔 𐤀𐤋𐤄𐤉𐤌 𐤀𐤕 𐤄𐤓𐤒𐤉𐤏 𐤅𐤉𐤁𐤃𐤋 𐤁𐤉𐤍 𐤄𐤌𐤉𐤌 1:7

𐤀𐤔𐤓 𐤌𐤕𐤇𐤕 𐤋𐤓𐤒𐤉𐤏 𐤅𐤁𐤉𐤍 𐤄𐤌𐤉𐤌 𐤀𐤔𐤓 𐤌𐤏𐤋

𐤋𐤓𐤒𐤉𐤏 𐤅𐤉𐤄𐤉 𐤊𐤍

𐤅𐤉𐤒𐤓𐤀 𐤀𐤋𐤄𐤉𐤌 𐤋𐤓𐤒𐤉𐤏 𐤔𐤌𐤉𐤌 𐤅𐤉𐤄𐤉 𐤏𐤓𐤁 1:8

𐤅𐤉𐤄𐤉 𐤁𐤒𐤓 𐤉𐤅𐤌 𐤔𐤍𐤉

𐤅𐤉𐤀𐤌𐤓 𐤀𐤋𐤄𐤉𐤌 𐤉𐤒𐤅𐤅 𐤄𐤌𐤉𐤌 𐤌𐤕𐤇𐤕 𐤄𐤔𐤌𐤉𐤌 1:9

𐤀𐤋 𐤌𐤒𐤅𐤌 𐤀𐤇𐤃 𐤅𐤕𐤓𐤀𐤄 𐤄𐤉𐤁𐤔𐤄 𐤅𐤉𐤄𐤉 𐤊𐤍

𐤅𐤉𐤒𐤓𐤀 𐤀𐤋𐤄𐤉𐤌 𐤋𐤉𐤁𐤔𐤄 𐤀𐤓𐤑 𐤅𐤋𐤌𐤒𐤅𐤄 𐤄𐤌𐤉𐤌 1:10

𐤒𐤓𐤀 𐤉𐤌𐤉𐤌 𐤅𐤉𐤓𐤀 𐤀𐤋𐤄𐤉𐤌 𐤊𐤉 𐤈𐤅𐤁

𐤅𐤉𐤀𐤌𐤓 𐤀𐤋𐤄𐤉𐤌 𐤕𐤃𐤔𐤀 𐤄𐤀𐤓𐤑 𐤃𐤔𐤀 𐤏𐤔𐤁 1:11

𐤌𐤆𐤓𐤉𐤏 𐤆𐤓𐤏 𐤏𐤑 𐤐𐤓𐤉 𐤏𐤔𐤄 𐤐𐤓𐤉 𐤋𐤌𐤉𐤍𐤅 𐤀𐤔𐤓

𐤆𐤓𐤏𐤅 𐤁𐤅 𐤏𐤋 𐤄𐤀𐤓𐤑 𐤅𐤉𐤄𐤉 𐤊𐤍

𐤅𐤕𐤅𐤑𐤀 𐤄𐤀𐤓𐤑 𐤃𐤔𐤀 𐤏𐤔𐤁 𐤌𐤆𐤓𐤉𐤏 𐤆𐤓𐤏 1:12

𐤋𐤌𐤉𐤍𐤄𐤅 𐤅𐤏𐤑 𐤏𐤔𐤄 𐤐𐤓𐤉 𐤀𐤔𐤓 𐤆𐤓𐤏𐤅 𐤁𐤅

למינהו וירא אלהים כי טוב
ויהי ערב ויהי בקר יום שלישי 1:13
ויאמר אלהים יהי מארת ברקיע השמים 1:14
להבדיל בין היום ובין הלילה והיו
לאתת ולמועדים ולימים ושנים
והיו למאורת ברקיע השמים להאיר 1:15
על הארץ ויהי כן
ויעש אלהים את שני המארת הגדלים את 1:16
המאור הגדל לממשלת היום ואת המאור
הקטן לממשלת הלילה ואת הכוכבים
ויתן אתם אלהים ברקיע השמים להאיר 1:17
על הארץ
ולמשל ביום ובלילה ולהבדיל בין האור 1:18
ובין החשך וירא אלהים כי טוב
ויהי ערב ויהי בקר יום רביעי 1:19
ויאמר אלהים ישרצו המים שרץ נפש חיה 1:20
ועוף יעופף על הארץ על פני רקיע השמים
ויברא אלהים את התנינם הגדלים ואת 1:21
כל נפש החיה הרמשת אשר שרצו המים
למינהם ואת כל עוף כנף למינהו
וירא אלהים כי טוב
ויברך אתם אלהים לאמר פרו ורבו ומלאו 1:22
את המים בימים והעוף ירב בארץ
ויהי ערב ויהי בקר יום חמישי 1:23
ויאמר אלהים תוצא הארץ נפש חיה למינה 1:24
בהמה ורמש וחיתו ארץ למינה ויהי כן
ויעש אלהים את חית הארץ למינה ואת 1:25
הבהמה למינה ואת כל רמש האדמה למינהו
וירא אלהים כי טוב

𐤅𐤉𐤀𐤌𐤓 𐤀𐤋𐤄𐤉𐤌 𐤍𐤏𐤔𐤄 𐤀𐤃𐤌 𐤁𐤑𐤋𐤌𐤍𐤅 1:26
𐤊𐤃𐤌𐤅𐤕𐤍𐤅 𐤅𐤉𐤓𐤃𐤅 𐤁𐤃𐤂𐤕 𐤄𐤉𐤌 𐤅𐤁𐤏𐤅𐤐 𐤄𐤔𐤌𐤉𐤌
𐤅𐤁𐤁𐤄𐤌𐤄 𐤅𐤁𐤊𐤋 𐤄𐤀𐤓𐤑 𐤅𐤁𐤊𐤋 𐤄𐤓𐤌𐤔 𐤄𐤓𐤌𐤔
𐤏𐤋 𐤄𐤀𐤓𐤑
𐤅𐤉𐤁𐤓𐤀 𐤀𐤋𐤄𐤉𐤌 𐤀𐤕 𐤄𐤀𐤃𐤌 𐤁𐤑𐤋𐤌𐤅 𐤁𐤑𐤋𐤌 𐤀𐤋𐤄𐤉𐤌 1:27
𐤁𐤓𐤀 𐤀𐤕𐤅 𐤆𐤊𐤓 𐤅𐤍𐤒𐤁𐤄 𐤁𐤓𐤀 𐤀𐤕𐤌
𐤅𐤉𐤁𐤓𐤊 𐤀𐤕𐤌 𐤀𐤋𐤄𐤉𐤌 𐤅𐤉𐤀𐤌𐤓 𐤋𐤄𐤌 𐤀𐤋𐤄𐤉𐤌 𐤐𐤓𐤅 1:28
𐤅𐤓𐤁𐤅 𐤅𐤌𐤋𐤀𐤅 𐤀𐤕 𐤄𐤀𐤓𐤑 𐤅𐤊𐤁𐤔𐤄 𐤅𐤓𐤃𐤅 𐤁𐤃𐤂𐤕
𐤄𐤉𐤌 𐤅𐤁𐤏𐤅𐤐 𐤄𐤔𐤌𐤉𐤌 𐤅𐤁𐤊𐤋 𐤇𐤉𐤄 𐤄𐤓𐤌𐤔𐤕
𐤏𐤋 𐤄𐤀𐤓𐤑
𐤅𐤉𐤀𐤌𐤓 𐤀𐤋𐤄𐤉𐤌 𐤄𐤍𐤄 𐤍𐤕𐤕𐤉 𐤋𐤊𐤌 𐤀𐤕 𐤊𐤋 𐤏𐤔𐤁 1:29
𐤆𐤓𐤏 𐤆𐤓𐤏 𐤀𐤔𐤓 𐤏𐤋 𐤐𐤍𐤉 𐤊𐤋 𐤄𐤀𐤓𐤑 𐤅𐤀𐤕 𐤊𐤋
𐤄𐤏𐤑 𐤀𐤔𐤓 𐤁𐤅 𐤐𐤓𐤉 𐤏𐤑 𐤆𐤓𐤏 𐤆𐤓𐤏 𐤋𐤊𐤌
𐤉𐤄𐤉𐤄 𐤋𐤀𐤊𐤋𐤄
𐤅𐤋𐤊𐤋 𐤇𐤉𐤕 𐤄𐤀𐤓𐤑 𐤅𐤋𐤊𐤋 𐤏𐤅𐤐 𐤄𐤔𐤌𐤉𐤌 𐤅𐤋𐤊𐤋 1:30
𐤓𐤅𐤌𐤔 𐤏𐤋 𐤄𐤀𐤓𐤑 𐤀𐤔𐤓 𐤁𐤅 𐤍𐤐𐤔 𐤇𐤉𐤄 𐤀𐤕 𐤊𐤋
𐤉𐤓𐤒 𐤏𐤔𐤁 𐤋𐤀𐤊𐤋𐤄 𐤅𐤉𐤄𐤉 𐤊𐤍
𐤅𐤉𐤓𐤀 𐤀𐤋𐤄𐤉𐤌 𐤀𐤕 𐤊𐤋 𐤀𐤔𐤓 𐤏𐤔𐤄 𐤅𐤄𐤍𐤄 𐤈𐤆𐤁 𐤌𐤀𐤃 1:31
𐤅𐤄𐤍𐤄 𐤏𐤓𐤁 𐤅𐤉𐤄𐤉 𐤁𐤒𐤓 𐤉𐤅𐤌 𐤄𐤔𐤔𐤉
𐤅𐤉𐤊𐤋𐤅 𐤄𐤔𐤌𐤉𐤌 𐤅𐤄𐤀𐤓𐤑 𐤅𐤊𐤋 𐤑𐤁𐤀𐤌 2:1
𐤅𐤉𐤊𐤋 𐤀𐤋𐤄𐤉𐤌 𐤁𐤉𐤅𐤌 𐤄𐤔𐤁𐤉𐤏𐤉 𐤌𐤋𐤀𐤊𐤕𐤅 𐤀𐤔𐤓 2:2
𐤏𐤔𐤄 𐤅𐤉𐤔𐤁𐤕 𐤁𐤉𐤅𐤌 𐤄𐤔𐤁𐤉𐤏𐤉 𐤌𐤊𐤋 𐤌𐤋𐤀𐤊𐤕𐤅
𐤀𐤔𐤓 𐤏𐤔𐤄
𐤅𐤉𐤁𐤓𐤊 𐤀𐤋𐤄𐤉𐤌 𐤀𐤕 𐤉𐤅𐤌 𐤄𐤔𐤁𐤉𐤏𐤉 𐤅𐤉𐤒𐤃𐤔 2:3
𐤀𐤕𐤅 𐤊𐤉 𐤁𐤅 𐤔𐤁𐤕 𐤌𐤊𐤋 𐤌𐤋𐤀𐤊𐤕𐤅 𐤀𐤔𐤓
𐤁𐤓𐤀 𐤀𐤋𐤄𐤉𐤌 𐤋𐤏𐤔𐤅𐤕

* * *

The following text is the same as the ancient text except that it is in the writing of *unaccented* or *unmarked* Biblical Hebrew. Traditional verses numbers are added for convenience. The text has been adapted from the *Biblia Hebraica*[381]—put into plain text.

1:1 בראשית ברא אלהים את השמים ואת הארץ
1:2 והארץ היתה תהו ובהו וחשך על־פני תהום ורוח אלהים מרחפת
על־פני המים
1:3 ויאמר אלהים יהי אור ויהי־אור
1:4 וירא אלהים את־האור כי־טוב ויבדל אלהים בין האור ובין
החשך
1:5 ויקרא אלהים לאור יום ולחשך קרא לילה ויהי־ערב ויהי־בקר
יום אחד
1:6 ויאמר אלהים יהי רקיע בתוך המים ויהי מבדיל בין מים למים
1:7 ויעש אלהים את־הרקיע ויבדל בין המים אשר מתחת לרקיע ובין
המים אשר מעל לרקיע ויהי־כן
1:8 ויקרא אלהים לרקיע שמים ויהי־ערב ויהי־בקר יום שני
1:9 ויאמר אלהים יקוו המים מתחת השמים אל־מקום אחד ותראה
היבשה ויהי־כן
1:10 ויקרא אלהים ליבשה ארץ ולמקוה המים קרא ימים וירא אלהים
כי־טוב
1:11 ויאמר אלהים תדשא הארץ דשא עשב מזריע זרע עץ פרי עשה
פרי למינו אשר זרעו־בו על־הארץ ויהי־כן
1:12 ותוצא הארץ דשא עשב מזריע זרע למינהו ועץ עשה פרי אשר
זרעו־בו למינהו וירא אלהים כי־טוב
1:13 ויהי־ערב ויהי־בקר יום שלישי
1:14 ויאמר אלהים יהי מארת ברקיע השמים להבדיל בין היום ובין
הלילה והיו לאתת ולמועדים ולימים ושנים
1:15 והיו למאורת ברקיע השמים להאיר על־הארץ ויהי־כן
1:16 ויעש אלהים את־שני המארת הגדלים את־המאור הגדל
לממשלת היום ואת־המאור הקטן לממשלת הלילה ואת הכוכבים
1:17 ויתן אתם אלהים ברקיע השמים להאיר על־הארץ

1:18 ולמשל ביום ובלילה ולהבדיל בין האור ובין החשך וירא אלהים
כי־טוב

1:19 ויהי־ערב ויהי־בקר יום רביעי

1:20 ויאמר אלהים ישרצו המים שרץ נפש חיה ועוף יעופף
על־פני רקיע השמים

1:21 ויברא אלהים את־התנינם הגדלים ואת כל־נפש החיה הרמשת
אשר שרצו המים למינהם ואת כל־עוף כנף למינהו וירא אלהים
כי־טוב

1:22 ויברך אתם אלהים לאמר פרו ורבו ומלאו את־המים בימים
והעוף ירב בארץ

1:23 ויהי־ערב ויהי־בקר יום חמישי

1:24 ויאמר אלהים תוצא הארץ נפש חיה למינה בהמה ורמש
וחיתו־ארץ למינה ויהי־כן

1:25 ויעש אלהים את־חית הארץ למינה ואת־הבהמה למינה ואת
כל־רמש האדמה למינהו וירא אלהים כי־טוב

1:26 ויאמר אלהים נעשה אדם בצלמנו כדמותנו וירדו בדגת הים
ובעוף השמים ובבהמה ובכל־הארץ ובכל־הרמש הרמש
על־הארץ

1:27 ויברא אלהים את־האדם בצלמו בצלם אלהים ברא אתו זכר
ונקבה ברא אתם

1:28 ויברך אתם אלהים ויאמר להם אלהים פרו ורבו ומלאו
את־הארץ וכבשה ורדו בדגת הים ובעוף השמים ובכל־חיה
הרמשת על־הארץ

1:29 ויאמר אלהים הנה נתתי לכם את־כל־עשב זרע זרע אשר
על־פני כל־הארץ ואת־כל־העץ אשר־בו פרי־עץ זרע זרע
לכם יהיה לאכלה

1:30 ולכל־חית הארץ ולכל־עוף השמים ולכל רומש על־הארץ
אשר־בו נפש חיה את־כל־ירק עשב לאכלה ויהי־כן

1:31 וירא אלהים את־כל־אשר עשה והנה־טוב מאד ויהי־ערב
ויהי־בקר יום הששי

2:1 ויכלו השמים והארץ וכל־צבאם

2:2 ויכל אלהים ביום השביעי מלאכתו אשר עשה וישבת ביום

השביעי מכל־מלאכתו אשר עשה
2:3 ויברך אלהים את־יום השביעי ויקדש אתו כי בו שבת
מכל־מלאכתו אשר־ברא אלהים לעשות

* * *

Ancient Ultra-Modern High-Tech DNA Editing Technology

This is the story, not of humanity's creation, but its *fabrication.* As it turns out in the biblical text, we, as a species, weren't created. We were *fabricated*—by a species of highly technological biological-entities. The story of *how* they fabricated our remote ancestors (bipedal primate hominids) can be more fully understood through the story of our own modern-day high-tech story of gene-editing technology known by its own acronym, CRISPR.

No one here will be expected to suffer through any detailed explanation about the intricacies of how the DNA-editing technology of CRISPR works. Anyone may do an internet search on that acronym. It will be enough to share the key concept. CAS-9 (of CRISPR CAS-9) works as an RNA-guided DNA endonuclease enzyme associated with the CRISPR technique—a high-tech tool of genetic engineers.[382] A CAS-9 "cleaver" breaks the double helix DNA like a pair of scissors at preprogramed places in order to make precision changes. The acronym "CAS" comes from the modified acronym "**C**RISPR **As**sociated." With that technology, it does not take a genetic scientist to see exactly how a species of advanced strange-biological-entities could modify and engineer the DNA as well as genetically edit the hominids they encountered here in our remote past.

There is another type of DNA-editing technology called CRISPR/Cpf 1. The designation "Cpf 1" stands for Clustered Regularly Interspaced Short Palindromic Repeats from Prevotella and Francisella 1. Like CAS-9, Cpf 1 is an endonuclease; but it is smaller and simpler.[383] For our purposes here, it is simply one of the two known CRISPR technologies.

Of additional critical importance, also by way of introduction, readers should be acquainted with a particular two-letter Hebrew word that designates one of two principle high-tech techniques used to *fabricate* the DNA alterations and genetic edits to the target species (our ancestors). We can use the idea behind the CRISPR/CAS technology, itself, as an analogy of how the Hebrew word, *ăt,*[384] pronounced as *ăht* and represented as "ᚷ ⫮" (*spelled ălăpf - tōō*) in the ancient Hebrew *anatomic alphabetic letters*, is used throughout the Reptilians' construction of the narrative text popularly known as Genesis.

Just as the CAS-9 protein cuts a double helix strand at a particular place so that a preprogramed strand of RNA may insert some other base-pair sequence into the target DNA for the one cut out, the ancient writers of the Genesis narrative inserted, at appropriate places, the letter-pair sequence, ᚷ ⫮ (*ăt*).

When we encounter that word in the ancient text it might stand for either one of two high-tech procedures that the Reptilian entities used to fabricate their hybrid—*that is*, us. We know which of the two high-tech procedures is referenced by the context in which the word ᚷ ⫮ appears. If ᚷ ⫮ appears in the context of DNA splicing, cutting, or editing, the concept to be translated into English is CRISPR analog technology—or CRISPR manipulation. If ᚷ ⫮ appears in the context of ICSI as associated with IVF, then the primary instrument of that procedure, an *injecting pipette*, may be the translation of the word, ᚷ ⫮ (*ăt*). In some verses the context may suggest that a more apt translation would be IVF—either as a noun or as a verb.

Readers might observe that the context of the actual narrative means that each of these technologies may be treated as verbs as well as nouns; and that as verbs they may be presented as present tense, past tense, or as a present participle (an "-ing" word). That treatment will happen as the word ᚷ ⫮ acts as a concept placeholder for the high-tech procedure called for by the context of the text itself. The writer of this ancient text used nouns that could act like verbs and verbs that could act like nouns. The ancient writer(s) as well used verbs that could be past, present, or ongoing—as determined by the context in which the concepts appeared. Be prepared for some unusual ways in which words and concepts are presented.

The text itself is going to be allowed to say what it wants to say and has said for up to—or over—three millennia—rather than its telling us what we have instructed, or programed, it to say. This volume is less concerned about what all of this "new" information means for all of humanity than about presenting, as exactly as possible, what the ancient text says and how it says what it says. With all the preceeding out of the way it is time to jump right into the actual Genesis text.

CHAPTER 7

The Researched Explanations of Each Hebrew Word Behind Each Word from the King James Version of Genesis 1

The Reptilian Aliens Introduce Their Hybridization Technologies

[Verses 1 – 4]

First up is the actual translation of the famous first verse:

> In your beginning, Cutting-*Strange Biological Entities* [aliens] CRISPR-manipulated The-Amazements and CRISPR-manipulated the I-Accomplish.

The first thing that may come to any reader is the question, "How in the dickens does all that come out of the Hebrew which experts and scholars have supposedly looked at for over two thousand years?" A short explanation is that they have never looked for anything other than what a committee of bought-and-paid-for "interpreters,"[385] some 2,200 years ago, wrote down in Greek as an asserted translation of the ancient Hebrew scriptural text. Their famous asserted translation is called [the] *Septuagint*. In Christianity it is known as the "Old Testament" in Greek.

What this present work is going to do, for the first time in history, is to reexamine each ancient Hebrew word behind the universally available King James Version of the Bible. Each verse is presented in order; and each ancient Hebrew word is dissected and explained—where an explanation is warranted—or sorely needed.

Let's first examine the first three words, *in the beginning*, as translated from the ancient Hebrew word, bĕrăshēt [𐤁𐤓𐤀𐤔𐤉𐤕]. Look in any standard Hebrew Dictionary of the Old Testament—the word, *bĕrăshēt* [𐤁𐤓𐤀𐤔𐤉𐤕 | בראשית] [Strong's H7725], is traditionally translated as "in the beginning". But there is no "the" prefix on this word; and the word's suffix, "*-ēt*", means, "your".

That word also may be bisected to be made of two "root words": *bĕra* and *shēt* [H1254 + H7896]. Think of each Hebrew word as being a concept-capsule. The word "*bĕră*" can mean *to create*; but it can also mean *to cut*. One of the meanings of the word, *shēt*, per the famous, and universally available, *Davidson's Analytical Hebrew and Chaldee Lexicon* (p. 712), is *to set a limit*.

This Hebrew word has double meanings. For the purposes of introducing this present-day translation, the more familiar introductory, "in your beginning", is being employed as the phrase that the Reptilians themselves probably selected to provide the full disclosure that the ancient text they wrote will presently provide.

The 17th Century King James Version *of* Genesis 1, Verse 1—
In the beginning God created the heaven and the earth.

Ancient Hebrew Anatomic Alphabet writing of that verse—
𐤁𐤓𐤀𐤔𐤉𐤕 𐤁𐤓𐤀 𐤀𐤋𐤄𐤉𐤌 𐤀𐤕 𐤄𐤔𐤌𐤉𐤌 𐤅𐤀𐤕 𐤄𐤀𐤓𐤑

An actual translation *with researched explanations below*—
In your beginning, Cutting-Strange Biological Entities [*aliens*] CRISPR-manipulated The-Amazements and CRISPR-manipulated the I-Accomplish.

The Researched Explanations—

in the beginning
As covered above.

God
The word, *ălăh·ēm* [𐤀𐤋𐤄𐤉𐤌][H430][386], is commonly defined as “of the supreme God”; and translated as “God”. The word, “God”, comes into English from the German word, “Gott”[387]. What is more important, and more to the point, is the functional meaning of the Hebrew word used in this ancient text. As previously explained, off-planet aliens are called (in official circles) by the acronym “EBENs”. That stands for, “**E**xtraterresterial **B**iological **EN**tities”[388]. The concept that ties the use of the word ălăhēm, when used here to describe them or by them to describe us, is the concept of “strange”. They are strange to us. We are strange to them. That is the concept that used here to define the ancient Hebrew word “ălăhēm”. The phrase *Strange Biological Entities* will be a fresh translation of that ancient word. However, the word “alien” also conveys the concept. As far as the grammar of the word goes, “-ē*m*”, is a common suffix, and generally serves to make a word plural.
TRANSLATED AS: strange-biological-entities [SBEs]

created
The word, *běra* [𐤁𐤓𐤀][H1254][389], has been traditionally translated as “to create”; but its second definition is “to *cut* down”. This definition seems to make more sense in the context of Reptilian specialists in splicing DNA or editing genes of their target species.
TRANSLATED AS: cutting

~a Hebrew word untranslated in the KJV~

The untranslated word from the ancient text here is, “ăt” [𐤀𐤕 | את]. Per any standard Hebrew Dictionary of the Old Testament, it can be found as Strong’s H855—defined as “coulter”[391]. A coulter is the part of a seed drill that cuts a furrow for the seed.

But, the Hebrew word here isn't standard and it isn't ordinary—per the previous explanation of the CRISPR system technology. The basic concept conveyed by this Hebrew word is the concept of *cutting* something. Given the context in which this word appears, we have to have something being cut with ultra-high technology. We are turning the acronym "CRISPR" into the verb form that fits the context of the narrative. [Fair-use credit to— https://en.wikipedia.org/wiki/Cas9]

TRANSLATED AS: CRISPR-manipulated

the heavens

The word, *hā·shĭm·ēm* [𐤄𐤔𐤌𐤉𐤌|השמים], has been traditionally translated as "the heavens". That word is defined as "*to be lofty*"[391]; but that word derives from H8047 ["*to ruin*"][392], which derives from H8074 [𐤔𐤌𐤌]["*to stun, to devastate;* or, *to be astonished*"][393]. Note: There are plenty of scriptural instances where the root word in "heavens" is translated as "amazed". This is a plural word.

TRANSLATED AS: the amazements

and

The word in the text here is "𐤅𐤀𐤕" as "*ōōă·ăt*". [See explanation above.] The prefix, 𐤅, means "and".

TRANSLATED AS: and CRISPR-manipulated

the earth

The word, *hā·ărĕtz* [𐤄𐤀𐤓𐤑] [H776[394]], has been traditionally defined as *ground* or *land*. It is *mis*translated as "earth" in this context. Our word here should be read as, "*hā·ă·rĕtzăh*" {[𐤄]𐤑𐤓𐤀𐤄 | [ה]הארצ} [H7521][395], "*to be pleased with, accomplish, et cetera*". The prefix, 𐤄, is "the". The letter, 𐤀, is "I".

TRANSLATED AS: the I-Accomplish

A researched translation of the ancient Hebrew Genesis 1:1—
In your beginning, Cutting-Strange Biological Entities [*aliens*] CRISPR-manipulated The Amazements and CRISPR-manipulated the I-Accomplish.

Summary:
The beginning of how our species got its start was because Strange Biological Entity (*alien*) scientists, called *cutting SBEs*, (*or Cutting-Aliens*) used a DNA-splicing technology called "CRISPR" on our ancient hominid ancestors. The SBEs had two designations for their programs. One was called *The-Amazements* and the other was called the *I-Accomplish.*

Conclusion:
The beginning of species Homo sapiens was on account of the direct scientific intervention of Strange Biological Entities by way of DNA-manipulating technology known today as **C**lustered **R**egularly **I**nterspaced **S**hort **P**alindromic **R**epeats [CRISPR].

The KJV of Genesis 1, Verse 2 (*first sentence*)
And the earth was without form, and void; and darkness was upon the face of the deep.

Ancient Hebrew Anatomic Alphabet writing of that phrase—
והארץ היתה תהו ובהו וחשך על פני תהום

An actual translation *with researched explanations below*—
And the I-Accomplish is your existence!—and voids it. And (the) restraining yoke [*the DNA molecules that form the "yoke", or "backbone", of DNA*]: my presence (is) their existence.

The KJV of Genesis 1, Verse 2 (*second sentence*)—
And the spirit of God moved upon the face of the waters.

Ancient Hebrew Anatomic Alphabet writing of that phrase—
ורוח אלהים מרחפת על פני המים

An actual translation *with researched explanations below*—
And (the) intent (of the) Strange Biological Entities (is to) effectually centrifuge my presence—the semen.

The Researched Explanations—

and the earth
The word, *ōōă·hā·ărĕtz* [והארץ] [H776], is traditionally defined as "ground *or* land", and mistranslated as "earth". The word should be read as, "*ōōă·hā·ă·rĕtz·ăh*" {והארצ[ה]} [H7521], "*to be pleased with, accomplish, et cetera*".

TRANSLATED AS: and the I-Accomplish

was
The word, *hā·ē·tōō·ăh* [היתה] [H1961][396], is traditionally translated as "was". *Translation note*: This word's root is היה (*hā·ē·ăh*); and is our

present tense word, "is". The inserted letter, *tōō* [𐤕], can mean "you" or "your".

TRANSLATED AS: is your

without form
The word, *tōō·hōō* [𐤕𐤄𐤅|תהו], given as H8414[397], is traditionally translated "without form". The word should be read as "*tōō·hōō·ăh*" {𐤕𐤄𐤅[𐤄]} [H1961], and is *actually* a form of the verb, "*to be*"[398]. *Translation note:* Per above, the letter, *tōō* [𐤕], can mean "you", "your"; or, it can act as an exclamatory emphatic—our exclamation point, "!".

TRANSLATED AS: !existence

and void
The word, *ōōă·bĕh·ōō* [𐤅𐤁𐤄𐤅|ובהו], traditionally is given as H922, and translated "and void"[399]. It is indeed Strong's H922; and is from an unused root, *to void*, or *to be empty.* The word "void" is being treated here as a present tense verb instead of a noun.

TRANSLATED AS: and voids

and darkness
The word, *ōōă·khĕshĭk* [𐤅𐤇𐤔𐤊|וחשך], traditionally cited as H2822, is translated as "and darkness"[400]. But, *khĕshĭk*, has a range of definitions: *to restrain*[401], *to refuse, to hinder, hold back, punish, withhold*; *dark, to be dark, darkness, cause darkness*; *misery, destruction, death, ignorance, sorrow,* and *wickedness*.

TRANSLATED AS: and restraining

upon
The word, *ōl* [𐤏𐤋], traditionally cited as H5927, is translated as "upon" [על]; *but*—that word *also* has several items on the menu of definitions—including H5923, "*yoke*"[402], as a *fastening framework* on two oxen pulling a plow. The word, as used here, is the original text-writer's chosen description of the *fastening framework* of the phosphate-deoxyribose "*yoke*" which

fastens together the other nucleotides of the DNA double helix molecular structure.

TRANSLATED AS: yoke

the face of

The word, *pfān·ē* [𐤐𐤍𐤉], traditionally cited as H6440[403], is translated "face". But that word's root, 𐤐𐤍𐤄 (*pfānāh*), also means "presence"[404]. The word's suffix, *yad* [𐤉], means "me", or "my".

TRANSLATED AS: my presence

the deep

The word, *tōō·hōōm* [𐤕𐤄𐤅𐤌|תהום], is traditionally given as H8415, and variously translated as "deep" or "the deep"[405]. But, this word *is also* a creative use of the noun form ("existence") of the verb derived from H1961, 𐤄𐤉𐤄 ("to exist"[406]). The word here is the derived root of the famous word, "YHWH" [𐤉𐤄𐤅𐤄[407].]. The prefix, *tōō* [𐤕], is the exclamatory emphatic [!]. The suffix, *mĕm* [𐤌], denotes third-person plural pronouns *they, them,* and *their*.

TRANSLATED AS: !their existence

and the spirit of

The word, *ōōă·rōōkh* [𐤅𐤓𐤅𐤇|ורוח], traditionally given as H7307. It is variously translated "wind", "breath", "spirit"[408], and "disposition" [Davidson's p. 678][409]. Here, the word being used is "intent"—as a synonym of "disposition".

TRANSLATED AS: and (the) intent (of the)

God

The word, *ălăh·ēm* [𐤀𐤋𐤄𐤉𐤌][H430], commonly translated "God", is the same word as found in the Book of Daniel—as "ălăh·ēn"[410]. Here it is treated as "*strange-biological-entities*". *Translation note*: the "-ēn" (or "-ē*m*") suffix on the Hebrew word "ălăh" makes the word plural. Literally, the word is "*alah-beings*".

TRANSLATED AS: strange-biological-entities

moved

The word, *mĕ·rĕkhĕpf·āt* [𐤌𐤓𐤇𐤐𐤕|מרחפת][H7363], the KJV translates as "moved"[411]; but this word appears only once in the Hebrew Bible—here in this verse[412]. The root word, 𐤓𐤇𐤐 [רחפ], never appears there[413]. A variant of this word appears twice: once in Deut. 32:11 as "flutters"; and in Jer. 23:9 as "shake". The prefix, *mĕm* [𐤌], acts as a utility determinative. It denotes the SBEs' utility of "shake". To centrifuge something is indeed to shake it.

TRANSLATED AS: centrifuged!

upon

The word, *ōl* [𐤏𐤋], as previously noted, is traditionally cited as H5927, as "upon"; and treated here previously as "yoke" [H5923][414]; but, in the word's context here, it can be read as a homonym, "ōl"—that is, "𐤏𐤋𐤋" [H5953] with the final 𐤋 dropped. Strong's defines the word as "to effect"[415]; and Davidson [p. 601], as "effectually"[416].

TRANSLATED AS: effectually

the face of

The word, *pfān·ē* [𐤐𐤍𐤉|פני] [H6440], could be "face"; *but*—that word's root, 𐤐𐤍𐤄 (*pfānāh*), also means "presence". The suffix, *yad* [𐤉], means "me", "my".

TRANSLATED AS: my presence

the waters

The word, *hā·mēm* [𐤄𐤌𐤉𐤌][417] [H4325], can be "waters" (or "sea"); *but*—it can also, by euphemism, mean "urine" or "semen"[418]. The prefix letter, *hāy* [𐤄], means "the"[419].

TRANSLATED AS: the semen

A researched translation of the ancient Hebrew Genesis 1:2—
And the I-Accomplish is your existence!—and voids it [*your existence*]. And (the) restraining yoke [*the DNA molecules that form the "yoke", or "back-bone", of DNA*]: my presence (is) their existence! And (the) intent (of the) strange-biological-entities (is to) effectually centrifuge my presence—the semen.

Genesis 1:2—*in plain English*

- ☆ The "I-Accomplish" is the strange-biological-entities own successful DNA modification project.
- ☆ Their modified DNA represents the strange-biological-entities' existence.
- ☆ They centrifuged their semen to obtain their sperm specimen.

The KJV of Genesis 1:3—
And God said Let there be light: and there was light.

Ancient Hebrew Anatomic Alphabet writing of that verse—
4Yǂ ZᕽZY 4Yǂ ZᕽZ ᘻZᕽᒪǂ 4ᘻǂZY

An actual translation *with researched explanations below*—
And strange-biological-entities said, It is I-Place [*the beveled injecting pipette*]; and it is I-Placed.

The Researched Explanations—

and said
The word, *ōōă·ē·ămĕr* [4ᘻǂZY|ויאמר], is traditionally cited as H559, as "said"; but it is a word used "with great latitude". For this space-age translation the traditional treatment of this word is valid; though technically, *ōōă·ē·ămĕr* [4ᘻǂZY], is "and it said".

TRANSLATED AS: and said

God
The word, *ălăh·ēm* [ᘻZᕽᒪǂ] [H430], commonly translated, "of the supreme God". Here it is treated as "*strange-biological-entities*". Note: The "-ēn" (or "-ēm") suffix on the Hebrew word "ălăh" makes the word plural. The word could be "*alah-beings*".

TRANSLATED AS: strange-biological-entities

let there be
The word, *ēă·hē* [ZᕽZ][420][H1961], is certainly of the root, "to be"; but here, under enhanced interrogation, confesses "let there". The grammar of this word, ēă·hē [ZᕽZ|יהי], is exceedingly simple. The word's prefix, *yad* [Z], is "it" or "he". Here it is, "it"[421]. The root, "to be", is "ᕽZᕽ"[422]. The word in the text has a *dropped letter, hay* [ᕽ]. The verb "be" is not used here; instead—the word "is".

TRANSLATED AS: it is

light

The word, *ă·ōōr* [𐤓𐤅𐤀] [H216], can be "light" (or variants) such as the word, "bioluminescence"[423]. *But*, this ancient Hebrew word needs to be treated as a *contracted modification* of "ă·ēr·ăh"[424] {[𐤄] 𐤓𐤉𐤀} [H3384]—*to lay, throw, or cast—especially an arrow*; *to teach* or *to instruct*. In the word, ă·ōōr [𐤓𐤅𐤀], the 𐤀 is the prefix, "I"; and the root modifier, "𐤅", is substituted for the letter, "𐤉", in the root "𐤄𐤓𐤉" with a dropped letter *hay* [𐤄]. Here, the modifier can make the verb, "to cast" into a synonym, "to place".

TRANSLATED AS: I-Place [-the-beveled-injection-pipette]

and there was

Again, the word, *ōōă·ē·hē* [𐤉𐤄𐤉𐤅][H1961], is from the root, "to be". But, as previously seen is simply the present tense, "is". Yes, there ought to be a final letter, *hay* [𐤄], on the root, "𐤄𐤉𐤄"[425]; but it is common among biblical writers to drop the final *hay*—just as it is in the word in the text. The word's first prefix is 𐤅, "and". The word's second prefix is 𐤉, "it". The verb is 𐤉𐤄 ("is")[426].

TRANSLATED AS: and it is

light

As from the discussion above, the word, *ă·ōōr* [𐤓𐤅𐤀] [H216], can be "light" (or variants) such as the word, "bioluminescence". *But*, this ancient Hebrew word needs to be treated as a *contracted modification* of "ă·ēr·ăh" {[𐤄] 𐤓𐤉𐤀} [H3384]—*to lay, throw, or cast—especially an arrow*; *to teach* or *to instruct*. In the word, ă·ōōr [𐤓𐤅𐤀], the 𐤀 is the prefix, "I"; and the root modifier, "𐤅", is substituted for the letter, "𐤉", in the root "𐤄𐤓𐤉" with a dropped letter *hay* [𐤄]. Here, the modifier can make the present tense verb, "cast" into a past tense synonym, "placed"[427].

TRANSLATED AS: I-Placed [-the-beveled-injection-pipette]

A researched translation of the ancient Hebrew Genesis 1:3—
And strange-biological-entities said, It is I-Place [*the beveled injecting pipette*]; and it is I-Placed.

Genesis 1:3—*in plain English*

- ☆ The strange-biological-entities utilize an injecting pipette to place sperm cells for their in-vitro fertilization [IVF] project.
- ☆ They had two names for their IVF project.
- ☆ An unidentified SBE gave the names: I-Place and I-Placed.

The KJV of Genesis 1:4 (*first phrase*)—
And God saw the light, that it was good:

Ancient Hebrew Anatomic Alphabet writing of that phrase—
𐤅𐤉𐤓𐤀 𐤀𐤋𐤄𐤉𐤌 𐤀𐤕 𐤄𐤀𐤅𐤓 𐤊𐤉 𐤈𐤅𐤁

An actual translation *with researched explanations below*—
And strange-biological-entities consider injection pipetting—the I-Place [*the beveled injection pipette*] because (it is) better [*as a technical solution*].

The KJV of Genesis 1:4 (*second phrase*)—
And God divided the light from the darkness.

Ancient Hebrew Anatomic Alphabet writing of that phrase—
𐤅𐤉𐤁𐤃𐤋 𐤀𐤋𐤄𐤉𐤌 𐤁𐤉𐤍 𐤄𐤀𐤅𐤓 𐤅𐤁𐤉𐤍 𐤄𐤇𐤔𐤊

An actual translation *with researched explanations below*—
And strange-biological-entities differentiated, distinguishing the I-Place [*the beveled injection pipette*], and distinguishing the restraint [*of the target species according to their agenda*].

The Researched Explanations—

and saw
The word here [*ōōă·ē·ra* | 𐤅𐤉𐤓𐤀] may be “and saw”[428]. It may also be “fear” [H3372][429]. The Hebrew root means “to see” [H7200—*to see (literally or figuratively)*]. This root is treated as “consider” at Exodus 33:13 and Leviticus 13:13 in the KJV Bible. The root is “𐤓𐤀𐤄”. The final letter, 𐤄, has been dropped by the ancient writer. The word’s prefix, 𐤅, is “and”. The word’s second prefix, 𐤉, is the third person singular subject pronoun, “it” (a collective reference to the strange-biological-entities). The verb is “𐤓𐤀”. The pronoun will be dropped from the final translation.

TRANSLATED AS: and consider

God
The word, *ălăh·ēm* [𐤌𐤉𐤄𐤋𐤀][H430], is traditionally translated "God". Literally, the word could be treated as "*alah-beings*"[430]; but here it refers to a collective of E.T. beings.

TRANSLATED AS: strange-biological-entities

the
This word, "the" [*ăt* |𐤕𐤀 | את], is out of context. It's rarely cited as any Strong's number. As previously discussed, it's H855—defined as "coulter". Again, the coulter is the part of a seed drill that cuts a furrow for the seed; and can be found at First Samuel 13:20 and 21. A modern synonym, used in IVF, is called an injecting pipette.

TRANSLATED AS: injection pipette

light
As from the previous discussion, the word, *ă·ōōr* [𐤓𐤅𐤀] [H216], can be "light" (or variants) such as the word, "bioluminescence". *But*, this ancient Hebrew word needs to be treated as a *contracted modification* of "ă·ēr·ăh" {[𐤄]𐤓𐤉𐤀} [H3384]—*to lay, throw, or cast—especially an arrow*; *to teach* or *to instruct.* In the word in the text is, *hā*· · ·ă·ōōr [𐤓𐤅𐤀𐤄]. The first prefix, 𐤄, is "the". The second prefix, 𐤀, is "I". The root modifier, "𐤅", is substituted for the letter, "𐤉", in the root "𐤄𐤓𐤉" with a dropped letter *hay* [𐤄]. Here, the modifier can make the verb, "cast" into a synonym, "place"[431].

TRANSLATED AS: the I-Place [-the-beveled-injection-pipette]

that it was
The key to understanding how "that it was" becomes "because" is because the word in the text is "*kē*" (pronounced "key") [𐤉𐤊][432]. It is Strong's H3588—and generally means "for" or "because". The words, "that it was" was conveniently inserted by traditionalist English translators. The Greek word selected 2,200 years ago by the Jewish interpreters who put together the *Septuagint* used the word, οτι[433] (*hŏtĭ*) [G3754][434], which means *that* or *because.*

TRANSLATED AS: because

good

The thing about the word, *thōōb* [𐤈𐤅𐤁|טוב] [H2896][435] is that it can mean *better*, *precious*, *merry*, *fair*, *bountiful*, and *pleasant*. Here, it is "better"—in the sense of the practical necessity of IVF.

TRANSLATED AS: better

and divided

The word, *ōōă·ē·bĕdăl* [𐤅𐤉𐤁𐤃𐤋|ויבדל][436], is cited as H914; *but* it's a word used "in various senses literally or figuratively". Other meanings are "separated" and "distinguish". The traditional "divided" is valid; but "differentiate" is more in context.

TRANSLATED AS: and it differentiated

God

The word, *ălăh·ēm* [𐤀𐤋𐤄𐤉𐤌][H430], is traditionally translated "God" [437]. Here there is no uber-being; only extraterrestrials.

TRANSLATED AS: strange-biological-entities

~a Hebrew word untranslated in the KJV~

The untranslated word in the text here is, "*bēn*" [𐤁𐤄𐤍|בין][438]. Per any Strong's Hebrew Dictionary, it can be found as Number 995—*to separate mentally or distinguish, be cunning.*

TRANSLATED AS: distinguishing

the light

The word, *ă·ōōr* [𐤀𐤅𐤓] [H216], can be "light" (or variants); *but*, this ancient word is treated here as a *contracted modification* of "*hā·ă·ēr·ăh*" {𐤄𐤀𐤉𐤓[𐤄]} [H3384]—*to lay, throw, or cast*. In the word, *hā·ă·ōōr* [𐤄𐤀𐤅𐤓], the 𐤄 is the prefix, "the"; the 𐤀 is a prefix, "I"; and the root modifier, "𐤅𐤓", *from* the root, "𐤉𐤓", with a *dropped hay* [𐤄]. The modification makes "cast" into "place".[439]

TRANSLATED AS: the I-Place [the beveled injection pipette]

from
The Hebrew word in the text is the same form as the untranslated word as given above. Here the word in the text is, "*ōōă·bēn*" [𐤅𐤁𐤉𐤍]. Per any edition of *Strong's*, it can be found as H995—*to separate mentally or distinguish.*

TRANSLATED AS: and distinguishing

the darkness
The word, *hā·khĕshĭk* [𐤄𐤇𐤔𐤊|החשך][H2820], has a range of cited definitions—from *dark* and *darkness*[440], to *refrain* and *restrain*[441]. Here, the ancient writer uses the word as a noun[442].

TRANSLATED AS: the restraint [of the target species according to their agenda]

A researched translation of the ancient Hebrew Genesis 1:4—
And strange-biological-entities consider injection pipetting—(the) I-Place [*the-beveled-injection-pipette*] because (it is) better [*as a technical solution*]. And strange-biological-entities differentiated, distinguishing the I-Place [*the beveled injection pipette*], and distinguishing the restraint [*of the target species according to their agenda*].

Genesis 1:4—*in plain English*

- ☆ The strange-biological-entities considered the "I-Place" a good technical solution.
- ☆ They knew that they had to do IVF of the egg of the female of the target species.
- ☆ They knew that they had to determine which ways to restrain the target species.

The Reptilians encounter technical problems

[Verses 5 – 10]

The KJV *of* Genesis 1:5 (*first sentence, first phrase*)—
And God called the light Day

Ancient Hebrew Anatomic Alphabet writing of that phrase—
𐤅𐤉𐤒𐤓𐤀 𐤀𐤋𐤄𐤉𐤌 𐤋𐤀𐤅𐤓 𐤉𐤅𐤌

An actual translation *with researched explanations below*—
And strange-biological-entities encountered, in regard to bioluminescent it-and-them [*the ovum (egg cell) is the "it", and the mass of sperm cells is the "them"*];

The KJV *of* Genesis 1:5 (*first sentence, second phrase*)—
and the darkness he called Night.

Ancient Hebrew Anatomic Alphabet writing of that phrase—
𐤅𐤋𐤇𐤔𐤊 𐤒𐤓𐤀 𐤋𐤉𐤋𐤄

An actual translation *with researched explanations below*—
and in regard to restraint [*of the target species according to their agenda*]—encountering (the) absolute state (of) the twisting spiral [*the DNA molecular structure*].

The KJV *of* Genesis 1:5 (*second sentence*)—
And the evening and the morning were the first day.

Ancient Hebrew Anatomic Alphabet writing of that phrase—
𐤅𐤉𐤄𐤉 𐤏𐤓𐤁 𐤅𐤉𐤄𐤉 𐤁𐤒𐤓 𐤉𐤅𐤌 𐤀𐤇𐤃

An actual translation *with researched explanations below*—
And it is to interbreed and it is to research unifying it-and-them

[*the egg cell is the "it", and the mass of sperm cells is the "them"*].

The Researched Explanations—

and called

Yes, the word, *ōōă·ē·qwōōră* [𐤅𐤉𐤒𐤓𐤀|ויקרא], can be "to call" [H7121][443]; but its other definition is "to encounter" [H7122][444]. The verb employed in this translation is that very usage.

TRANSLATED AS: and it encountered

God

As previously seen, *ălăh·ēm* [𐤀𐤋𐤄𐤉𐤌] [H430], has been explained as being some speices of E.T.'s.[445]

TRANSLATED AS: strange-biological-entities

the light

Previously treated as a *contracted modification* of "ă·ēr·ăh", here, the word, *lă·ăōōr* [𐤋𐤀𐤅𐤓|לאור][H216], is prefixed by the letter, *lămĕd* [𐤋], meaning "to", "toward", *or* "in regard to"[446]. The word here is treated as a *variant* of "light"[447]—as "bioluminescence". Note: there is no "the" prefix on this Hebrew word.

TRANSLATED AS: in regard to bioluminescent

day

Appearing some 2,300 times in the biblical text as Strong's H3117, the word ĕăōōm [𐤉𐤅𐤌|יום] is "day". That word also appears, (much less often), as: *space (as a period of time), days, year, when, while, long, whole, ever,* and *always*[448]. We're informed by Dr. Strong that this word is from *an unused root—meaning "to be hot*". As—*get this*, a day, he lectures, is when our "warm hours" are[449]. The problem is that none of these words-in-translation are in context here.

What *is* in context? CRISPR-manipulation in the first verse, the phosphate-deoxyribose sugar backbone (yoke) of the DNA molecule and centrifuged semen in the second verse, injection pipette placement in the third verse, IVF in the fourth verse; and thus far in the fifth verse, bioluminescence.

To translate the word, it must be revisualized—not as traditional grammarians or lexicographers have instructed the texts author(s) what their words means—but in the context of what the entities themselves were doing and were working to accomplish. It is in this verse that they are going to do exactly that.

In their grammar (deduced from years of study as to how it *actually* operates) this three-letter word is made of three different "units of grammar". These *grammar units* are not dissimilar to grammar as it is traditionally conceived and explained[450]. The word will represent, as a description (in words), what the entities are seeing under their electron microscope.

The word is spelled, *yăd-ōōă*-["vav"]-*mĕm* [𐤉𐤅𐤌|יום]. The grammar-function of the first letter, *yăd* [𐤉|י], here is that it is a common prefix which represents the third person singular subject pronoun "he" or "it" (sometimes "she"). Here, the prefix-letter means "it". In the context of the entirety of the entities' *executive summary* (*Genesis One*) the "it" here refers to the ovum—the solitary egg of their laboratory homind female readied for conceptive penetration by one sperm cell among a broiling mass of sperm cells swimming toward the solitary egg cell—as visualized under an electron microscope.

The grammar-function of the second letter, *ōōă* ["vav"] [𐤅|ו], is that of another common prefix—the conjunction "and". The sighting of the prefix "and" as a second prefix may be as rare as a hen's tooth in traditional Hebrew grammar books. Here, the entities are teaching *us* how their language functions. This translation will not presume to tell the authors of the ancient text how their language is to function.

The grammar function of the third letter, *mĕm* [𐤌|ם], is that of a common suffix which represents the third person plural object pronoun "them". The "them" refers to the mass of sperm cells surrounding the solitary ovum awaiting conceptive penetration by the fastest strongest swimmingest sperm cell.

TRANSLATED AS: it-and-them

and the darkness

First off, in the Hebrew text there isn't a "the" prefix on this word, encountered as the last word of Verse 4. There, the word was, "*hā·khĕshĭk*" [𐤄𐤇𐤔𐤊]—*the restraint*. Here it appears as, *ōōă·lă·khĕshĭk* | 𐤅𐤋𐤇𐤔𐤊 |ולחשך. It's still the same *restraint*[451]—but now it has *two* prefixes: 𐤅, "and"; *and* 𐤋, which, in this context means *in regard to*.

TRANSLATED AS: and in regard to restraint

he called

Again, first off—there is no "he" personal pronoun prefix on this word. The first word of this verse "and-it-encountered" appears here without any prefixes, as "𐤒𐤓𐤀"[452]; so it's *just* the verb form.

TRANSLATED AS: encountering

night

Buckle the seatbelt in your flying-saucer simulator because we're going to be encountering some serious word-turbulence. First up is the word in the ancient text, *lēl·ăh* [𐤋𐤉𐤋𐤄|לילה][H3915], defined as "*a twist (away from the light), i.e. night*". Did you get that? Next, Dr. Strong refers us to H3883, where we encounter "*an unused root meaning to fold back; a spiral step—winding stair*". You seeing what I'm seeing? Next, Dr. Strong refers us to H3924, where we encounter "*from the same as H3883—a loop*". *Well*—a loop, a twist, a fold back, a spiral step, a winding stair. That's a pretty good description of the famous DNA double-helix molecular structure. The suffix on this word, a *hāy* [𐤄|ה], per another famous Hebrew wordsmith, Ben Davidson, is "silent" and "inconsequential"[453]. *But* Professor Davidson informs us elsewhere that *hāy* [𐤄] as a suffix may refer to the "the absolute state" of the word upon which the *hay* is suffixed. We're landing on that *absolute state*.

TRANSLATED AS: the absolute state (of the) twisting spiral

and the
This is the same Hebrew word encountered in Verse 3 as, *ōōă·ē·hē* [𐤅𐤉𐤄𐤉] [H1961]. Here, "and"[454], is the word's prefix.

TRANSLATED AS: and it is

evening
Better retighten that seatbelt. Sure, *ōrĕb*[455] [𐤏𐤓𐤁|ערב] [H6153] can be "evening" *through the idea of covering as with a texture*[456] [H6150]. How romantic is *that* imagery? If you like that, you'll love this: Strong's H6148 [𐤏𐤓𐤁][457] and H6154 [𐤏𐤓𐤁][458] are more on-point—as, *to intermix*—as with a *mingled people*. Professor Davidson doesn't mince words. He says, "*to have intercourse*"[459]. That's what the word, "intermix" really getting at.

TRANSLATED AS: interbreed

and the
This is the same Hebrew word encountered above—as, *ōōă·ē·hē* [𐤅𐤉𐤄𐤉|ויהי][H1961]. The conjunction, "and" is the context here.

TRANSLATED AS: and it is

morning
As was with the word, "evening", so it is similar with the word here. The word, *bĕ·qwōōr* [𐤁𐤒𐤓|בקר][*given as* H1242], is properly "dawn"[460]—through the idea of *breaking forth*[461] [H1239]. Another meaning is to "*search*" [Leviticus 27:33][462]. Here, we're going to use a synonym of that word, but which is identified with a scientific search—as "research".

TRANSLATED AS: to research

were the
These two words were not translated from Hebrew, as they are not in the Hebrew text[463]. They come from a word in the Greek fake-out translation of the ancient Hebrew scripture—the word, "εγένετο"[464] (*egeneto*) [G1096],

meaning "*to cause to be*". No translation is needed here: these words are not in the original text.

day

Previously treated in this verse, the word *ĕăōōm* [𐤌𐤅𐤉|יוֹם] [H3117], functions as a three *letter-units* of grammar (as previously explained). The word is the description of what the entities are observing under electron microscopy.

TRANSLATED AS: it-and-them

first

This word, *ăkhĕd* [𐤃𐤇𐤀|אחד] [H258/H259] means, in context, "to unify", "united", "one", *and* "first". This Hebrew word appears some 952 times as translated into the KJV Bible—most often as the word, "one". But it also appears as "every", ''each", "only", "other", "alone", "altogether", and "together". Here it is being used as a present participle—*an "ing" word.*

TRANSLATED AS: unifying

A researched translation of the ancient Hebrew Genesis 1:5—

And entities encountered, in regard to bioluminescent it-and-them [*the ovum (egg cell) is the "it", and the mass of sperm cells is the "them"*]; and in regard to restraint [*of the target species according to their agenda*]—encountering (the) absolute state (of) the twisting spiral [*the DNA molecular structure of the egg and sperm cell*]. And it is to interbreed and it is to research unifying it-and-them.

Genesis 1:5—*in plain English*

- ☆ The entities' technology made it possible for them to see tiny points of light at the molecular level.
- ☆ They knew they had to figure out how to restrain the target species at the DNA level.
- ☆ Their intention is to interbreed and to conduct research on how to optimally unify DNA-manipulated cells of reproduction to achieve conception and fertilization.

The KJV *of* Genesis 1:6 (*first phrase*)—
And God said, Let there be a firmament in the midst of the waters,

Ancient Hebrew Anatomic Alphabet writing of that phrase—
𐤅𐤉𐤀𐤌𐤓 𐤀𐤋𐤄𐤉𐤌 𐤉𐤄𐤉 𐤓𐤒𐤉𐤏 𐤁𐤕𐤅𐤊 𐤄𐤌𐤉𐤌

An actual translation *with researched explanations below*—
And strange-biological-entities said, "It is spread out—in among the semen;

The KJV *of* Genesis 1:6 (*second phrase*)—
and let it divide the waters from the waters.

Ancient Hebrew Anatomic Alphabet writing of that phrase—
𐤅𐤉𐤄𐤉 𐤌𐤁𐤃𐤉𐤋 𐤁𐤉𐤍 𐤌𐤉𐤌 𐤋𐤌𐤉𐤌

An actual translation *with researched explanations below*—
and it is sorted out—distinguishing semen [*the alien sperm cells rejected by the human egg cell*] in regard to semen [*SBE's spermatozoa that are accepted*].

The Researched Explanations—

and said
The word, *ōōă·ē·ămĕr* [𐤅𐤉𐤀𐤌𐤓], is previously cited [H559] as "said". It is a word used "with great latitude". For this modern translation the traditional treatment of this word is valid; though to be grammatically exact, it is: "and-it-said".

TRANSLATED AS: and it said

God
As previously seen, *ălăh·ēm* [𐤀𐤋𐤄𐤉𐤌] [H430], is traditionally treated in English as "God". Again, literally, they are "alah-beings"; and translated here similar to how *aliens* are described in official government circles.[465]

TRANSLATED AS: strange-biological-entities

let there be

The word, *ēă·hē* [𐤉𐤄𐤉][H1961], is from the root, “to be”. Look at the word’s simple grammar: ēă·hē [𐤉𐤄𐤉]. 𐤉 is “it”; 𐤄𐤉 is “is”.

TRANSLATED AS: it is

a firmament

In some translations, the word, *rĕqwēō*[466] [𐤓𐤒𐤉𐤏|רקיע] [H7549 from H7554] is “expanse”[467]—which comes from the idea of being “spread out”—what we find at Job 37:18, “…spread out the sky”[468]. That is the translation used here. The real-life consideration for the strange-biological-entities’ scientists (as well as for our fertility doc’s) is that of assessing the sperm specimen for fertility. That includes checking for unusually high semen volume which would dilute, or *spread out*, the sperm specimen and decrease the concentration of spermatozoa. As well, the E.T.’s must be concerned about the hominid egg’s anti-sperm antibodies. The grammar note is that the presence, or use, of the inserted *yăd* [𐤉][469] simply means that the writer intended to modify his verb, to spread, in some way, which would be understood—in context—as it is here.

TRANSLATED AS: spread out

in the midst

This word will need only slight treatment. It is *bĕ·tōōk*[470] [𐤁𐤕𐤅𐤊|בתוך] [H8432]—which is *to sever,* is *a bi-section, the center,* or *among.* Of the 415 times that Strong’s H8432 is cited in the KJV, the word, “among”, appears 134 times in translation[471]. Note: the *bet* [𐤁] prefix can mean: “in”, “among”, or “against”[472].

TRANSLATED AS: in among

of the waters

If you look up Strong’s *Hebrew* Number 4325 [*hā·mēm* | 𐤄𐤌𐤉𐤌| המים] you’ll find “water” alright; but you’ll also find “juice”, and “*by extension, urine*” and “*semen*”[473]. Grammar note: the prefix, *hay* [𐤄], is “the”; and the root word, *mēm* [𐤌𐤉𐤌], is “semen”—specifically, *spermatozoa.*

TRANSLATION: the semen [spermatozoa]

and let it

We just saw this word as "let there be". Only, here it has a one-letter prefix, 𐤅, "and". The verb is, "to be" [H1961], *ōōă·ē·hē* [𐤅𐤉𐤄𐤉|ויהי]—where 𐤅 *is* "and", 𐤉 is "it"; *and* 𐤄𐤉 is "is".

TRANSLATED AS: and it is

divide

This word can be "divide". The word in the text is *mĕ·bĕdēl*[474] [𐤌𐤁𐤃𐤉𐤋|מבדיל][H914]—divide (*"in various senses, literally and figuratively"*), separate, *and* distinguish. Since the letter *yad* [𐤉] is inserted into the root, the writer intends the meaning to be modified—here, as *past tense*. While translated in Verse 4 as "differentiated", the word here has a *mem* [𐤌] prefix—a utility determinative. The *various sense* utility here is "sorted out".

TRANSLATED AS: sorted out

~a Hebrew word untranslated in the KJV~

The untranslated word in the text here is, "*bēn*" [𐤁𐤉𐤍|בין]. Per any standard Hebrew Dictionary of the Old Testament, it can be found as Strong's H996—defined as "*a distinction*".

TRANSLATED AS: distinguishing

the waters

The word in the text here does not have the *hāy* [𐤄] prefix, "the"; and has been previously explained. It is only: *mēm* [𐤌𐤉𐤌|מים].

TRANSLATED AS: semen [spermatozoa]

from the waters

Obviously, this is the same word. Here it has the *lămĕd* [𐤋] prefix, *in regard to*. Our word is *lă·mēm* [𐤋𐤌𐤉𐤌|למים].

TRANSLATED AS: in regard to [fully functional] semen [spermatozoa]

A researched translation of the ancient Hebrew Genesis 1:6—
And strange-biological-entities said, "It is spread out—in among the semen; and it is sorted out—distinguishing semen [*the entities' sperm cells rejected by the hominid egg cell*] in regard to semen [*alien spermatozoa that will be accepted*].

Genesis 1:6—*in plain English*

- ☆ The strange-biological-entities knew that their own semen wasn't concentrated enough to fertilize a hominid egg.
- ☆ They knew their sperm cells were rejected by the hominid egg cell and that they had to solve the technical problems.

The KJV *of* Genesis 1:7 (*first phrase*)—
And God made the firmament,

Ancient Hebrew Anatomic Alphabet writing of that phrase—

ויעש אלהים את הרקיע

An actual translation *with researched explanations below*—
And strange-biological-entities did in-vitro fertilization (of) the spread out.

The KJV *of* Genesis 1:7 (*second phrase*)—
and divided the waters which were under the firmament
from the waters which were above the firmament:

Ancient Hebrew Anatomic Alphabet writing of that phrase—

ויבדל בין המים אשר מתחת
לרקיע ובין המים אשר מעל לרקיע

An actual translation *with researched explanations below*—
And it differentiated: distinguishing the semen [*sperm cells*]. I solve [*the problem of*] useful fertility in regard to [*sperm*] being spread out [*decreased concentration of sperm cells which necessitated IVF*]. And it differentiated—distinguishing the semen [*sperm*], I solve [*the problem of the*] fastening framework [*the molecular 'yoke' holding the DNA structure together*] in regard to being spread out.

The KJV *of* Genesis 1:7 (*third phrase*)—
and it was so.

Ancient Hebrew Anatomic Alphabet writing of that phrase—

ויהי כן

An actual translation *with researched explanations below*—
And it is true.

The Researched Explanations—

and made

This word is translated as "did"—the past tense of "do". The word in the text is *ōōă·ē·ōsh* [WOZY|ויעש][H6213]—to do *or* to make (*"in the broadest sense and widest application"*). The letter *yad* [Z] is not inserted into the root word here—it is the *second* prefix, "it"; the *first* prefix is, *"ōōă"* [*aka the more well-known Hebrew letter, "wav"*], "and". The "it" refers collectively to the sentence's subject, the strange-biological-entities.

TRANSLATED AS: and it did

God

As previously seen, *ălăh·ēm* [MZ𐤄L𐤀|אלהים] [H430], is traditionally treated in English as "God". Again, literally, they are "alah-beings"; and similarly translated here according to how *aliens* are described in official government circles.[475]

TRANSLATED AS: strange-biological-entities

the

This word, "the", is part of the traditional *translational fake-out*. It is not attached to the word "firmament" (which is next up on the translation chopping block). Again, we have *ăt* | X𐤀|את]. Rarely cited as any Strong's number—it's H855. It's a "coulter"—the part of a seed drill that cuts a furrow for the seed. (Find this word at 1 Samuel 13:20 and 21.[476]) A space-age synonym of that tool, used in IVF [in-vitro fertilization], is an injecting pipette. Here, *ăt*, in translation, is being treated as the process in which an injecting pipette is used.

TRANSLATED AS: in-vitro fertilization

firmament

As seen in the previous verse, the word in the text, *hā·rĕqwēō*[477] [OZ𐤒𐤓𐤄|הרקיע] [H7549 from H7554] is "expanse"[478]—which comes from the idea of being "spread out"—what we find at Job 37:18, "...spread out the sky”[479]. The grammar here is that the inserted *yăd* [𐤉] modifies this verb, to spread in a way which would be understood in context. The *hāy* [𐤄] is the prefix, *the*.

TRANSLATED AS: the spread out

and divided

Seen in Verse 4, it’s the same here: *ōōă·ē·bĕdăl* [𐤅𐤉𐤁𐤃𐤋][H914]. Traditionally rendered as “divided”; but is used in a different—though similar sense. The “it” is a collective reference to the actors here, *the strange biological entities.*

TRANSLATED AS: and it differentiated

~a Hebrew word untranslated in the KJV~

This word was also seen in Verses 4 and 6. It is “*bēn*” [𐤁𐤉𐤍]. It is found as Strong’s H995—*to separate mentally* or *to distinguish.*

TRANSLATED AS: distinguishing

the waters

Seen in Verse 2 and three times in Verse 6, the word here is *hā·mēm* [𐤄𐤌𐤉𐤌] [H4325]. Yes, it can be *waters* or *sea*. But can also be *urine* or *semen*[480]. Here, it refers to—or *is*, “sperm”. The word has a prefix [𐤄], meaning “the”.

TRANSLATED AS: the semen

which

Used 111 times as H834 [*ăshĭr*] throughout the KJV, is a word chameleon. It can be a relative pronoun used as *which*, *whose*, *wheresoever*, *where*, and *whereas*, among others. The word in the text is ăshĭr [𐤀𐤔𐤓|אשר]. Here it is read as ă·shĭr·ăh [𐤀𐤔𐤓𐤄][H8281—“*to free*”], with the root word *shĭrăh* [𐤔𐤓𐤄][481]. It has a prefix *alapf* [𐤀], “I”; and a dropped *hāy* [𐤄]. Defined as “to free”, it is traditionally translated as “solving” at Daniel 5:12[482], though as root “𐤔𐤓𐤀” [*shĭră*] [שְׁרֵא], a perfect homonym of “𐤔𐤓𐤄” [*shĭrăh*]. That is how it is used here. The tacked-on "the problem of" [in brackets] is understood—in the context of *solving.*

TRANSLATED AS: I solve [the problem of]

were under

The word in the text is *mě·tōōkhět*[483] [𐤕𐤇𐤕𐤌|מתחת][H8478], most often seen here as "under". Our word here is from root "𐤕𐤇𐤕" [H8480][484]. The word, *tōōkhět* [𐤕𐤇𐤕|תחת] appears six times in the Hebrew Bible, and only as the name of a place: an oasis in the desert—from which we get the word "fertility"—as an oasis *is* a place of fertility. The prefix, *měm* [𐤌], is a utility determinative. The *měm* is translated, as a *utility*, as *"useful*".

TRANSLATED AS: useful fertility

the firmament

There is no "the" as a prefix on the Hebrew word. It is the exact word previously seen in this verse.

TRANSLATED AS: in regard to (being) spread out

from

Previously, our untranslated word, *bēn*, here appears as "*ōōă·bēn*" [𐤍𐤉𐤁𐤅], *to distinguish*. Here it has a prefix, [*ōōă* | 𐤅], as "and".

TRANSLATED AS: and distinguishing

the waters

Seen in Verse 2, three times in Verse 6, and now twice in this verse, the word here is *hā·mēm* [𐤌𐤉𐤌𐤄][H4325]. *Water, waters,* or *sea*—it can also be *urine* or *semen*. Here, it refers to sperm in semen[485].

TRANSLATED AS: the semen

which

The word "which" is traditionally derived from the word, *ă·shĭr* [𐤓𐤔𐤀] when it is treated as the root associated with Strong's H834. Here it is treated as *ă·shĭr·ăh* [𐤀𐤔𐤓𐤄][H8281—"*to free*"]—the way it is used in Book of Daniel 5:12—as "*solving*"[486]. Putting the word's dropped letter *hāy* back on gives it a prefix—the letter 𐤀, which means "I".

TRANSLATED AS: I solve [the problem]

were above
The word "above" is traditionally derived from the word, *ōl* [𐤏𐤋], when associated with Strong's H5920 or 5921—where it pretends association with "Highest", "top", "God", or "Jehovah". Here, the word in the text is *mě·ōl* [𐤌𐤏𐤋|מעל]. The associated Strong's Number is H5923—yoke. The prefix, *měm* [𐤌], as a utility determinative, allows "yoke" to be treated as the *utility* of a yoke—a fastening framework.

TRANSLATED AS: fastening framework

the firmament
There's no, "the" here as a prefix on the word in the text. It is the exact word, *lă·rě·qwēō* [𐤋𐤓𐤒𐤉𐤏], previously seen in this verse[487].

TRANSLATED AS: in regard to (being) spread out

and it was so
The two words in the text here are *ōōă·ē·hē kăn* [𐤅𐤉𐤄𐤉 𐤊𐤍| ויהי־כן]. They are associated with H1961 and H3651. The prefix, *ōōă* [𐤅], is "and"; the *yăd* [𐤉] is the *second* prefix, "it". The root fragment, *hē* [𐤄𐤉], is "is". The second word, *kăn* [𐤊𐤍] can mean "so"; but it also can mean "thus" and "true".

TRANSLATED AS: and it is true

A researched translation of the ancient Hebrew Genesis 1:7—
And strange-biological-entities did in-vitro fertilization (of) the spread out [*decreased concentration of sperm cells which necessitated IVF*]. And it differentiated: distinguishing the semen [*sperm cells*]. I solved [*the problem*] of useful fertility in regard to [*sperm*] being spread out. And distinguishing

the semen [*sperm*], I solved (*the problem of the*) fastening framework [*the molecular 'yoke' holding the DNA structure together*] in regard to being spread out. And it is true.

Genesis 1:7—*in plain English*

- ☆ Strange-biological-entities used an injecting pipette for in-vitro fertilization of their viable sperm cells as a solution to their problem of low sperm concentration.
- ☆ The entities solved the technical problem of holding their own DNA together inside viable sperm cells.
- ☆ The account states that what they are relating is true.

The KJV *of* Genesis 1:8 (*first sentence*)—
And God called the firmament Heaven.

Ancient Hebrew Anatomic Alphabet writing of that phrase—

ויקרא אלהים לרקיע שמים

An actual translation *with researched explanations below*—
And strange-biological-entities encountered it in regard to [*sperm cells*] spread out [*decreased concentration of sperm cells which necessitated IVF*]. [*And they were*] amazed.

The KJV *of* Genesis 1:8 (*second sentence*)—
And the evening and the morning were the second day.

Ancient Hebrew Anatomic Alphabet writing of that phrase—

ויהי ערב ויהי בקר יום שני

An actual translation *with researched explanations below*—
But it is to interbreed; and it is to research my duplicating it-and-them [*the ovum (egg cell) is the "it", and the mass of sperm cells is the "them"*].

The Researched Explanations—

and called

As previously treated, the word, *ōōă·ē·qwōōră* [ויקרא], can be "to call" [H7121]; but its other definition is "to encounter" [H7122]. That is how that word is employed here.

TRANSLATED AS: and it encountered

God

As previously seen, *ălăh·ēm* [אלהים] [H430], is traditionally treated as "God". Again, they could be thought of as "alah-beings"; but in this context it is more accurate to think of them as "SBEs".[488]

TRANSLATED AS: strange-biological-entities

the firmament
There's no "the" here in the ancient text. It is the exact word, *lă·rĕ·qwēō* [OZϘ4𐤋], previously seen in Verse 7. This word is encountered at Job 37:18 as, "...spread out the sky". The grammar of the word is that the inserted *yăd* [Z] modifies this verb, *to spread*, in a way which would be understood in context. The prefix, *lămĕd* [𐤋], is *in regard to*.

TRANSLATED AS: in regard to (being) spread out

heaven
First seen in the KJV Verse 1 as "the heavens"—here it is just "heaven". The word, *shĭm·ēm* [𐤌Z𐤌W|שמים][H8064], has been traditionally translated as "heaven", as that word is defined as "*to be lofty*". The fly in the heavenly ointment, however, is that word derives from H8047 ["*to ruin*"], which derives from H8074 ["*to stun, to devastate;* or, *to be astonished*"]. There are other scriptural instances where the root word, "*shĭ·mēm*", is translated as "astonished"[489]. Here, a synonymous noun is used; and the word is a plural something, not a singular something.

TRANSLATED AS: amazements

and the
For sure, the prefix "and" is in the ancient word in the text; but there is no "the" in the phrase, "and the evening". Spoiler alert: there's not going to be any "evening" either. The word here is *ōōă·ē·hē* [Z𐤄ZY][H1961] from the root, "to be". For a review, look back at "Let there be" in Verse 3. The prefix here is *ōōă* [Y], "and"; the second prefix is *yăd* [Z], "it"; and the root word is, "is".

TRANSLATED AS: and it is

evening
Yes, the word *ōrĕb* [𐤁4O] is generally given as "evening" [H6153]. Here is given as H6148—"braid" (per Dr. Strong) and "intermix"—in the sense of *mingled seed*. It is properly translated here as "interbreed".

TRANSLATED AS: interbreed

and the
This is the same word as "*And the*" previously explained. The prefix, *ōōă* [𐤅], on the word, 𐤅𐤉𐤄𐤉, may also be the word "but".

TRANSLATED AS: but it is

morning
Sure, the word *bĕqwōōr* [𐤁𐤒𐤓] can be "morning". That's Strong's Number H1242. But the eminent authority, Dr. Strong, tells us that H1242 is derived from H1239, which is *to seek, seek out, inquire,* and *inquiry*. H1240 is *to seek* or *to inquire* in all five places where it appears in the text. Here, "to seek out", is treated as *to research.*

TRANSLATED AS: to research

were the
These words do not appear at this place in the ancient text.

second
The number, "second", in this ancient language comes from the idea of *duplication.* The word, *shĭnē* [𐤔𐤍𐤉][H8145—from H8138 (𐤔𐤍𐤄|"שנה")—*to duplicate*]. The suffix, *yăd* [𐤉], can be the pronouns *me* or *my*. The final letter, 𐤄|ה, was dropped by the original writer.

TRANSLATED AS: my duplicating

day
This word is the same as we saw twice in Verse 5.

TRANSLATED AS: it-and-them

A researched translation of the ancient Hebrew Genesis 1:8—
And entities encountered [*sperm*] in regard to (being) spread out [*a decreased concentration of sperm cells necessitating IVF*]. [*And they were*] amazed. But it is to interbreed; and it is to research my duplicating it-and-them [*the ovum (egg cell) is the "it", and the mass of sperm cells is the "them"*].

Genesis 1:8—*in plain English*

- ☆ Strange-biological-entities again recognize that they have a problem of low sperm concentration which IVF will solve.
- ☆ They state their amazement at that fact.
- ☆ They restate their intention to interbreed and to conduct research on how to optimally unify DNA-manipulated cells of reproduction to achieve conception and fertilization.

The KJV *of* Genesis 1:9 (*first phrase*)—
And God said, Let the waters under the heaven be gathered

Ancient Hebrew Anatomic Alphabet writing of that phrase—
𐤅𐤉𐤀𐤌𐤓 𐤀𐤋𐤄𐤉𐤌 𐤉𐤒𐤅𐤅 𐤄𐤌𐤉𐤌 𐤌𐤕𐤇𐤕 𐤄𐤔𐤌𐤉𐤌

An actual translation *with researched explanations below*—
And strange-biological-entities commanded, It binds it [*to the human egg*], the semen usefully fertile. The-Amazements—

The KJV *of* Genesis 1:9 (*second phrase*)—
unto one place, and let the dry land appear:

Ancient Hebrew Anatomic Alphabet writing of that phrase—
𐤀𐤋 𐤌𐤒𐤅𐤌 𐤀𐤇𐤃 𐤅𐤕𐤓𐤀𐤄 𐤄𐤉𐤁𐤔𐤄

An actual translation *with researched explanations below*—
through accomplishing unity [*of DNA modified egg and sperm cell*]. And discerned the absolute shame-cause!

The KJV *of* Genesis 1:9 (*third phrase*)—
and it was so.

Ancient Hebrew Anatomic Alphabet writing of that phrase—
𐤅𐤉𐤄𐤉 𐤊𐤍

An actual translation *with researched explanations below*—
And it is true.

The Researched Explanations—

and said
The word, *ōōă·ē·ămĕr* [𐤅𐤉𐤀𐤌𐤓], is previously cited [H559] as "said". It is a word used "with great latitude". For the translation in this verse the word

is “command” is taken from Exodus 8:27. The traditional “said” is also past tense; and the grammar of the word is, “and-it-commanded”.

TRANSLATED AS: and it commanded

God
As previously seen, *ălăh·ēm* [אלהים] [H430], is traditionally treated in English as “God”. Again, literally, they are “alah-beings”; and translated here according to how *aliens* are described in official government circles.[490]

TRANSLATED AS: strange-biological-entities

let the waters under the heaven be gathered
The challenge of matching the traditional presentation of this phrase is that in some verses there is only a loose word-for-word relationship between the well-known famous *false* narrative and the Hebrew words in the ancient text. The KJV English words that follow will be in the original word order in Hebrew[491].

let be gathered
The Hebrew word here is *ēă·qwōō·ōō* [יקוו|יקוו] [H6960]. Its root word is *qwōō·ăh* [קוה]—*to bind together*. The prefix, *yăd* [י], is “it”. The root word is “bind”[492]. The final letter [ה] of the three-letter root word was dropped by the original author or by a subsequent scriptural editor. The suffix is *ōōă* [ו], “it”. The implied subject and implied object are in brackets; and the translation is, “it [*the injection pipette*] is to bind it [*the selected sperm cell inside the human egg cell*]”.

The word “let” comes to us as a translational necessity of the KJV translators when they, in the translating their KJV Bible in 1611, had to juggle the wording of the Latin Vulgate[493], the Greek Septuagint[494], and possibly the first English translation done in 1382 by martyred Englishman John Wycliffe[495]. It was Professor Wycliffe who first translated into literal English the biblical text from the Latin Vulgate[496].

The Greek-language laundering occurred in the time-frame of 285—246 BCE during the reign of the Greek pharaoh of Egypt, Ptolemy Philadelphus[497].

As part of the fake narrative imposed on the actual text, there had to be (in Greek) an imperative command from God (Theos) regarding a collection, or gathering, of water. The ancient Greek word chosen for that task was the word, "συναχθητω"[498] (*sunachtheto*), which conveys the idea of something (the water) being collected together[499]. For it is from this very word in Greek that the concept of "be gathered" comes in the first place. The linguistic relationship between the Greek word's "base" (*sun*) [Strong's G4862] is that the word "sun" denotes *union*. Obviously, the union of a viable sperm cell (*spermatazoom*) and an egg cell (*ovum*) was someplace the Third Century BCE Jewish interpreters couldn't go. It is in the disposing of the word, "Let", that this incursion into the ancient Greek wording has been undertaken. Next, the Latin word that conveyed the concept of a collected gathering together will be tackled.

Sometime between the time Pope Damasus commissioned him in 382 of our common era[500] and the end of his life some 38 years later, an ascetic monk-scholar by the name of Eusebius Hieronymus took on putting into common-use Latin what he held out to be a translation directly from Hebrew[501]. The word he chose for his "Vulgate" ("vulgar", or "common" Latin) to convey the Hebrew word, יקוו (*ēă·qwōō·ōō*), was "congregentur"—as in "dixit vero Deus congregentur aquae"[502]. A Latin dictionary doesn't have to be cracked to inform us that "congregentur" is closer to letting waters congregate (or gather) just as it is in Greek than it is to the concept of "bind" in Hebrew.

In 1382 John Wycliffe published his hand-written literal translation of the Latin Vulgate[503]. Here's how he wrote this verse, "Forsooth God said, The waters, that be under heaven, be gathered into one place, and a dry place appear; and it was done so."[504]

TRANSLATED AS: it [the injection pipette] is to bind it [the selected sperm cell inside the human egg cell]

let the waters
This word appears in Verses 2, 6, and 7—*hā·mēm* [𐤄𐤌𐤉𐤌|המים] translated here again as, "the semen"[505].

TRANSLATED AS: the semen

under

The idea of "under" is a mistranslation—pure and simple. The Hebrew word behind that idea is *mĕ·tōō·khĕt* [𐤌𐤕𐤇𐤕|מתחת] [H8478], seen in Verse 7. Here, the SBEs are only dealing with the utility of fertile semen combined with the practical necessity of IVF. The word's prefix, a letter (*mĕm*) [𐤌], is a utility determinative. The root, 𐤕𐤇𐤕 [תחת], means *fertility*[506].

TRANSLATED AS: useful [for in-vitro] fertility

the heaven

The words, "the heaven" are another mistranslation. As previously seen in Verses 1 and 8, the heaven [*hā·shĭm·ēm* |𐤄𐤔𐤌𐤉𐤌] is translated here from the actual Hebrew root word, "𐤔𐤌𐤌" (*shĭmĕm*) [H8074], *to amaze*[507].

TRANSLATED AS: the amazements

unto

The word in the text here is *ăl* [𐤀𐤋|אל] [H413]. That usage of this word, as Strong's H413 in the KJV Bible, is rendered as 33 different words in its 38 appearances[508]. Here's what's on the definitional menu: unto, with, against, at, in, into, before, to, of, upon, by, toward, hath, for, beside, from, where, after, within, through [Numbers 25:8—*as in* "and thrust both of them through"], over, them, according, concerning, that, because, under, near, about, out, touching [Jer. 22:11], both, *and* seemeth. Here, the word is treated as *through*.

TRANSLATED AS: through

place

The Hebrew word here is *mĕ·qwōōm* [𐤌𐤒𐤅𐤌][H4725–*from* H6965 (קוֹם)]—*to rise; to accomplish*. The presence of the *inserted letter* [𐤅] serves to modify the word—in this instance to a gerund (an "ing" word).

TRANSLATED AS: accomplishing

one
This word here, *ăkhĕd* [𐤀𐤇𐤃|אחד] [H258/H259], means (in context) "to unify", "united", "one", *and* "first". This Hebrew word appears close to a thousand times as translated into the KJV Bible—most often as the word, "one". Here, the verb "unify" is being used in its noun form.

TRANSLATED AS: unity

and let...appear
The word here in the text is not about something appearing. It is about *seeing something*—that is, discernment. The word in the text is, *ōōă·tōō·ră·ăh* [𐤅𐤕𐤓𐤀𐤄|ותראה] [H7200]—*to see, to discern,* and so forth. The letter, 𐤕, is an "inserted letter". It means "you", "your", or it can be and "exclamatory emphatic" (our exclamation point).

TRANSLATED AS: and !discerned

the dry land
The actual word is *hā·ēbĕsh·ăh* [𐤄𐤉𐤁𐤔𐤄|היבשה][H3004—*from* H3001]. Strong's H3001 appears 78 times[509] in the text; and there are quite a few words in the definition derby: "wither" and "up" appear most often in translation; the word "dry" only appears three times. The word "ashamed" appears three times; and the word "shame", two times. "Confounded" appears seven times; and "clean", once. Its prefix, *hāy* [𐤄], is "the"; and its suffix, also a letter, *hāy* [𐤄], denotes "the absolute state" of a root word.

TRANSLATED AS: the absolute cause of shame

and it was so
The two ancient words in the text here are *ōōă·ē·hē kăn* [𐤅𐤉𐤄𐤉 𐤊𐤍|כן-ויהי]. They are associated with H1961 and H3651. The prefix, *ōōă* [𐤅], is "and"; the *yad* [𐤉] is the *second* prefix, "it"; and the root fragment, *hē* [𐤄𐤉], is "is". The second word, *kăn* [𐤊𐤍] can mean "so"; but it also can mean "thus" and "true".

TRANSLATED AS: and it is true

A researched translation of the ancient Hebrew Genesis 1:9—
And strange-biological-entities commanded, It [*the injection pipette*] is to bind it [*inside the human egg cell*]. The semen (is to be) useful (for in-vitro) fertility. The Amazements—through accomplishing unity [*of DNA modified egg and sperm cell*]. And discerned the absolute cause of shame! And it is true.

Genesis 1:9—*in plain English*

- ☆ Strange-biological-entities recognized the success of the injecting pipette for putting their sperm cell inside the egg of the female of the target species.
- ☆ The account states that the entities knew their actions could be viewed as shameful.
- ☆ The account states that what they are relating is true.

The KJV *of* Genesis 1:10 (*first phrase*)—
And God called the dry land Earth;

Ancient Hebrew Anatomic Alphabet writing of that phrase—
𐤅𐤉𐤒𐤓𐤀 𐤀𐤋𐤄𐤉𐤌 𐤋𐤉𐤁𐤔𐤄 𐤀𐤓𐤑

An actual translation *with researched explanations below*—
And strange-biological-entities encountered, in regard to the absolute cause of shame, [the] I-Accomplish;

The KJV *of* Genesis 1:10 (*second phrase*)—
and the gathering together of the waters called he Seas:

Ancient Hebrew Anatomic Alphabet writing of that phrase—
𐤅𐤋𐤌𐤒𐤅𐤄 𐤄𐤌𐤉𐤌 𐤒𐤓𐤀 𐤉𐤌𐤉𐤌

An actual translation *with researched explanations below*—
and in regard to [*the injection pipette*] binding [*inside the hominid egg cell*] the spermatozoa called spermatozoon.

The KJV *of* Genesis 1:10 (*third phrase*)—
and God saw that it was good.

Ancient Hebrew Anatomic Alphabet writing of that phrase—
𐤅𐤉𐤓𐤀 𐤀𐤋𐤄𐤉𐤌 𐤊𐤉 𐤈𐤅𐤁

An actual translation *with researched explanations below*—
And strange-biological-entities saw that (it was a) good [*technical solution*].

The Researched Explanations—

and called
Yes, the word, *ōŏă·ē·qwōōră* [𐤅𐤉𐤒𐤓𐤀], can be "to call" [H7121]; but its other definition is "to encounter" [H7122].

TRANSLATED AS: and it encountered

God

As previously seen, *ălăh·ēm* [𐤀𐤋𐤄𐤉𐤌] [H430], is traditionally treated in English as "God". Again, literally, they are "alah-beings"; and translated here according to how *aliens* are described in official government circles.[510]

TRANSLATED AS: strange-biological-entities

the dry land

The actual word here is *lă·ēbĕsh·ăh* [𐤋𐤉𐤁𐤔𐤄][H3004—*from* H3001]. Previously treated in the Verse 9—the word "shame" is traditionally translated (in context) twice in the Hebrew text. Its prefix, *lămĕd* [𐤋], means "in regard to"; and its suffix, the letter *hāy* [𐤄] denotes "the absolute state" of a root word.

TRANSLATED AS: in regard to (the) absolute cause of shame

earth

The word, *ărĕtz* [𐤀𐤓𐤑] [H776], traditionally mistranslated as "earth", could as easily be read as "ă·rĕtz·ăh" {[𐤄]𐤑𐤓𐤀}[H7521], "*to be pleased with* or *accomplish, et cetera*". The rereading of the word gives the prefix is 𐤀, meaning "I".

TRANSLATED AS: I-Accomplish

and the gathering together

The word in the text is *ōōă·lă·mĕ·qwōōăh* [𐤅𐤋𐤌𐤒𐤅𐤄|ולמקוה], treated in similar form in Verse 9. The Strong's number for this word's is H6960, 𐤒𐤓𐤄, which is "*to bind together*". This word has three prefixes: a 𐤅, *and*; a 𐤋, *in regard to*; and a 𐤌, meaning *from*.

TRANSLATED AS: and in regard to from [the injection pipette] binding [inside the hominid egg cell]

of the waters

Seen in Verse 2, three times in Verse 6, and twice Verse 7, the word here is *hā·mēm* [𐤄𐤌𐤉𐤌][H4325]. Here, "waters", read as "semen", is treated as "*spermatozoa*". That's the word's context.

TRANSLATED AS: the spermatozoa

called he

The Hebrew word here is *qwōōră* [𐤒𐤓𐤀]. We encountered this word in Verse 5. There is no personal pronoun "he" on this word.

TRANSLATED AS: called

seas

As seen previously, the same root word here in the text has a prefix, *yăd* [𐤉], on the word, *ēă·mēm* [𐤉𐤌𐤉𐤌][H4325]. This prefix means "it". Just as "*seas*" is a variant of "waters", the variant of semen is treated here as "spermatozoon"—the sperm cell that fertilizes the egg cell[511].

TRANSLATED AS: it spermatozoon

and saw

The word, [*ōōă·ē·ră* | 𐤅𐤉𐤓𐤀|וירא][H7200], may be "and saw". Literally, it is "and-it-saw". The root, 𐤓𐤀𐤄, may also be translated as *to see, to exist, to live, to view, to regard,* or *to observe*. Here it will be given almost as traditionally translated. The letter, 𐤉, is the pronoun, "it", refers collectively to the strange-biological-entities.

TRANSLATED AS: and it saw

God

As previously seen, *ălăh·ēm* [𐤀𐤋𐤄𐤉𐤌] [H430], is traditionally treated in English as "God". Again, literally, they are "alah-beings"; and translated here close to the way that *aliens* are described in official government circles.[512]

TRANSLATED AS: strange-biological-entities

that

The word in the text is *kē* (pronounced "key") [𐤊𐤉]. It is Strong's H3588. Commonly rendered as "for" or "because", here it is "that".

TRANSLATED AS: that

it was good
The word, *thōōb* [𐤁𐤅𐤈|טוב][H2896] means "good" in the widest sense. Here it is given as traditionally translated—in the sense of the practical necessity of in vitro fertilization.

TRANSLATED AS: good [technical solution]

A researched translation of the ancient Hebrew Genesis 1:10—
And strange-biological-entities encountered, in regard to the absolute cause of shame, (the) I-Accomplish; and in regard to [*the injection pipette*] binding [*inside the hominid egg cell*] the spermatozoa called spermatozoon. And strange-biological-entities saw that (it was a) good [*technical solution*].

Genesis 1:10—*in plain English*

☆ The entities would not be shamed because their experiments with IVF were successful.

☆ They recognized that they had developed successful technical solutions.

The Reptilians' technical solutions

[Verses 11 through 13]

The KJV *of* Genesis 1:11 (*first phrase*)—
And God said, Let the earth

Ancient Hebrew Anatomic Alphabet writing of that phrase—

ויאמר אלהים תדשא הארץ

An actual translation *with researched explanations below*—
And strange-biological-entities commanded, To germinate[!] (is) The I-Accomplish.

The KJV *of* Genesis 1:11 (*second phrase*)—
bring forth grass, the herb yielding seed, and the fruit tree

Ancient Hebrew Anatomic Alphabet writing of that phrase—

דשא עשב מזריע זרע עץ פרי עשה פרי

An actual translation *with researched explanations below*—
Germinate green ejaculated spermatozoa—to close the increase—to affect the increase—

The KJV *of* Genesis 1:11 (*third phrase*)—
after his kind, whose seed is in itself, upon the earth:

Ancient Hebrew Anatomic Alphabet writing of that phrase—

למינו אשר זרעו בו על הארץ

An actual translation *with researched explanations below*—
in regard to our semen. I solved [*the low concentration of*] his spermatozoa in it effectually—The I-Accomplish.

The KJV *of* Genesis 1:11 (*fourth phrase*)—
and it was so.

Ancient Hebrew Anatomic Alphabet writing of that phrase—

𐤅𐤉𐤄𐤉 𐤊𐤍

An actual translation *with researched explanations below*—
And it is true.

The Researched Explanations—

and said

The word, *ōōă·ē·ămĕr* [𐤅𐤉𐤀𐤌𐤓], is previously cited [H559] as "said". It is a word used "with great latitude". For this translation in this verse the word is "commanded". The grammar of the word is, "and-it-commanded" [*ōōă*·ē·ămĕr [𐤅𐤉𐤀𐤌𐤓|ויאמר].

TRANSLATED AS: and it commanded

God

As previously seen, *ălăh·ēm* [𐤀𐤋𐤄𐤉𐤌] [H430], is traditionally treated in English as "God". Again, literally, they are "alah-beings"; and translated here close to how *aliens* are described in official government circles.[513]

TRANSLATED AS: strange-biological-entities

let

The Hebrew word at this place in the ancient text is *tōō·dăshă* [𐤕𐤃𐤔𐤀|תדשא][H1876]. The root means *to sprout*—which is to germinate. That's the translation here. The word's prefix, the letter *tōō* [𐤕], is an exclamatory emphatic—our exclamation point[!).

TRANSLATED AS: !to germinate (is)

the earth

The word, *hā·ărĕtz* [𐤄𐤀𐤓𐤑] [H776], is traditionally defined as "ground *or* land" and mistranslated as "earth". Here it is read as "*hā·ă·rĕtz·ăh*" {[𐤄] 𐤀𐤓𐤑} [H7521], "*to be pleased with* or *accomplish*". The prefix *hāy* [𐤄] is the indefinite article, "the". The letter, *alăpf* [𐤀] is "I".

TRANSLATED AS: the I-Accomplish

bring forth grass

The word here is simply the root [𐤃𐤔𐤀] of *tōō·dăshă* (above).

TRANSLATED AS: germinate

the herb

The word is *ōshĭb* [𐤏𐤔𐤁][H6212]. The word means *to glisten* or *to be green.* Note: there is no "the" prefix, *hāy* [𐤄], on this word.

TRANSLATED AS: green

yielding

Here's an interesting word that fits perfectly into a narrative about IVF. It's *mĕ·zărēō* [𐤌𐤆𐤓𐤉𐤏|מזריע]. It has two meanings: Strong's H2232—*to sow* or *to disseminate*; and H2233—*seed, posterity,* or *carnality.* There are two grammatic components which modify this word's meaning. The first is the word's prefix, *mĕm* [𐤌], a utility determinative. The noun, "ejaculate", is the *utility* of "disseminate" when dealing with the kind of seed dissemination going on in this narrative. The second is the *inserted letter*, *yăd* [𐤉], inserted into the root—which serves to alter the root's meaning—in this instance, making it *past tense* (which is in context).

TRANSLATED AS: ejaculated

seed

Here we have the root, *zărō* [𐤆𐤓𐤏|זרע], of the previous word. It is H2233. It is translated as the technical word, spermatozoa, which is the operative part of the word "seed" as regards human cross-breeding with the species of strange biological entities.

TRANSLATED AS: spermatozoa

and the fruit tree
At this point in the text there is no "and the". The two words appearing in the Hebrew text are, *ōtz pfār·ē* [עץ פרי|𐤏𐤑 𐤐𐤓𐤉]. They are falsely given as "fruit tree". Here, the word for "tree" [*ōtz*] is treated as if the word is *ōtz·ăh* [𐤏𐤑𐤄] [H6095], *to close*; and its final letter, *hāy* [𐤄], dropped by the original writer or lost over the ages. Here, "ōtz" is being translated as "to close". The word "fruit" is *pfār·ē* [from root, 𐤐𐤓𐤄][H6509]—*to increase*—as in "fruitful". The suffix, *yăd* [𐤉], is usually "he" or "it". Only rarely is this suffix seen, in context, as "the".

TRANSLATED AS: to close the increase

-untranslated words from the Hebrew text-
Two untranslated words from the ancient text here are, "*ōshăh pfār·ē*" [עשה פרי|𐤏𐤔𐤄 𐤐𐤓𐤉]. The word "ōshăh" is Strong's H6213, *to do* or *to make*, used—as dictionary lingo goes, *in the broadest sense and widest application*. That word is being translated as *to affect*. The word, *pfār·ē*, per the treatment above, is the *increase*.

TRANSLATED AS: to affect the increase

after his kind
Here, the context is less about "kind" than it is about "seed". The Hebrew word here [למינו|𐤋𐤌𐤉𐤍𐤅] has been traditionally treated as if it were "*lă·mēn·ōō*" [ל·מינ·ו][H4327—*kind*]. In its actual context, however, the word should be treated as "*lă·mē·nōō*" [ל·מי·נו][H4325—*water*]. Our root here is the two-letter abbreviation, *mĕm-yăd* [𐤌𐤉] for the three-letter root, *mĕm-yăd- mĕm* [𐤌𐤉𐤌]. That word is used here in the sense of *water* as a biblical

euphemism for "semen"[514]. The prefix, *lămĕd* [𐤋], is *in regard to*. The suffix, *nōō* [𐤍𐤅], is "our"[515].

TRANSLATED AS: in regard to our semen

whose
Previously seen in Verse 7 as "*which*", the word in the text is ăshĭr [𐤀𐤔𐤓], from the root, *shĭrăh* [𐤔𐤓𐤄][H8281][516] with prefix ă*lăpf* [𐤀], "I"; and a dropped final letter, *hāy* [𐤄].

TRANSLATED AS: I solved [*the problem of*]

seed
As previously seen, *zărō* is the word "seed". 𐤆𐤓𐤏𐤅 (*zărō·ōō*) is translated here by the technical name of the cells that constitute the "seed" of the SBE's. The suffix, *ōōă* [𐤅], is "it", "its", or "his".

TRANSLATED AS: his spermatozoa

is in itself
There is no "is", in the Hebrew word, *bōō* (yes, "boo") [𐤁𐤅|בוֹ]. The word is a prefix, *bĕt* [𐤁], "in"; and has a suffix, *ōōă* [𐤅], "it".

TRANSLATED AS: in it

upon
The word, *ōl* [𐤏𐤋|עַל], as seen in Verse 2, is traditionally cited as H5927, "*upon*"; and treated previously here as "yoke" [H5923]. In the word's context here, however, it can be read as a homonym, "ōl"—from the root, "𐤏𐤋𐤋" (*ōlăl*) [H5953] with the final *lămĕd* [𐤋] dropped. Dr. James Strong defines H5953 "to effect"; and Professor Benjamin Davidson defines it as "effectually"[517].

TRANSLATED AS: effectually

the earth
The word, *hā·ărĕtz* [𐤄𐤀𐤓𐤑][H776], is traditionally translated as "ground *or* land". It is read here as "*hā·ă·rĕtz·ăh*" {𐤄𐤀𐤓𐤑[𐤄]} [H7521], "*to accomplish.* The prefix *hāy* [𐤄] is the indefinite article, "the". The prefix *alăpf* [𐤀] is "I".

TRANSLATED AS: the I-Accomplish

and it was so
The two words in the text here are *ōōă·ē·hē kăn* [𐤅𐤉𐤄𐤉 𐤊𐤍]. They are associated with H1961 and H3651. The prefix, *ōōă* [𐤅], is "and"; the *yăd* [𐤉] is the *second* prefix, "it"; and the root fragment, *hē* [𐤄𐤉], is "is". The second word, *kăn* [𐤊𐤍] can mean "so"; but it also can mean "thus" and "true".

TRANSLATED AS: and it is true

A researched translation of the ancient Hebrew Genesis 1:11—
And strange-biological-entities commanded, To germinate[!] is The I-Accomplish. Germinate green ejaculated spermatozoa—to close the increase [*the concentration differential between viable spermatozoa and the volume of semen*], to affect the increase—in regard to our semen. I effectively solved [*the low concentration of*] his spermatozoa in it [*his semen*]—the I-Accomplish. And it is true.

Genesis 1:11—*in plain English*

- ☆ The strange-biological-entities' successful germination of a hominid egg by their sperm is a major accomplishment.
- ☆ They directed that their own green sperm be used for their in-vitro fertilization (IVF) project; and solve their sperm concentration problem through the use of IVF.

The KJV *of* Genesis 1:12 (*first phrase*)—
And the earth brought forth grass, and herb yielding seed

Ancient Hebrew Anatomic Alphabet writing of that phrase—
ותוצא הארץ דשא עשב מזריע זרע

An actual translation *with researched explanations below*—
And gone out! The I-Accomplish. Germinate green ejaculated spermatozoa

The KJV *of* Genesis 1:12 (*second phrase*)—
after his kind, and the tree yielding fruit, whose seed was in itself,

Ancient Hebrew Anatomic Alphabet writing of that phrase—
למינהו ועץ עשה פרי אשר זרעו בו

An actual translation *with researched explanations below*—
in regard to its species [*that is, the hybrid creature to be genetically engineered*] to close [*the gap between the concentration of spermatozoa to semen*]—making my increase [*concentration of spermatozoa*]. I solve [*the problem of*] its spermatozoa in it.

The KJV *of* Genesis 1:12 (*third phrase*)—
after his kind: and God saw that it was good.

Ancient Hebrew Anatomic Alphabet writing of that phrase—
למינהו וירא אלהים כי טוב

An actual translation *with researched explanations below*—
in regard to its [*the hybrid creature to genetically engineered*] species. And strange-biological-entities saw that (it was a) good [*technical solution*].

The Researched Explanations—

and the earth brought forth

In the ancient text here, the action word came first, then the subject word. The action word here is *ōōă·tōō·ōōtză* [𐤅𐤕𐤅𐤑𐤀|ותוצא][H3318]. The root word is *ēătză* [𐤉𐤑𐤀]—*to go out* in a great variety of uses. Here it is "gone out" The first prefix, *ōōă* [𐤅] is "and"; the second prefix, *tōō* [𐤕] is an exclamatory emphatic—an "!". The letter, *ōōă* [𐤅] (substituted by the original author for the letter 𐤉) serves to make the word *past tense*.

THE ACTION WORD TRANSLATED AS: and !gone out

the earth

This Hebrew word has been dealt with here as previously as in Verse 11. The word, *hā·ărĕtz* [𐤄𐤀𐤓𐤑][H776], is traditionally translated as "the earth". It is treated here as "*hā·ă·rĕtz·ăh*" {[𐤄]𐤀𐤓𐤑𐤄} [H7521], "*to accomplish*. The prefix *hāy* [𐤄] is the indefinite article, "the". The prefix *alăpf* [𐤀] is "I".

THE SUBJECT WORD TRANSLATED AS: the I-Accomplish

grass

Our word, "grass" was seen in Verse 11 as the phrase, "*bring forth grass*". The word in the text there is the same word here. It is simply *dăshă* [𐤃𐤔𐤀]—*to germinate*.

TRANSLATED AS: germinate

and herb

Seen in Verse 11 as "*the herb*", our word here is the same. It is *ōshĭb* [𐤏𐤔𐤁|עשב][H6212]. The word means *to glisten* or *to be green*. There is no prefix letter *ōōă* [𐤅|ו] to be translated as "and".

TRANSLATED AS: green

yielding

This word was last seen in Verse 11—as itself, "yielding". The very same word also appears here in the ancient text. It's still a perfect fit in a narrative all about IVF. It's *mĕ·zărēō* [𐤌𐤆𐤓𐤉𐤏|מזריע]. It has two meanings:

Strong's H2232—*to sow* or *to disseminate*; and H2233—*seed, posterity,* or *carnality*. There are two grammar components modifying this word's meaning. The first is the word's prefix, *měm* [𐤌], a utility determinative. The noun, "ejaculate", is the *utility* of "disseminate" when dealing with the kind of seed dissemination going on in the narrative. The second is the letter, *yăd* [𐤉], inserted into the root—serving to alter the root's meaning. In this instance it makes it *past tense*.

TRANSLATED AS: ejaculated

seed
As seen in Verse 11, *zărō* [𐤆𐤓𐤏] is "seed"; and is translated here by the technical name of the "seed" of bipedal hominids.

TRANSLATED AS: spermatozoa

after his kind
Naturally, a person might expect that the Hebrew word for "after his kind" as seen in Verse 11 would be the same Hebrew word here. It's not. In that verse it was "*lă·mē·nōō*" [𐤋𐤌𐤉𐤍𐤅|למינהו] [H4325—*water-as-semen*]. In this verse it *is* the word for "kind"—that is, *kind of*. Our word here is *lă·mēn·hōō* [𐤋𐤌𐤉𐤍𐤄𐤅|לְמִינֵהוּ][H4327—*to portion out, kind,* or *species*]. The prefix *lăměd* [𐤋] is *in regard to*; and the suffix, *hōō* [𐤄𐤅] is "it".

TRANSLATED AS: in regard to it-species [that is, the hybrid creature to be genetically engineered]

and the tree
Traditionally given as "tree", *ōtz* [H6086][𐤅𐤏𐤑], seen in Verse 11, per the first definition offered by Davidson [p. 609][Strong's H6095—*to fasten; close*], for root 𐤏𐤑𐤄 [עצה], is "to close" (and is linked to "the eyes"). Note: The word here is *ōōă·ōtz* [𐤅𐤏𐤑|ועץ]; the prefix is the letter *ōōă* [𐤅], "and".

TRANSLATED AS: and to close [the gap between the concentration of spermatozoa to semen] *yielding*

It's logical to think that the Hebrew word for "yielding" here would be the same as for "yielding" (above); but it's not. Here, the word, *ōshăh* [𐤏𐤔𐤄] [H6213], means to do or to make.

TRANSLATED AS: making

fruit

"Fruit" is used as a noun in all the traditional renditions of the Genesis story. Here, its verb form is used also as a noun. In the text it is "*pfăr·ē*" [𐤐𐤓𐤉] [H6529 (the noun, *fruit*)—from H6509 [𐤐𐤓𐤄] (the verb, *to be fruitful* or *to increase*)]. The suffix, *yăd* [𐤉], is "my"

TRANSLATED AS: my increase

whose

Previously seen in Verse 11 as "*whose*", the word in the text is the same: ăshĭr [𐤀𐤔𐤓] It is from the root, *shĭrăh* [𐤔𐤓𐤄][H8281] with prefix *ălăpf* [𐤀], "I"; and a dropped letter, *hāy* [𐤄].

TRANSLATED AS: I solve [the problem of]

seed was

As seen in Verse 11, *zărō* is the word "seed". Here the word is 𐤆𐤓𐤏𐤅 (*zărō*·ōō) [זרעו]. It is translated here by the technical name of the cells that constitute the "seed" of bipedal hominids. The suffix, *ōōă* [𐤅], is "it".

TRANSLATED AS: its spermatozoa

in itself

Also seen in Verse 11, the Hebrew word here is *bōō* [𐤁𐤅]. The word consists of a prefix, *bĕt* [𐤁], "in"; and a suffix, *ōōă* [𐤅], "it".

TRANSLATED AS: in it

after his kind

This phrase was seen previously in this verse; and the Hebrew word here is the same: *lă·mēn·hōō* [𐤋𐤌𐤉𐤍𐤄𐤅] [H4327—*to portion out, kind,* or *species*]. The prefix *lamed* [𐤋] is *in regard to*; and the suffix, *hōō* [𐤄𐤅] is "it".

TRANSLATED AS: in regard to it-species [that is, the hybrid creature to be genetically engineered]

and God saw that it was good

and saw

The word, [*ōōă·ē·ră* | 𐤅𐤉𐤓𐤀] [H7200], may be "and saw". Literally, it is "and-it-saw". The root, 𐤓𐤀𐤄, may also be translated as *to see, to exist, to live, to view, to regard,* or *to observe*. Here it will be given as traditionally translated. The pronoun, "it", refers collectively to the strange biological entities.

TRANSLATED AS: and it saw

God

The word, *ălăh·ēm* [𐤀𐤋𐤄𐤉𐤌][H430], commonly translated "God". Here it is treated as "*strange-biological-entities*". *Translation note*: the "-ēn" (or "-ēm") suffix on the Hebrew word "ălăh" makes the word plural. The word could be thought of as "*alah-beings*".[518]

TRANSLATED AS: strange-biological-entities

that

The word in the text is *kē* (pronounced "key") [𐤊𐤉]. It is Strong's H3588; and it can act to connect all kinds of causes in a sentence, including "for" and "because". Here it will be given as traditionally translated.

TRANSLATED AS: that

it was good
There is no "it was" on this word in the text. The word, *thōōb* [𐤈𐤅𐤁] [H2896] means "good" in the widest sense. Here It will be given as traditionally translated—in the sense of the practical necessity of in vitro fertilization.

TRANSLATED AS: good [technical solution]

A researched translation of the ancient Hebrew Genesis 1:12—
And gone out! The I-Accomplish. Germinate green spermatozoa in regard to it-species [*the hybrid creature to be genetically engineered*]; and to close [*the gap between the concentration of spermatozoa to semen*]—making my increase [*concentration of spermatozoa*]. I solved [*the problem of*] spermatozoa—in regard to it-species. And strange-biological-entities saw that (it was a) good [*technical solution*].

Genesis 1:12—*in plain English*

- ☆ The strange-biological-entities obtained their own green sperm for their IVF project.
- ☆ They directed that their green sperm be germinated in the target species—referring to as the "it-species".
- ☆ They developed successful technical solutions.

The KJV *of* Genesis 1:13—
And the evening and the morning were the third day.

Ancient Hebrew Anatomic Alphabet writing of that phrase—
ZWZ𐤋W 𐤌YZ 4𐤒9 Z𐤄ZY 94O Z𐤄ZY

An actual translation *with researched explanations below*—
And it is to intermix and it (is) to research it-and-them [*the ovum (egg cell) is the "it", and the mass of sperm cells is the "them"*]: my intense (work to accomplish).

The Researched Explanations—

and the
For sure, the prefix "and" is in the ancient word in the text; but there is no "the" in the phrase, "and the evening". The word here is *ōōă·ē·hē* [Z𐤄ZY] [H1961]. It's from the root, "to be". For a review, look back "Let there be" in Verse 3. The prefix here is *ōōă* [Y], "and"; the second prefix is *yăd* [Z], "it". The root word fragment [Z𐤄 (from 𐤄Z𐤄] is, "is".

TRANSLATED AS: and it is

evening
Yes, the word *ōrĕb* [94O] is generally given as "evening" [H6153]. Here is given as H6148—"braid" and "intermix"—in the sense of mingled seed; and properly treated here as "interbreed".

TRANSLATED AS: interbreed

and the
Again, the prefix "and" is in the text. This is the same word as "*and the*" previously explained. There's no "morning" either.

TRANSLATED AS: and it is

morning
Sure, the word *bĕqwōōr* [4P9] can be "morning". That's Strong's Number H1242; but the eminent authority, Dr. Strong, tells us that H1242 is derived from H1239, which is to *seek, seek out, inquire,* and *inquiry*. H1240 is *to seek* or *to inquire* in all five places where it appears in the biblical text. To *research* is "to seek out".

TRANSLATED AS: to research

were the
These words do not appear at this place in the ancient text.

day
This word is the same as we saw twice in Verse 5 and in Verse 8.

TRANSLATED AS: it-and-them

third
By now we must realize that every word put forth in traditional Bibles must be scrubbed clean with a metaphoric wire brush. This word is no exception. The word in the text is *shĭl·ē·shĕ* [ZWZ∠W|שלישי]. Usually cited as Strong's H7992, "*third*"; it is cited as being from H7969, also "*third*". But the root cited there is "WY∠W"[519] [Note the inserted letter, *ōōă* (Y).] The detail we must not lose sight of is the word in the text, "ZWZ∠W" (*shĭl-ē-shĕ*), has an inserted *yăd* [Z]. The actual root here is "W∠W", Strong's H8027, which Dr. Strong states is "*perhaps originally to intensify*"[520]. The word, WZ∠W, appears one time in the Hebrew Bible—at Psalm 80:6[521], in the context of *intensity*[522, 523]. In our word in the text here we encounter an inserted *yăd* [Z], which is being treated so as to modify the noun form (*intensity*) of the verb infinitive, *to intensify*, to its adjective form. The work to be accomplished is understood (in context). The suffix, *yăd* [Z], is the pronoun, "my".

TRANSLATED AS: my intense (work to accomplish)

A researched translation of the ancient Hebrew Genesis 1:13—

And it is to intermix and it (is) to research it-and-them [*the ovum (egg cell) is the "it", and the mass of sperm cells is the "them"*]: my intense (work to accomplish).

Genesis 1:13—*in plain English*

- ☆ The entities state that their program of research into the integration of their DNA into that of the egg and sperm cells of the target species is intense.

Reptilians manipulate DNA

[Verses 14 through 18]

The KJV *of* Genesis 1:14 (*first phrase*)—
And God said, Let there be lights in the firmament of the heaven

Ancient Hebrew Anatomic Alphabet writing of that phrase—
ויאמר אלהים יהי מארת ברקיע השמים

An actual translation *with researched explanations below*—
And strange-biological-entities said, "It is cursedly frustrating in being spread out—[*the decreased concentration of sperm cells which necessitated IVF*] The Amazements!

The KJV *of* Genesis 1:14 (*second phrase*)—
to divide the day from the night;

Ancient Hebrew Anatomic Alphabet writing of that phrase—
להבדיל בין היום ובין הלילה

An actual translation *with researched explanations below*—
toward the differentiation—distinguishing the it-and-them and distinguishing the absolute state of the twisting spiral [*the DNA molecular structure*].

The KJV *of* Genesis 1:14 (*third phrase*)—
and let them be for signs, and for seasons, and for days, and years:

Ancient Hebrew Anatomic Alphabet writing of that phrase—
והיו לאתת ולמועדים ולימים ושנים

An actual translation *with researched explanations below*—
And it is in regard to [*enzyme*] appearances and in regard to useful positional directions and in regard to it-semen [*spermatozoa*] and them duplicating it."

The Researched Explanations—

and God said
This phrase has been previously seen in Verses 3, 6, 9, and 11.

TRANSLATED AS: and strange-biological-entities said

let there be
This phrase has been previously seen in Verses 3 and 6.

TRANSLATED AS: it is

lights
It is no exaggeration to say that we have been systematically and deliberately *alien*ated from literacy regarding the sacred scripture of the western world. The word, "lights", serves up yet another excellent, if curse-worthy, example. The word in the text is *mě·ărět* [𐤕𐤓𐤀𐤌|מארת].

It is traditionally cited as Strong's H3974 [*light*][524]. But—that is ***not*** the word in the Hebrew text. Dr. Strong associates the "modern Hebrew" word, "מָאוֹר", with that Strong's Number. Professor Benjamin Davidson cites two roots for this word[525]: one for the *traditional* light, "אור" [𐤓𐤅𐤀] and another, "ארר" [𐤓𐤓𐤀]. Since *traditional light* [H3974] does not fit into the context here, the root must be ărěr [𐤓𐤓𐤀], which means *to bitterly curse*[526].

Our word in the text, 𐤕𐤓𐤀𐤌, has as a root, 𐤓𐤓𐤀, with its final letter [𐤓] dropped by the text writer. The word's suffix, the letter *tōō* [𐤕], is an exclamatory emphatic—our exclamation point [!]. The prefix, the letter *měm* [𐤌], is a utility determinative. What is the "utility" of a *bitter* curse? Its utility is in the expression of extreme and intense frustration. The concept here is that what the entities were trying to do was a matter of great technical difficulty. This exact word appears in only one other place in the Hebrew Bible—as "curse"[527, 528]. The translation here is just as on-point.

TRANSLATED AS: cursedly frustrating!

in the firmament
A variant of this word was previously encountered twice in Verse 7 and once in Verse 8. There is no "the" prefix. Here it is *bĕ·rĕqwēō* [𐤁𐤓𐤒𐤉𐤏|ברקיע]. This word is encountered at Job 37:18 as, "...spread out [the sky]". The grammar is that the inserted *yăd* [𐤉] modifies this verb, *to spread*, in a way which would be understood in context. The prefix, *bĕt*[𐤁], is *in.*

TRANSLATED AS: in being spread out [the decreased concentration of sperm cells which necessitated IVF]

of the heaven
As seen in Verses 1, 8, and 9, *the heaven* [*hā·shĭm·ēm* |𐤄𐤔𐤌𐤉𐤌] is translated from the Hebrew root, "𐤔𐤌𐤌" [H8074], *to amaze.*

TRANSLATED AS: the amazements

to divide
Seen in Verse 4 as "𐤅𐤉𐤁𐤃𐤋" ("and separated"), it shares the very same root, "𐤁𐤃𐤋", with our Hebrew word here in this verse. The word is *lă·hā·bĕd·ēl* [𐤋𐤄𐤁𐤃𐤉𐤋|להבדיל] [H914]—*separated, divided,* or *distinguished.* The first prefix, 𐤋, is *toward.* The second prefix, 𐤄, is "the". The root word, 𐤁𐤃𐤋 [בדל], is *to distinguish,* with an inserted 𐤉—which changes the verb to something else, such as a noun. Our noun here is "differentiation", which is synonymous with "to distinguish".

TRANSLATED AS: toward the differentiation

~a Hebrew word untranslated in the KJV~
Some English translations employ the word "between" at this place in the verse—as the Hebrew word in the text here is *bēn* [𐤁𐤉𐤍]. That word is Strong's H996—*to separate mentally, distinguish,* or *to be cunning*. It appears about 2,300 times in the Hebrew Bible.

TRANSLATED AS: distinguishing

the day

The word here in the text is *hā·ēōōm* [𐤌𐤅𐤉𐤄|היום]. The word, "day" was seen twice in Verse 5, once in Verse 8, and in Verse 13. In those places its translation is "it-and-them" (as explained). The only difference here is that there is a common prefix letter, *hăy* [𐤄|ה], which means "the"[529].

There is another way of handling this word—in a way which will become a significant feature of the being's narrative starting in Genesis Two. That way would be to treat the word's first two letters as the first two letters of the verb "to be"[530]. The complete three-letter root word is "𐤄𐤉𐤄" ("היה").

That word is the same root word of the famous four-letter "Tetragrammaton". Dr. James Strong gives his definition of "יהוה", popularly known as "Jehovah" (or known by its acronym, YHVH or YHWH), as "Self-Existent"[531]. The contracted root here (𐤉𐤄) could be translated as "exists", since the text is informing us that the "it-them" *do* exist. Certainly, the "it-them" exist. But viewed, in real time, under their electron microscope, the sight will appear not only to *exist*, but to be *alive*! Such *aliveness* could well exist as the being's description of the moment of conception.

TRANSLATED AS: the it-and-them

from

The Hebrew word here is the same as the untranslated word, above; except here, it has a prefix. Our word here is *ōōă*·bēn [𐤍𐤉𐤁𐤅], *to distinguish.* The prefix, *ōōă* [𐤅], is "and".

TRANSLATED AS: and distinguishing

the night

Given the full treatment when it was seen in Verse 5, the word here has a prefix, 𐤄, "the". As a refresher, our here word is *hā·lēl·ăh* [𐤄𐤋𐤉𐤋𐤄|הלילה] [H3915], defined as "*a twist (away from the light), i.e. night*". Strong's refers us to H3883, where we encounter "*an unused root meaning to fold back; a spiral step—winding stair*". It then refers us to H3924 where we encounter "*from the same as H3883—a loop*". What have we got here?—a loop, a twist, a spiral step, a winding stair, and to fold back. That's a *spot-on* description of the famous DNA double-helix molecular structure. The suffix on this word, a *hāy* [𐤄], which, per the late Professor Benjamin Davidson, is "silent" and "inconsequential"[532]. *But*, elsewhere, Professor Davidson informs us that a *hāy* [𐤄] suffix can refer to the "the absolute state" of the word upon which the *hay* is suffixed. We're utilizing that understanding of the *absolute state*.

TRANSLATED AS: the absolute state (of) the twisting spiral

and let them be

This word is straightforward. It is *ōōă·hē·ōō* [𐤅𐤄𐤉𐤅][H1961]—*to be*. The prefix, 𐤅, is "and". The root, 𐤄𐤉 [from 𐤄𐤉𐤄], is "is"; and the suffix, 𐤅, is "his" or "it".

TRANSLATED AS: and it is

for signs

The Hebrew word here is *lă·ăt·ōōt* [𐤋𐤀𐤕𐤕|לאתת] refers to *the sense of appearing; a signal (literally or figuratively)*. The prefix, 𐤋, is *in regard to*. The root, 𐤀𐤕 [from 𐤀𐤅𐤕] means *appearances*[533]. The suffix, 𐤕, is the exclamatory emphatic, "!". The word "enzyme" is added inside the brackets as the word's *apparent* context.

TRANSLATED AS: in regard to [enzyme] appearances!

and for seasons

Keep in mind that the context of Genesis 1 is about the technicalities of these entities' high-tech manipulation of the DNA of the resident bipedal hominids they encountered on our planet. In that context we won't be dealing with "seasons", but with the behavior of enzymes such as DNA gyrase and DNA polymerase.

The word in the ancient text, in the ancient way of writing, is, 𐤅𐤋𐤌𐤅𐤏𐤃𐤉𐤌 (*ōōă·lă·mĕ·ōō·ōd·ēm*). For any who may be familiar with Biblical Hebrew, the word in the text is, "ולמועדים". There's quite a bit going on inside this somewhat complex word. It has three prefixes. It has an "*ōōă-yăd*" [ו / י] letter swap in the first letter of the root word; and it has a two-letter suffix. The Strong's Number associated with the word in the text is H4150—*an appointment*. Its translation here comes from its actual root word, H3259 [ΔOZ (*ēăōd*)]—*to fix upon by agreement, to meet, to summon, to direct (in a certain quarter or position).* Its first prefix is "and". Its second prefix means "in regard to". Its third prefix is a utility determinative. The letter swap indicates that the meaning of the root word is being changed by the author—here the presumptive meaning is "useful". Its suffix makes the word plural.

TRANSLATED AS: and in regard to useful positional directions

and for days

The word "day" was seen twice in Verse 5 and once in Verses 8 and 13. Here, we're supposed to see the word as containing the Hebrew word for "days" [ᙏYZ|יום][Strong's H3117] in it. We're supposed to see it there even though it's in a form where the middle letter, Y|ו, is supposedly to have been dropped from the word by the ancient author.

The word in the text is ᙏZᙏZᏞY|ולימים. The actual root word and the actual grammar of the word must be taken into consideration. The root word here is not the word for "day"; but the word for "water"—or rather, semen[534] [*mēm*|ᙏZᙏ|מים]. The first prefix is the letter, *ōōă* [Y], "and". The second prefix is the letter, *lăměd* [Ꮭ], is "in regard to". The third prefix (or *inserted letter*), *yăd* [Z], means "it".

TRANSLATED AS: and in regard to it-semen [spermatozoa]

and years

If you look up Strong's H8141 you will see the Biblical Hebrew writing, "שָׁנֶה" [*shĭn-nŭn-hāy* ("*shaw-neh*")]. You will also see what appears to be a smack-down definition, "a year". The word here in the original text would have been in the ancient (actual) Hebrew writing as, "ᙏZ1WY" [ושנים]. The "actual" root word is Strong's Number H8138—which is *to fold; i.e. duplicate*[535]. The prefix, Y, is "and". The two suffixes, "Z" and "ᙏ", mean "it" and "them" respectively.

TRANSLATED AS: and duplicate it them

A researched translation of the ancient Hebrew Genesis 1:14—
And entities said, "It is cursedly frustrating in being spread out [*decreased concentration of sperm cells which necessitated IVF*]. The Amazements! Toward the differentiation—distinguishing the it-and-them [*the ovum (egg cell) is the "it", the mass of sperm cells (even in decreased concentration) are the "them"*]; and distinguishing the absolute state of the twisting spiral [*the DNA molecular structure of the egg and of the sperm cells*]. And it is in regard to [*enzyme*] appearances and in regard to useful positional directions; and in regard to it-semen [*hominid spermatozoa*]: and them [*Messenger RNA, Transfer RNA (tRNA), Ribosomal RNA, and MicroRNA*[536]] duplicating it [*"it" is the long-chain DNA molecular structure conveying the entities' modified genetic information*]."

Genesis 1:14—*in plain English*

- ☆ The entities cursed about their problem of low sperm concentration requiring IVF.
- ☆ They were amazed by their own frustration.
- ☆ They thoroughly studied the physical nature and characteristics of hominid DNA. They did an analysis of the enzymes and of the role that molecular positioning plays in RNA to aid in the duplication of DNA.
- ☆ All their reseach is toward genetically engineering a fully self-reproducing hybrid-being.

The KJV *of* Genesis 1:15 (*first phrase*)—
And let them be for lights in the firmament of the heavens

Ancient Hebrew Anatomic Alphabet writing of that phrase—

𐤅𐤄𐤉𐤅 𐤋𐤌𐤀𐤅𐤓𐤕 𐤁𐤓𐤒𐤉𐤏 𐤄𐤔𐤌𐤉𐤌

An actual translation *with researched explanations below*—
And it is in regard to bioluminescence in spreading out The Amazements

The KJV *of* Genesis 1:15 (*second phrase*)—
to give light upon the earth: and it was so.

Ancient Hebrew Anatomic Alphabet writing of that phrase—

𐤋𐤄𐤀𐤉𐤓 𐤏𐤋 𐤄𐤀𐤓𐤑 𐤅𐤉𐤄𐤉 𐤊𐤍

An actual translation *with researched explanations below*—
in regard to the bioluminescent yoke [*as a fastening framework in the form of the phosphate-deoxyribose 'yoke'—yoking the other structural nucleotides of the DNA double helix molecule structure*]: The I-Accomplish. And it is true.

The Researched Explanations—

and let them be
We've already seen variations of these words in English in Verses 3, 6, and 14. They derive from the ancient Hebrew word, *ōōă·hē·ōō* [𐤅𐤄𐤉𐤅|והיו]. The root word is *hē·ăh* [𐤄𐤉𐤄][H1961], meaning "*to be*". The present tense of "to be" is expressed as the word, "is". The prefix, 𐤅, is "and". The root word has its terminal letter [𐤄] dropped in the original text. The suffix, 𐤅, is "his" or "its".

TRANSLATED AS: and it is

for lights

It would be logical to think that the lights here would be the same as the lights in Verse 14; but each of these traditional "lights" is the product of a deliberate fraud. The Hebrew word in the text at this location has more built into it than the two English words, "for lights". The word in the text is *lă·mĕ·ăōōr·ĕt* [𐤋𐤌𐤀𐤅𐤓𐤕|למאורת] from the root, "𐤀𐤅𐤓" [H215]; and is defined as *to be luminous*. The letters built onto the root word are in its two prefixes (the 𐤋 and the 𐤌) and one suffix (the 𐤕). The most important *meaning modifier* here is the *mĕm* [𐤌], which acts as a utility determinative. In the context DNA manipulation, the utility of *to be luminous* is luminescence. These prefix and suffix letters have been previously explained. The literal translation of *lă·mĕ·ăōōr·ĕt* is *in regard to bioluminescence!* Biological luminescence is bioluminescence.

TRANSLATED AS: in regard to bioluminescence!

in the firmament

A variant of this word was previously encountered twice in Verse 7 and once in Verse 8; and as the exact same word in Verse 14. There's no "the" prefix here. Our word is *bĕ·rĕqwēō* [𐤁𐤓𐤒𐤉𐤏| ברקיע]. It is encountered at Job 37:18 as, "…spread out [the sky]". The grammar is that the inserted *yăd* [𐤉] modifies the verb, *to spread*, in a way understood in context. The prefix, *bĕt* [𐤁], is *in*.

TRANSLATED AS: in (being) spread out [the decreased concentration of sperm cells which necessitated IVF]

of the heavens

As previously seen in Verses 1, 8, 9, and 14, *the heavens* [*hā·shĭm·ēm* |𐤄𐤔𐤌𐤉𐤌] is translated from the Hebrew root, *shĭ·mēm* ["𐤔𐤌𐤌" | H8074], *to amaze.* The word here has a prefix, 𐤄, "the". The third letter [𐤌] of the root was dropped in the original text. The suffix, 𐤉𐤌-, pluralizes.

TRANSLATED AS: the amazements

to give light

In this word, *lă·hā·ăēr* [𐤋𐤄𐤀𐤉𐤓], we will get "bioluminescent", but by way of a slightly different grammatical route. We all know that any bioluminescence is, of course, light. But all light isn't *bio*luminescence. Of course: the metabolic reactions inside the DNA molecular structure, taking into consideration that the energy molecules, *adenosine triphosphate* (ATP), are present in every biological action of living organisms—means that the entities observed it—and now are describing it.

In the previous word for light, *lă·mĕ·ăōōr·ĕt* [𐤋𐤌𐤀𐤅𐤓𐤕], the "heavy lifting" of modifying the understanding of "light" is the prefix, *mĕm* [𐤌], which acts as a utility determinative. In our word in this verse [𐤋𐤄𐤀𐤉𐤓|להאיר] we can see that there is no *mĕm* [𐤌] prefix. In our word here the root-word is still *ăōōr* "𐤀𐤅𐤓" ["אור"]; except that we can see that the middle letter, *ōōă* [𐤅/"ו"] is swapped for the letter *yăd* [𐤉/"י"] by the ancient writer. It is the *swap* of these two particular letters, one for the other, that "signals" to the reader (or hearer) that the usual meaning of the word is being changed. There is no grammar to give us "give".

TRANSLATED AS: in regard to (the) bioluminescent

upon

Although this word [*ōl* |𐤏𐤋] has been explained previously; it is helpful to know that when Strong's Number H5923 is looked up, there is a one-word definition—*yoke*. An eternal irony is that the actual word in the text, whether represented in the ancient way as "𐤏𐤋" or in the "modern" way as "על", the definition of "yoke" exactly fits the context here.

TRANSLATED AS: yoke [as a fastening framework of the phosphate-deoxyribose yoking the double helix structure together]

the earth

Last sighted in Verse 11, the word, *hā·ărĕtz* [𐤄𐤀𐤓𐤑][H776], has been traditionally defined as *ground* or *land,* and translated (rather, mistranslated) as "earth". It is read here as "*hā·ă·rĕtz·ăh*" [𐤄]𐤄𐤀𐤓𐤑], from Strong's H7521, "*to accomplish*. The prefix *hāy* [𐤄] is the indefinite article, "the". The prefix *ălăpf* [𐤀] is "I".

TRANSLATED AS: the I-Accomplish

and it was so
This phrase has been seen in Verses 7, 9, and 11. The two words in the text here are *ōōă·ē·hē kăn* [𐤅𐤉𐤄𐤉 𐤊𐤍]. They are associated with Strong's H1961 and H3651. The prefix, *ōōă* [𐤅], is "and". The *yăd* [𐤉] is the *second* prefix, "it". The root fragment, *hē* [𐤄𐤉 from the root 𐤄𐤉𐤄], means "is". The second word, *kăn* [𐤊𐤍] can mean "so"; but it also means "true". That's the choice here.

TRANSLATED AS: and it is true

A researched translation of the ancient Hebrew Genesis 1:15—

And it is in regard to bioluminescence in spreading out The Amazements in regard to the bioluminescent yoke [*as a fastening framework in the form of the phosphate-deoxyribose 'yoke'—yoking the other structural nucleotides of the DNA double helix molecule structure*]: The I-Accomplish. And it is true.

Genesis 1:15—*in plain English*

- ☆ The entities noted some significant observations.
- ☆ At the molecular level there are tiny points of light in their semen.
- ☆ Their semen has a low concentration of sperm cells.
- ☆ The tiny points of light were seen where the phosphate-sugar bond connects the DNA spiral ladder to DNA base pairs.
- ☆ The account states that what they are relating is true.

The KJV of Genesis 1:16 (*first phrase*)—
And God made two great lights:

Ancient Hebrew Anatomic Alphabet writing of that phrase—
ויעש אלהים את שני המארת הגדלים

An actual translation *with researched explanations below*—
And strange-biological-entities [*the alien lab technicians*] made ready the preferred CRISPR analog [*technology*]. The cursedly frustrating[!] The-Twists [*the DNA*]:

The KJV of Genesis 1:16 (*second phrase*)—
the greater light to rule the day,

Ancient Hebrew Anatomic Alphabet writing of that phrase—
את המאור הגדל לממשלת היום

An actual translation *with researched explanations below*—
CRISPR manipulating the bioluminosity (of) The-Twist [*at a site on the DNA molecular structure*] in regard to replicating [*DNA self-replication*] the it-and-them [*the DNA-manipulated egg and sperm cells*]:

The KJV of Genesis 1:16 (*third phrase*)—
and the lesser light to rule the night: he made the stars also.

Ancient Hebrew Anatomic Alphabet writing of that phrase—
ואת המאור הקטן לממשלת הלילה
ואת הכוכבים

An actual translation *with researched explanations below*—
and CRISPR manipulating the bioluminosity (by) the cutting off [*segments*]—in regard to replicating [*in DNA self-replication*]! The CRISPR-manipulated twisting spiral [*the DNA*]—and CRISPR manipulating the tiny blazings.

The Researched Explanations—

and God made

and made

The root word here, WOZY [ויעש], could be translated here as "made". But the word may also be a variety of other similar verbs, such as: *to work, to labor, to fabricate, to create, to produce, to yield, to get, to acquire, to make ready, to prepare, to dress, to execute, to accomplish, to perform, to act, to press,* and *to squeeze.* The eminent Dr. Strong writes that this word may be used, "*in the broadest sense and widest application*". The word's first prefix, Y, means "and". The second prefix, Z, means "it".

TRANSLATED AS: and it made ready

God

The word "God" is associated with the English rendering of the Germanic *gott*, *got*, or *gud*. Here it is treated as "*strange-biological-entities*"—or simply "entities". *Note*: the suffix on the Hebrew word makes the word plural.[537]

TRANSLATED AS: strange-biological-entities

~a Hebrew word untranslated in the KJV~

The untranslated word in the text here is, "*ăt*" [X 4]. Per any standard Hebrew Dictionary of the Old Testament, it can be found as Strong's H855—defined as "coulter". A coulter is the part of a seed drill that cuts a furrow for the seed. That word can be found at 1 Samuel 13:20 and 21. Modern synonyms of that ancient tool could be an *injecting pipette* as used in IVF or a "CRISPR analog" technology used for splicing sections of the DNA.

TRANSLATED AS: CRISPR analog [technology]

two

Traditionally given as "two", the word in the text, *shĭnē* [Z 7W], is from the root *shĭnăh* [𐤄 7W][Strong's H8138]. The Strong's Number is given as: *to fold, to duplicate, to transmute, to pervert,* or *to do the second time*. Strong's

H8138 appears 22 times in the King James Bible text; and appears at Esther 2:9 as “preferred”. The suffix, the letter *yăd* [𐤉] can stand for *me, my,* (rarely *I*); and occasionally for article, “the”[538]. This word is such an instance.

TRANSLATED AS: the preferred

lights

The Hebrew word order here requires us to first take on the word, “lights”—which isn’t “lights”, and then the word, “great”—which isn’t “great”. We saw the same word misrepresented as “lights” in Verse 14 in the word, “*mĕ·ărĕt* [𐤌𐤀𐤓𐤕]”.

Here it is *hā·mĕ·ărĕt* [𐤄𐤌𐤀𐤓𐤕|המארת][H779], which means *to bitterly curse*. The only difference in the word here is the addition of another prefix, *hāy* [𐤄], as “the”. The presence of the letter, *mĕm* [𐤌], is a reference to the *utility* of intense frustration.

TRANSLATED AS: the cursedly frustrating!

great

Sure, the Strong’s Number associated with the word “great” is H1419; and the Hebrew word given for H1419 is “גדול” (“*gadowl*”). But that word, however, is *not* the word in the text. The word in the text here is *hā·gĭdăl·ēm* [𐤄𐤂𐤃𐤋𐤉𐤌|הגדלים]. It is from the root, “גדל” (“*gadol*”)] H1431, “*a primitive root, properly to twist*”. The suffix *ēm* [𐤉𐤌-] makes the word plural.

TRANSLATED AS: the twists [a visual description of the DNA molecule]

the greater light

—as rearranged in the Hebrew word order,

the light greater

the

Often left untranslated, the Hebrew word at this place in the text is the same word encountered four words previous. It is the word, “ăt” [𐤀𐤕 | “את”]. It is Strong’s H855, and defined as “coulter”—which is the part of a seed drill that cuts a furrow for the seed. The modern translation, in context, is the

"CRISPR" technology. In context, the word is translated as a verb in present participle form.

TRANSLATED AS: CRISPR-manipulating

light

If we track with the word order in the actual Hebrew text the word that follows is "light". Why isn't "light" here going to be the same "light" as seen just three words previous? The word there was, "*mĕ·ărĕt* [X𐤓𐤀𐤌]". Here, *hā·mĕ·ăōōr* [𐤓𐤅𐤀𐤌𐤄|המאור][H215], is the root word seen in Verse 15 (as *for lights*). This word's first prefix, 𐤄, means "the". Its second prefix, *mĕm* [𐤌], acts as a utility determinative. The utility of luminescence in context here is *cellular luminosity*—which is bioluminescent.

TRANSLATED AS: the bioluminosity

greater

The word "greater" here is the same as the word "great" just three words previous—except this Hebrew word is singular. The word in the text is *hā·gĭdăl* [𐤋𐤃𐤂𐤄].

TRANSLATED AS: the twist [at a site on the DNA molecular structure]

to rule

Very conveniently, the context of the traditional scriptural psy-op provided Dr. James Strong, (for whom the famous Strong's Numbers are named), the cover for his definition of H4475. His meaning for that numbered word is, "*the realm of a ruler, i.e. dominion*". It is from his Strong's H4474, "*to rule, ruler*", which is from H4910, that we have, "*to rule*" and "*to have dominion*".

But, and this is a big but, Strong's H4911 (the same root word as H4910), is *to resemble*. The word is used five times in KJV as "like" (as in, *to resemble*). Strong's H4915 (same root word) is supposed to be *from* H4911. Its meaning is given as "*parallel*"; and is used only three times in KJV—one time as "like" (as in, *to resemble*).

The actual word here is *lă-mĕ-mĕshĭl-ăt* [X𐤋𐤔𐤌𐤌𐤋| לממשלת]. We have previously encountered each of the two prefixes—the *lămĕd*, meaning "in regard to"; and the *mĕm* as a utility determinative, which may be taken as giving us *resemblance*. In translation, that would be our word, "replicate" (as a synonym of "resemblance"). The suffix, *tōō* [X], may act as an exclamatory emphatic—our "!". Here the word is used as a verb.

TRANSLATED AS: in regard to replicating [in DNA self-replication]!

the day
The Hebrew word "the day" [ᗰYZ𐤄] was fully explained when last seen in Verse 14.

TRANSLATED AS: the it-and-them [the DNA-manipulated egg and sperm cells]

and the
Our word here, *ōōă·ăt* [X𐤀Y |"ואת"], is the same root [*ăt* [X𐤀 | "את"], as seen previously. It is Strong's H855, defined as "coulter"; and used here as a modern-day synonym, "CRISPR technology". The prefix Y is "and". Here also the word is in verb form.

TRANSLATED AS: and CRISPR manipulating

light
Here we have the exact word as in "light" just previously seen.

TRANSLATED AS: the bioluminosity

lesser
This word in the KJV is associated with Strong's H6996. That Strong's Number appears 101 times[539] in the KJV—variously as, *little, least, small, smallest, younger,* and *youngest*; and once as "lesser". H6996 ["קָטָן"] is defined as *abbreviated* or *diminutive*. It is from the root H6962 ["קוט"], defined as "to cut off"[540]. It is understandable how *abbreviated* or *diminutive* can come from the idea of "to cut off". It can also be seen how *little, least, small, smallest, younger,* and *youngest* can come from the idea of *abbreviated* or *diminutive*.

The word in the text is *hā·qwōōthĕn* [𐤄𐤒𐤈𐤍][הקטן]. H6962 appears seven times[541] in the KJV—variously as "grieved", "loathe", and "little". *However*, the wording "cut off" serves each scriptural context just as well. The prefix, *hāy*, is the article, "the".

TRANSLATED AS: the cutting off

to rule
This "to rule" is the exact same word as just previously treated.

TRANSLATED AS: in regard to replicating [in DNA self-replication]!

the night
Seen in Verses 5 and in 14, our here word is *hā·lēl·āh* [𐤄𐤋𐤉𐤋𐤄] [H3915], defined as "*a twist (away from the light), i.e. night*". Strong's refers us to H3883, where we encounter "*an unused root meaning to fold back; a spiral step—winding stair*". It then refers us to H3924 where we encounter "*from the same as H3883—a loop*". What are these definitions describing? They're pretty much a description of the famous DNA double-helix molecule. The suffix, *hāy* [𐤄], can refer to the "the absolute state" of a word—here understood as having been CRISPR-manipulated.

TRANSLATED AS: the CRISPR-manipulated twisting spiral

~a Hebrew word untranslated in the KJV~
Our word here, *ōōă·ăt* [𐤅𐤀𐤕 |ואת][H855], has been explained.

TRANSLATED AS: and CRISPR manipulating

he made the stars also

As in the example of many previous words, the meaning-information provided by a legitimate study of the actual Hebrew word may give us something contextually quite different. The differences are, however, completely in context with the actual ancient document.

In the word in the text here we will encounter a root word, *kăkăb*, a letter (𐤅) inserted into the word, a prefix (𐤄), "the"; and a common suffix (𐤉𐤌-) which makes the word plural. Our word here is *hā-kōōkăb-ēm* [𐤄𐤊𐤅𐤊𐤁𐤉𐤌|הכוכבים][H3556]. The root of *that* Strong's Number is *kōōkăb* [𐤊𐤅𐤊𐤁]. It is described as being *probably from H3522 in the sense of rolling; or H3554 in the sense of blazing.* "𐤊𐤅𐤄" is the root cited for Strong's H3554; but the roots, "𐤊𐤅𐤄" and "𐤊𐤊𐤁" never appear in the biblical text; and the word, "𐤊𐤅𐤊𐤁" (*kōōkăb*) appears only twice—each time as *star*.

The inserted letter, *ōōă* [𐤅], signals that the writer is modifying the word to mean what he has in mind; and what the hybrid (or *strange entity*) writer must have had in mind is what was *observed* under the entities' microscope—since they undoubtedly had an entire scientific laboratory for their IVF and DNA-manipulation research and development project.

The word "blazing" does not appear in the KJV; but we must also know that the ancients did not use our word "stars" either. How do stars appear to the naked eye? They appear as tiny blazings or as tiny twinklings in the sky. The words, "blazings" or "tiny blazings" would just as well fit the contexts in which the English word "stars" appears in the Bible.

TRANSLATED AS: the tiny-blazings

A researched translation of the ancient Hebrew Genesis 1:16—

And strange-biological-entities [*the alien lab technicians*] made ready the preferred CRISPR analog [*technology*]. The cursedly frustrating[!] The-Twists [*the DNA*]: CRISPR manipulating the bioluminosity (of) The-Twist [*at a site on the DNA molecular structure*] in regard to replicating [*DNA self-replication*] the it-and-them [*the DNA-manipulated egg and sperm cells*]: and CRISPR manipulating the bioluminosity (by) the cutting off [*segments*]—in regard to replicating [*in DNA self-replication*]! The CRISPR-manipulated twisting spiral [*the DNA*]—and CRISPR manipulating the tiny blazings.

Genesis 1:16—*in plain English*

- ☆ CRISPR technologies play a staring role in this verse; and the entities refer to the complexity of the DNA structure, which they call "The Twist" or "the twisting spiral".

- ☆ They refer directly to copying DNA and to cutting off segments of DNA.
- ☆ Molecular bioluminosity plays a role in their determination where to cut DNA segments.

The KJV of Genesis 1:17 (*first phrase*)—
And God set them in the firmament of the heaven

Ancient Hebrew Anatomic Alphabet writing of that phrase—
𐤅𐤉𐤕𐤍 𐤀𐤕𐤌 𐤀𐤋𐤄𐤉𐤌 𐤁𐤓𐤒𐤉𐤏 𐤄𐤔𐤌𐤉𐤌

An actual translation *with researched explanations below*—
And it [*alien spermatozoa*] (is) elongated: in-vitro fertilize them. Strange-biological-entities (intervened) against being spread out [*decreased concentration of sperm cells in their semen which necessitated IVF*]—The-Amazements—

The KJV of Genesis 1:17 (*second phrase*)—
to give light upon the earth,

Ancient Hebrew Anatomic Alphabet writing of that phrase—
𐤋𐤄𐤀𐤉𐤓 𐤏𐤋 𐤄𐤀𐤓𐤑

An actual translation *with researched explanations below*—
in regard to the bioluminescent yoke [*as a fastening framework (the phosphate-deoxyribose "yoke") holding the double helix structure together—yoking the other structural nucleotides of the DNA together]*: The I-Accomplish.

The Researched Explanations—

and God set them

and set

Here is the first appearance of the word, *ōōā-ētōōn* [𐤅𐤉𐤕𐤍|ויתן]. It is traditionally given as H5414, and is, presumptuously enough, presumed to be from the verb, "𐤍𐤕𐤍" (*nōōtōōn*), *to give, to cause*, or *to set*. The fly in *this* ointment, however, is that the actual root word here is "𐤕𐤍" (*tōōn*, rhymes with "moon"). It is Strong's H8565—"*from an unused root probably meaning* to elongate; *a monster (as preternaturally formed)*".

Let's first dispense with the twenty-five cent word, "preternaturally". This word's prefix is from the Latin "præter", which means "outside"—by which Dr. Strong (and every preceding as well as subsequent theologian and academician) has meant "outside" of the natural order of things—or what we would call, "supernatural".

We should allow the word's traditional (and contextual) definitions to give us some clues as to what this Hebrew word has been, *and is*, attempting to say. The first clue is "elongate". An internet search on "elongated sperm in IVF" will provide just about all the information needed to connect this word with its definition. The second clue is the word, "monster".

You see, the medical condition the strange entities dealt with here goes by a modern-day medical term, "teratospermia"—where the prefix "terato" is from the Latin, "monster"—*monster sperm cells*. Their green sperm cells were of the abnormal type known as "elongated"—that is, their cells were afflicted by an abnormal condition known as "tapering"[542].

That cause of male infertility, *elongated sperm*, has a remedy—if fertility is the issue—*in vitro fertilization* by way of a procedure known as *intracytoplasmic sperm injection* [ICSI]. In that current-day medical procedure an *injection pipette* inserts the best sperm cell available into a readied female ovum (egg)[543].

Armed with that information, and knowledge of Hebrew prefixes, our word in the text here easily reveals itself. The word, again, is *ōōă-ētōōn* [𐤅𐤉𐤕𐤍]. The common prefix, *ōōă* [𐤅], (its first prefix) is "and". The common prefix, *yăd* [𐤉], (its second) is "he" or "it". The root word, *tōōn* [𐤕𐤍], is "elongated"—a condition of *teratospermia.*

TRANSLATED AS: and it (is) elongated

them

This word has been seen several times throughout the text—it is Strong's H855 [*coulter*]. The entities are using a modern medical synonym—an "injecting pipette". Our word here is *ăt·ōōm* [𐤀𐤕𐤌 | אתם]. The word's suffix, the letter *mĕm* [𐤌], means *they, their,* or *them*. Here, the noun, injecting pipette, is being used (in context) as a verb implied by the procedure in which it is used.

TRANSLATED AS: in-vitro fertilize them

God
The word "God" is associated with the English rendering of the Germanic *gott*, *got*, or *gud*. Here it is treated as "*strange-biological-entities*". *Translation note*: the "-ēn" (or "-ē*m*") suffix on the Hebrew word "ălăh" makes the word plural.[544]

TRANSLATED AS: strange-biological-entities

in the firmament
Last seen in Verse 15 and 14, variants of the word, "firmament", were also seen in Verses 7 and 8. Again, no "the" prefix. Here again is our word, *bĕ·rĕqwēō* [𐤁𐤓𐤒𐤉𐤏]. This word is encountered at Job 37:18 as, "…spread out [the sky]". The grammar is that the inserted *yăd* [𐤉] modifies this verb, *to spread*, in a way which is understood in context. The prefix, *bĕt*[𐤁], may be *in, among,* or *against.* Here it is being used as "in"—as, *in response to a problem.* The "problem" here is known among today's doctors who specialize in fertility matters as *oligospermia* [a low concentration of spermatozoa in the semen].

TRANSLATED AS: in [response to a problem] being spread out [decreased concentration of sperm cells in their semen which necessitated IVF]

of the heaven
We have encountered this Hebrew word in Verses 1, 8, 9, 14, and 15. The word *hā·shĭm·ēm* [𐤄𐤔𐤌𐤉𐤌] is translated from the Hebrew root, *shĭ·mēm* ["𐤔𐤌𐤌" | H8074], *to amaze.* This word's suffix ("-ēm") makes the word plural.

TRANSLATED AS: the amazements

to give light
The metabolic reactions inside the DNA molecular structure, along with the actions and activities of the energy molecules, *adenosine triphosphate* (ATP), are present in every biological action of living organisms. That means that the strange entities were observing *bioluminescence*—here expressed by the word, *lă·hā·ăēr* [𐤋𐤄𐤀𐤉𐤓|להאיר]—last encountered in Verse 15.

Here, the root-word is *ăōōr* "𐤀𐤅𐤓" ["אור"][H215]. It can be seen that there is a swap (by the ancient writer) of the middle letter, *ōōā* [𐤅]["ו"], for the letter *yăd* [𐤉]["י"]. It is the *swap* of these two particular letters, one for the other, that "signals" to the reader (or hearer) that the usual meaning of the word is being changed. The word's prefix, 𐤋, means "in regard to". There is no "give" in the grammar of this word.

TRANSLATED AS: in regard to (the) bioluminescence

upon
Last seen in Verse 15, this word [*ōl* |𐤏𐤋] has been explained. It is helpful to know that this Strong's Number (H5923) is looked up, there is a one-word definition—*yoke*. An eternal irony is that the actual word in the text, whether represented in the ancient writing as "𐤏𐤋", or in the "modern" way as "על", the definition of "yoke" fits exactly the context here.

TRANSLATED AS: yoke [as a phosphate-deoxyribose fastening framework yoking the double helix structure together]

the earth
Last seen in Verse 12, the words "*the earth*" have been given as "the earth" since put into Greek as "*tos ges*" (*the earth*) about 2,200 years ago. The word is treated here as "*hā·ă·rĕtz·ăh*" [𐤄𐤀𐤓𐤑𐤄][הארצה], "*to accomplish*—the root being "𐤓𐤑𐤄" [רָצָה][545] with presumption of a commonly dropped letter *hāy* [𐤄]["ה"]. The prefix *hāy* [𐤄] is the indefinite article, "the". The prefix *ălăpf* [𐤀] is "I".

TRANSLATED AS: the I-Accomplish

A researched translation of the ancient Hebrew Genesis 1:17—
And it [*the entities' spermatozoa*] is elongated: in-vitro fertilize them. Strange-biological-entities (intervened) against being spread out [*decreased concentration of sperm cells in semen which necessitated IVF*]—The-Amazements—in regard to the bioluminescent yoke [*as a fastening framework (the phosphate-deoxyribose "yoke") holding the double helix structure*

together—yoking the other structural nucleotides of the DNA together]: The I-Accomplish.

Genesis 1:17—*in plain English*

- ☆ The strange entities discover that their sperm cells are abnormally elongated.
- ☆ They again acknowledge their problem of low sperm concentration.
- ☆ They use IVF technology to solve both problems.
- ☆ They comment that the bioluminescent bonds in the DNA double helix to its base-pairs is amazing; and that their successful IVF procedures are an accomplishment.

The KJV of Genesis 1:18 (*first phrase*)—
And to rule over the day and over the night,

Ancient Hebrew Anatomic Alphabet writing of that phrase—
𐤅𐤋𐤌𐤔𐤋 𐤁𐤉𐤅𐤌 𐤅𐤁𐤋𐤉𐤋𐤄

An actual translation *with researched explanations below*—
And in regard to resembling [*the template DNA molecular structure*] in it-and-them [*the ovum (egg cell) is the "it", and the mass of sperm cells is the "them"*] and in CRISPR-manipulated twisted spiraling [*the DNA molecular structure*],

The KJV of Genesis 1:18 (*second phrase*)—
and to divide the light from the darkness:

Ancient Hebrew Anatomic Alphabet writing of that phrase—
𐤅𐤋𐤄𐤁𐤃𐤉𐤋 𐤁𐤉𐤍 𐤄𐤀𐤅𐤓 𐤅𐤁𐤉𐤍 𐤄𐤇𐤔𐤊

An actual translation *with researched explanations below*—
and in regard to differentiation—distinguishing the light [*as literal bioluminescence, a phenomena associated with a living organism*], and distinguishing the absence of light [*where "absence-of-light" is literally an absence of bioluminescence, a phenomena associated with an organism no longer living*].

The KJV of Genesis 1:18 (*third phrase*)—
and God saw that it was good.

Ancient Hebrew Anatomic Alphabet writing of that phrase—
𐤅𐤉𐤓𐤀 𐤀𐤋𐤄𐤉𐤌 𐤊𐤉 𐤈𐤅𐤁

An actual translation *with researched explanations below*—
And strange biological entities saw that (it was a) good [*technical solution*].

The Researched Explanations—

and to rule over

Here, the word *ōōā·lă·měshǐl* [𐤅𐤋𐤌𐤔𐤋], given in the text is similar to the word previous used Verse 16. The word in the text, 𐤅𐤋𐤌𐤔𐤋, has two prefixes, 𐤅 (*and*) and 𐤋 (*in regard to*). It has a root, [Strong's H4911], "to resemble".

TRANSLATED AS: and in regard to resembling [the template DNA molecular structure]

the day

The word here is *bě·ēōōm* [𐤁𐤉𐤅𐤌|ביום]. It is traditionally given as "the day". It is similar to the "the day" as previously seen. There is no "root word" here. Each of the word's four letters (*bět, yăd, ōōă* [*văv*] and *hāy*) is an element of ancient grammar. The letter 𐤁 (*as a prefix*) here means "*in*". The letter 𐤉 (*as a prefix*) here means "*it*". The letter 𐤅 (*as a prefix*) means "*and*". The letter 𐤌 (*as a suffix*) means "*them*".

TRANSLATED AS: in it-and-them

and over the night

Here, the word *ōōā·bě·lă·ēl·ăh* [𐤅𐤁𐤋𐤉𐤋𐤄|ובלילה], is similar to the word previously used in Verses 5, 15, and 16. The word, "𐤅𐤁𐤋𐤉𐤋𐤄" has two prefixes: 𐤅 (*and*) *and* 𐤁 (*in, among,* or *against*). It has a root word, "𐤋𐤉𐤋" [H3915], "*twisting spiral*". It has one suffix, 𐤄, denoting "the *absolute state* of the root word". Here, that state is in having been CRISPR-manipulated.

TRANSLATED AS: and in CRISPR-manipulated twisted spiraling [the DNA molecular structure]

and to divide

The root word, or *base word*, here in the ancient text we have seen previously. In Verse 4 it was as "𐤅𐤉𐤁𐤃𐤋" (*and it separated*), it shares the very same root, "𐤁𐤃𐤋", with our Hebrew word here. In Verse 14 it was as "𐤋𐤄𐤁𐤃𐤉𐤋" (*toward the differentiation*). It was able to become "differentiation" because of the inserted letter, 𐤉, which changed the verb to something else, such as a noun.

Again, our base word is *bĕdăl* [𐤁𐤃𐤋]. It is Strong's H914, *separated, divided,* or *distinguished*. Here, we have the same base—with the same letter [𐤉] inserted. Here, we have *three* prefixes on the word, *ōōă·lă·hā·bĕd·ē·l* [𐤅𐤋𐤄𐤁𐤃𐤉𐤋][ולהבדיל]. The first prefix is "and". The second prefix is "in regard to". The third prefix is "the". The root, 𐤁𐤃𐤋, has an inserted letter [𐤉]. Note: a noun-form, such as "differentiation", is a synonym of "distinguished"—and is the noun following the article, "the".
Translation: and in regard to the differentiation

~a Hebrew word untranslated in the KJV~
The untranslated word in the text here is, "*bēn*" [𐤁𐤉𐤍], which word we saw twice in Verse 4. It is Strong's H995—*to separate mentally or distinguish, be cunning.*

TRANSLATED AS: distinguishing

the light
The ancient Hebrew for "the light" is, *hā·aōōr* [𐤄𐤀𐤅𐤓|האור].

TRANSLATED AS: the light [as literal bio-luminescence, a phenomena associated with a living organism]

from
It is from the ancient Hebrew compound word *ōōă·bēn* [𐤅𐤁𐤉𐤍][H995—*distinguish*] that the word "from" is wrestled. Our untranslated word, *bēn*, (from two words previous), here has a prefix—the letter *ōōă* [𐤅], meaning "and".

TRANSLATED AS: and distinguishing

the darkness
Although the word that appears here, *hā·khĕshĭk* [𐤄𐤇𐤔𐤊|החשך], is the same word we saw in Verses 4 and 5. Here it is used in a different sense. There are homonyms by the boatload in Hebrew. We can see that in the

Strong's Number system when there are several number entries for a given word.

This is such a word. In Verses 4 and 5 our word under study was Strong's H2820—*to restrain*. The word is being used here in the sense of *withholding light* [H2821].

TRANSLATED AS: the absence of light [a literal absence of bioluminescence, a phenomenon associated with an organism no longer living]

and saw

The word, [*ōŏă·ē·ra* | 𐤅𐤉𐤓𐤀] [H7200], could be treated as "and saw". Literally, it is "and-it-saw". The root, 𐤓𐤀𐤄, may also be translated as *to see, to exist, to live, to view, to regard,* or *to observe*. Here it will be translated as traditionally read. The pronoun, "it", refers collectively to the strange-biological-entities.

TRANSLATED AS: and it saw

God

The word, *ălăh·ēm* [𐤀𐤋𐤄𐤉𐤌|אלהים][H430], commonly translated "God", is the same word as found in the Book of Daniel—as "ălăh·ēn" [אלהין]. Here it is treated as "*strange-biological-entities*". *Note*: the "-ēn" (or "-ēm") suffix on the Hebrew word "ălăh" makes the word plural. The word could also be "*alah-beings*".[546]

TRANSLATED AS: strange biological entities

that

The word in the text is *kē* (pronounced "key") [𐤊𐤉]. It is Strong's H3588; and it can act to connect all kinds of causes in a sentence, including the words "for" and "because".

TRANSLATED AS: that

it was good
There is no "it was" on this word in the text. The word, *thōōb* [𐤁𐤅𐤈] [H2896] means "good" in the widest sense. Here it will be given as traditionally translated—in the sense of the practical necessity of the SBE's DNA manipulation and genetic engineering.

TRANSLATED AS: good [technical solution]

A researched translation of the ancient Hebrew Genesis 1:18—
And in regard to resembling [*the template DNA molecular structure*] in it-and-them [*the ovum (egg cell) is the "it", and the mass of sperm cells is the "them"*], and in the CRISPR-manipulated twisted spiraling [*the DNA molecular structure*], and in regard to differentiation—distinguishing the light [*as literal bio-luminescence, a phenomena associated with a living organism*], and distinguishing the absence of light [*a literal absence of bio-luminescence, a phenomenon associated with an organism no longer living*]. And strange biological entities saw that (it was a) good [*technical solution*].

Genesis 1:18—*in plain English*

- ☆ Strange entities described that RNA works with DNA to reproduce DNA.
- ☆ The entities distinguished between living organisms which had bioluminescent properties at the molecular level and non-living organisms which are no longer bioluminescent.

Reptilians, called Remesh, sexually subjugate the hominids

[Verses 19 through 22]

The KJV of Genesis 1:19—
And the evening and the morning were the fourth day.

Ancient Hebrew Anatomic Alphabet writing of that phrase—
ZOZ94 ᎷYZ 4P9 ZᎸZY 940 ZᎸZY

An actual translation *with researched explanations below*—
But it is to interbreed; and it is to research it-and-them [*the ovum (egg cell) is the "it", and the mass of sperm cells is the "them"*]. I will copulate [*as the next aspect of the beings R&D program*].

The Researched Explanations—

and the

For sure, the prefix "and" is in the ancient word in the text; but there is no "the" in the phrase, "and the evening". The word here is *ōōă·ē·hē* [ZᎸZY] [H1961]. It's from the root, "to be". For a review, look back at Verse 1's "Let there be". The prefix here is *ōōă* [Y], "and"; the second prefix is *yăd* [Z], "it". The root word is, "is".

TRANSLATED AS: and it is

evening

Yes, the word *ōrĕb* [940] is generally given as "evening" [H6153]. Here is given as H6148—"braid" and "intermix"—in the sense of mingled seed; and properly treated here as "interbreed".

TRANSLATED AS: to interbreed

and the
Again, the prefix "and" is in the text. This is the same word as "*and the*" previously explained. Sorry—there's no "morning" either.

TRANSLATED AS: and it is

morning
Sure, the word *bĕqwōōr* [𐤁𐤒𐤓] can be "morning". That's Strong's Number H1242; but the eminent authority, Dr. Strong, tells us that H1242 is derived from H1239, which is to *seek, seek out, inquire,* and *inquiry.* H1240 is *to seek* or *to inquire* in all five places where it appears in the text. Here, we treat "to seek out" as "to research".

TRANSLATED AS: to research

were the
These words do not appear at this place in the ancient text.

day
This word is the same seen twice in Verse 5 and once in Verse 8.

TRANSLATED AS: it-and-them [*the ovum (egg cell) is the "it", and the mass of sperm cells is the "them"*]

fourth
The word in the Hebrew text is *rĕbēōē* [𐤓𐤁𐤉𐤏𐤉|רביעי]. It is associated with Strong's H7243, defined as "fractionally". It is from H7251 [𐤓𐤁𐤏|רבע], defined as, "*a root identified with* H7250 *through the idea of sprawling 'at all fours'*". Strong's H7250 [𐤓𐤁𐤏] is defined as, "*to squat or lay flat out (specically) in copulation—lie down*".

We must note that our word under study is used only in two places in the Hebrew Bible—here and in Genesis 15:16—as "fourth". As for a "real" word for "fourth", we can find that in the famous Ten Commandments (or "Ten Words" in Judaism) at Exodus 20:5. The word there is the same root, 𐤓𐤁𐤏, with a common pluralizing suffix in Hebrew, "-ēm" [-𐤉𐤌], as "𐤓𐤁𐤏𐤉𐤌".

Note also that there is an inserted letter, *yăd* [Z], in the word under study here: ZOZ94. Such an inserted letter changes the meaning of the word—sometimes to an adjective, sometimes as past-tense, sometimes as an "-ing" word, and sometimes changes it to a closely related concept.

The root [H7250 (O94)] is used three times in the first five books of the Bible—in Leviticus: 18:23, 19:19, and 20:16. Each appearance is in the context of copulation. The root [H7251 (O94)] appears six times—each time in Exodus—with the letter Y (*ōōă aka* the letter *waw*) inserted as, "OY94". That word is traditionally treated as "foursquare".

The word, *rĕbēō* [OZ94], never appears in the Hebrew Bible as a stand-alone word. The grammar, then, of this word is of having a root (or base) of, "O94", with an inserted Z, as "ZOZ94" (*rĕbēōē*). It has a suffix, Z, which denotes, as appropriate to the context, the personal pronouns *me* or *my*. This word, in translation, is "I will copulate". The SBE's own long-term R&D project includes copulation with the resident bipedal hominids—*our ancestors*. Literally, the word in translation is "copulate-me"; but here the translation in line with the way English speakers are used to seeing subects before action words.

TRANSLATED AS: I will copulate

A researched translation of the ancient Hebrew Genesis 1:19—
But it is to interbreed; and it is to research it-and-them [*the ovum (egg cell) is the "it", and the mass of sperm cells is the "them"*]. I will copulate [*as the next aspect of the beings' R&D program*].

Genesis 1:19—*in plain English*

☆ The strange entities now incorporate copulation with the hominids in their research on to how to successfully combine their DNA with that of the target species.

The KJV of Genesis 1:20 (*first phrase*)—

And God said,
Let the waters bring forth abundantly the moving creature that hath life,

Ancient Hebrew Anatomic Alphabet writing of that phrase—

𐤅𐤉𐤀𐤌𐤓 𐤀𐤋𐤄𐤉𐤌 𐤉𐤔𐤓𐤑𐤅 𐤄𐤌𐤉𐤌 𐤔𐤓𐤑 𐤍𐤐𐤔 𐤇𐤉𐤄

An actual translation *with researched explanations below*—
And strange-biological-entities said, It wriggles him—the ejaculate. Wriggle. Refresh. Revive.

The KJV of Genesis 1:20 (*second phrase*)—
and fowl that may fly above the earth

Ancient Hebrew Anatomic Alphabet writing of that phrase—

𐤅𐤏𐤅𐤐 𐤉𐤏𐤅𐤐𐤐 𐤏𐤋 𐤄𐤀𐤓𐤑

An actual translation *with researched explanations below*—
And exhausted: it-is-exhausted [*the result of genetically engineered hypersexuality*] yokes the I-Accomplish.

The KJV of Genesis 1:20 (*third phrase*)—
in the open firmament of heaven.

Ancient Hebrew Anatomic Alphabet writing of that phrase—

𐤏𐤋 𐤐𐤍𐤉 𐤓𐤒𐤉𐤏 𐤄𐤔𐤌𐤉𐤌

An actual translation *with researched explanations below*—
Yoke—My presence (is) die-casted. The Amazements.

The Researched Explanations—

and God said

This phrase has been previously seen in Verses 3, 6, 9, 11, and 14.

TRANSLATED AS: and strange-biological-entities said

let the waters bring forth abundantly the moving creature

There are no waters here in the traditional sense bringing forth an idealized vision of all manner of sea creatures. *Unless* we consider that here, "waters", is less like abundant seas than it is like semen. If we rearrange the traditional *non*translation word order into the order in which the original Hebrew words appear we might better be able to understand how the actual translation is derived.

let bring forth abundantly the waters the moving creature

let bring forth abundantly

Considering that Verse 19 closed with one of the SBE's "R&D statements", which was "I-will-Copulate"—we ought to expect more references to copulation. The ancient text meets expectation. There is no bring forth—unless it is the bringing forth of semen; and there is nothing attached to the actual Hebrew word which indicates abundance.

The text's five-letter word is "𐤅𐤑𐤓𐤔𐤉" [ישרצו]. It is pronounced, ēă·shĭrĕtz·ōō. It is associated with Strong's H8317; and its simple definition is *to wriggle*. The word has a prefix, *yăd* [𐤉], meaning "it". It has a root, "wriggle". It has a suffix, *ōōă* [𐤅], meaning "him" or "it". This translation has the verb, wriggle, in the present tense, as *wriggles*—the ancient text's way of referring to the spasmodic muscular contractions associated with ejaculation. The next word is *what* wriggles the entity, "I-will-copulate".

TRANSLATED AS: it wriggles it

the waters

The word, *hā·mēm* [𐤌𐤉𐤌𐤄], previously appeared as "the semen". Here, it is semen as the noun form of the action verb, *ejaculate* [ē·jac′·ū·lāt].

TRANSLATED AS: the ejaculate [ē·jac′·ū·lăt]

the moving
There is no “the” prefix on the Hebrew word here, which is simply the root word of “it wriggles him”. The root word here is “𐤔𐤓𐤑” (*shĭrĕtz*) [H8317]. It simply means, “wriggle”.

TRANSLATED AS: wriggle

creature
The actual ancient Hebrew text here has a three-letter word spelled *nōōn-pfăy-shĭn.* It is pronounced *nōōpfăsh* [𐤍𐤐𐤔]; and the Strong’s number is H5315—*to breathe, to breathe upon,* and *to be refreshed.* This translation simply uses the present tense of *to be refreshed.*

TRANSLATED AS: refresh

that hath life
The phrase, “that hath life”, does have a relationship to the meanings of the Hebrew word here, *khēăh* [𐤇𐤉𐤄][H2421—*to live, to revive,* or, *to be vigorous*]. This translation simply uses the present tense of *to revive.*

TRANSLATED AS: revive

and fowl

There is another Hebrew word for “birds” that is used throughout the ancient text—it is “𐤑𐤐𐤅𐤓” [*tzăpfōōr*]. The word in the text here is *ōōă·ō·ōōpf* [𐤅𐤏𐤅𐤐|ועוף]. It is associated with Strong’s H5775—*a bird. However*, our word here is treated as a homonym, even by traditionalists, and its other meaning is “to faint” [H5774]. What’s going on here is that in the context of *to faint*, ō·ōōpf [𐤏𐤅𐤐], is *not* our root word. Our root word here is actually *ōēpf* [𐤏𐤉𐤐], which is H5888/H5889—*languid, faint,* and *weary*. To be *languid* is to be exhausted or weak. *Faint* and *weary* are synonyms.

To modify a word in some way, ancient Hebrew writers would insert a *yăd* [𐤉] or a *ōōă* [𐤅] into a root word. The modified word may be a similar word (a synonym) or it may indicate that the word is in past tense (ending in “-ed”) or may be a present participle—such as a word ending in “-ing”.

In our word here, *ōōă·ō·ōōpf* [7YOY][H5888], the root is *ōēpf* [7ZO]. The ancient writer substituted the root's middle letter, *yăd* [Z], for an *ōōă* [Y], in order to indicate that the verb is in the past tense. The prefix, *ōōă* [Y], is "and".

Don't we all know that in the aftermath of sexual relations there is, or can be, a sense of feeling faint, or weary, or exhausted, or simply *spent*?

TRANSLATED AS: and exhausted

that may fly

The words "that may fly" will run afoul of the actual word in the ancient text, which is from the very same root word just examined. The word is *ēă·ō·ōōpfāpf* [77YOZ|יעופף]. It is the very same Strong's Number, H5888/H5889. This word's prefix, the letter *yăd* [Z] is *he* or *it.* There is no stand-alone word, "77YO" [*ō·ōōpfāpf*] in the Hebrew Bible; but our word here only appears in one other place, at Isaiah 6:2 in the context of flying. Our root word here, [7ZO], can be found multiple times in the Hebrew text as "faint" and several times as "weary". This one word also puts emphasis on the alien entities' sense of feeling faint, weary, and exhausted in the aftermath of copulation. Of notable interest is that the last letter, *pfāy* [7] is doubled—for emphasis—which is treated here as an exclamatory emphatic—our exclamation mark.

TRANSLATED AS: it-is-exhausted! [the result of genetically engineered hypersexuality]

above

The word, *ōl* [LO], traditionally cited as H5927, is translated as *upon*, *above*, or *in*. That word, however, *also* has several other items on the menu of definitions—including H5923—"*yoke*". A yoke is the *fastening framework* on two oxen pulling a plow. Used here, the word, *ōl*, is the original writer's chosen word describing the *fastening framework* of the phosphate-deoxyribose "*yoke*" which fastens together the other nucleotides of the DNA molecular structure. In its context here, "yoke" is a present tense verb.

TRANSLATED AS: yokes

the earth

Last seen in Verse 17, the words "the earth" have been previously explained. It is treated here as "*hā·ă·rĕtz·ăh*" {[ה]ץראה} [H7521], "to accomplish—the root being "הץר" with the presumption of a commonly dropped letter *hāy* [ה]. The prefix *hāy* [ה] is the indefinite article, "the". The prefix *ălăpf* [א] is "I".

TRANSLATED AS: the I-Accomplish

in

Just as with the word, *above*, our Hebrew word here is "*ōl*".

TRANSLATED AS: yoke

the open

The last time we saw this Hebrew word was in Verse 2. There it role-played as the word, "face"—as in *the face of the deep* and *the face of the waters*. It is the exact same word here, *pfān·ē* [ינפ]. It is traditionally cited as H6440 ("face"); *but*—that word's root, הנפ, also means "presence". The suffix, *yăd* [י], here is "my".

TRANSLATED AS: my presence

firmament

We have seen variants of this word in Verses 7, 8, 14, and 15—and in those verses the Hebrew root was translated as *spread out*—a reference to the entities' problem with *oligospermia* (a low concentration of spermatozoa in the semen). Here, however, we have the phosphate-deoxyribose *yoke* as *the I-Accomplish*; so we must look to our Hebrew word here, *rĕqwēō* [עיקר], as a homonym. Other definitions of H7554 (the root being, "עקר") include *to pound*, *to stamp*, and *to beat*. We know that an inserted letter, such as the inserted letter, *yăd* [י], modifies the verb in a way which is understood in context.

Here the context is the entities' seemingly successful micro-manipulation of the hybrid DNA phosphate-deoxyribose yoke. After their laboratory success, the next step would be for the hybrid DNA to self-reproduce in the exact same with each successive self-replication—into the indefinite future of the hybrid species. The translation here is *die-cast mold*, in the sense of a mass-produced stamped-out die casted mold: each die casted mold being the exact same as the previous and as the next.

TRANSLATED AS: die-casted

of heaven
We have encountered this Hebrew word in Verses 1, 8, 9, 14, 15, and 17. The word *hā·shĭm·ēm* [𐤌𐤉𐤌𐤔𐤄] is translated from the Hebrew root, *shĭ·mēm* ["𐤌𐤌𐤔" | H8074], *to amaze.*

TRANSLATED AS: the amazements

A researched translation of the ancient Hebrew Genesis 1:20—
And strange-biological-entities said, It wriggles him—the ejaculate. Wriggle. Refresh. Revive. And exhausted: it-is-exhausted [*the result of genetically engineered hypersexuality*] yokes the I-Accomplish. Yoke—My presence (is) die-casted. The Amazements.

Genesis 1:20—*in plain English*

- ☆ The biological entities noted mild spasmodic activity associated with orgasm.
- ☆ They noted associated sensations of feeling refreshed and revived followed by exhaustion.
- ☆ Their hybrids will be yoked by overpowering sex drive.
- ☆ The beings assert that their presence is in the DNA of every hominid DNA replication.
- ☆ They restate their amazement.

The KJV of Genesis 1:21 (*first phrase*)—
And God created great whales,

Ancient Hebrew Anatomic Alphabet writing of that phrase—
𐤅𐤉𐤁𐤓𐤀 𐤀𐤋𐤄𐤉𐤌 𐤀𐤕 𐤄𐤕𐤍𐤉𐤍𐤌 𐤄𐤂𐤃𐤋𐤉𐤌

An actual translation *with researched explanations below*—
And strange-biological-entities cut: CRISPR manipulated the Elongated Twistings [*a visual description of an elongated DNA molecule*].

The KJV of Genesis 1:21 (*second phrase*)—
and every living creature

Ancient Hebrew Anatomic Alphabet writing of that phrase—
𐤅𐤀𐤕 𐤊𐤋 𐤍𐤐𐤔 𐤄𐤇𐤉𐤄

An actual translation *with researched explanations below*—
And in-vitro fertilized to perfect Refresh [*that is, to perfect the ability of the genetically engineered hybrid creature to reproduce its own kind through their own copulation*]—the Revive [*another euphemism for copulation*].

The KJV of Genesis 1:21 (*third phrase*)—
that moveth, which the waters brought forth abundantly, after their kind,

Ancient Hebrew Anatomic Alphabet writing of that phrase—
𐤄𐤓𐤌𐤔𐤕 𐤀𐤔𐤓 𐤔𐤓𐤑𐤅 𐤄𐤌𐤉𐤌 𐤋𐤌𐤉𐤍𐤄𐤌

An actual translation *with researched explanations below*—
The reptile I-Dwell wriggles it. The ejaculate in regard to portion them out [*the spermatozoa for IVF*];

The KJV of Genesis 1:21 (*fourth phrase*)—
and every winged fowl after his kind:

Ancient Hebrew Anatomic Alphabet writing of that phrase—

𐤅𐤀𐤕 𐤊𐤋 𐤏𐤅𐤐 𐤊𐤍𐤐 𐤋𐤌𐤉𐤍𐤄𐤅

An actual translation *with researched explanations below*—
and in-vitro fertilized to make perfect exhaustion, lateral projection, and withdraw [*a euphemism for copulation-aftermath is "exhaustion"; a direct reference to active copulation is "lateral projection" (of the ejaculate from the erect male phallus), and linked with the post-copulative withdrawal of the flaccid phallus—toward perfecting the self-replication of the hybrid species through copulation*] in regard to the portion out it [*their way of expressing intracytoplasmic sperm injection (ICSI) through in-vitro fertilization (IVF) with the spermatozoon (the fertilizing sperm cell) of the sperm-donor*].

The KJV of Genesis 1:21 (*fifth phrase*)—
and God saw that it was good.

Ancient Hebrew Anatomic Alphabet writing of that phrase—

𐤅𐤉𐤓𐤀 𐤀𐤋𐤄𐤉𐤌 𐤊𐤉 𐤈𐤅𐤁

An actual translation *with researched explanations below*—
And strange-biological-entities saw that (there were) good [*technical solutions*].

The Researched Explanations—

and created
As we saw in Verse 1, the word, *bĕra* [𐤁𐤓𐤀][H1254], traditionally given as "to create", may also be a form of the action word, *to cut*. This definition makes more sense in the context of alien specialists in cutting (tissue micro-cutting, gene splicing and DNA manipulation via CRISPR CAS-9 technique analogs) to set limits on the target species. Our word here at this place is,

ōōă·ē·bĕră [𐤅𐤉𐤁𐤓𐤀|ויברא]. It is Strong's H1254—*to create; to cut down.* The prefix, 𐤅, is *and.* The second prefix, 𐤉, is *it.*

TRANSLATED AS: and it cut

God
As previously covered, the plural word is, *ălăh·ēm* [𐤀𐤋𐤄𐤉𐤌].[547]

TRANSLATED AS: strange-biological-entities

~a Hebrew word untranslated in the KJV~
The *ăt* [𐤀𐤕|את][H855], has been explained as their analog of what we today refer to as the CRISPR CAS-9 procedure. Here it is expressed, in context, in verb form.

TRANSLATED AS: CRISPR manipulated

great whales

The Hebrew word order here has the whales (that are not whales) coming before "great" (again—no "great"). The word that appears here is *hā·tōōnēn·ōōm* [𐤄𐤕𐤍𐤉𐤍𐤌|התנינם]. It is associated with Strong's H8577, which is defined as "a marine or land monster". That number, per Dr. Strong, is *from the same as* H8565. Well, Strong's H8565 is "𐤕𐤍" (*tōōn*), and is from an *unused root, to elongate*. The *unused root* here is "𐤕𐤍𐤍" (*tōōnōōn*). Professor Davidson defines that root, as being *ascribed the sense of stretching out or extending*[548]. There we have it: *elongate* and *extending*. The word's prefix is a *hāy* [𐤄], meaning *the*. The inserted letter is a *yăd* [𐤉] which modifies the meaning or understanding of the word.

We last saw this root, "𐤕𐤍" (*tōōn*) in Verse 17 as an abnormally elongated sperm cell. The modification here may be credited to the word becoming an adjective in order to modify the word that follows. There is a suffix, 𐤌, which denotes the pronoun "they" or "them". The translation that results is "the elongated them". The identity of "them" will be revealed by the translation of the word that follows.

TRANSLATED AS: the elongated them

great – of "great whales"

We saw the word "great" in Verse 16 as "great lights". The Hebrew word here is exactly the same as there. It is *hā·gĭdăl·ēm* [𐤄𐤂𐤃𐤋𐤉𐤌|הגדלים] H1431, "a primitive root, properly *to twist*". The suffix *ēm* [𐤉𐤌-] makes the word plural.

Translation: the-twists [a visual description of an elongated DNA molecule]

and every living creature that moveth

—as rearranged in the Hebrew word order,

and every creature living that moveth

and

Our word here, *ōōă·ăt* [𐤅𐤀𐤕 |ואת], is as previously explained in this verse. It is Strong's H855—defined as "coulter". It is used here as one of its space-age synonyms, "*injecting pipette*"—which is a device chiefly consisting of a hollow sharply beveled needle for injecting a sperm cell microscopically into a readied ovum (egg) of the target female of the species. The prefix *ōōă* [𐤅] is "and". Here again, the word is a utilitarian verb form of injection pipetting.

TRANSLATED AS: and in-vitro fertilized

every

Generally translated as "all", the word here is *kăl* [𐤊𐤋|כל]. It is associated with Strong's H3605, which is from H3634, "𐤊𐤋𐤋" (*kălăl*). H3634 is *to complete (to make perfect) properly, the whole—hence, all or every*. The word here is "𐤊𐤋𐤋" with a dropped (by the original author) final letter, 𐤋 [*lămĕd*].

TRANSLATED AS: to make perfect

creature

Last seen in Verse 20, the Hebrew word, *nōōpfāsh* [𐤍𐤐𐤔], is associated with Strong's H5315—*to breathe, to breathe upon,* and *to be refreshed*. For any who may be used to seeing this Hebrew word as "soul", as in *living soul*, a homonym of that word—*to be refreshed*—is used three times in the Hebrew Bible in exactly that context[549]. It is here in present tense. "Refresh" must have been employed as a metaphor for the act of copulation with the target species—the genetically engineered bi-pedal hominids. The hybrids are being engineered to replicate themselves through the observed act of "refresh"—or, as we know it, *sexual intercourse*.

TRANSLATED AS: refresh

living
Seen in Verse 20 as "that hath life", the word here has a *hāy* [𐤄] prefix giving us "the". The word is *hā·khēăh* [𐤄𐤇𐤉𐤄|החיה] [H2421—*to live, to revive,* or, *to be vigorous*]. This translation uses the verb infinitive, *to revive*, as a noun.

TRANSLATED AS: the revive [another of the beings' euphemisms for copulative relations]

that moveth
Seen here for the first time is the word *hā·rĕmĕsh·ĭt* [𐤄𐤓𐤌𐤔𐤕| הרמשת]. It is traditionally associated with Strong's H7430—*to glide swiftly*; but is actually H7431—"*a reptile*". The suffix, *tōō* [𐤕], acts here as an exclamatory emphatic—an exclamation point. The word, transliterated, is "Remesh". That's what they called themselves—"Remesh". Words will not be sugar-coated here.

TRANSLATED AS: the reptile! ***or*** the Remesh!

which the waters brought forth abundantly after their kind
—as rearranged in the Hebrew word order,
which brought forth abundantly the waters after their kind

which
This versatile pronoun is traditionally associated with Strong's H834—*a relative pronoun of every gender and number*. Dr. Strong follows the

traditional definition with a long laundry-list of English words which have been used to convey meaning.

The word in the text is *ăshĭr* [𐤀𐤔𐤓|אשר], but it is being treated here as *ă·shĭrăh* [[𐤄] 𐤀𐤔𐤓 | [ה]אשר]—presuming a dropped letter *hāy* [𐤄|ה] in the text. When the eminent Professor Ben Davidson is consulted about the meaning of the root, *shĭrăh* [𐤔𐤓𐤄|שרה], we see a wide range of definitions. There's *contend* and *wrestle*; as well as *to be a prince with* and *to prevail*. There is also *to loose* and *to set free*; as well as *to dwell*. Professor Davidson cites the Book of Daniel 2:22[550], where this root appears as "dwelleth" in the KJV[551]. That is the definition used in this translation—as it seems to fit the context more aptly than the other definition contenders. The prefix, *ălăpf* [𐤀], is the first person singular pronoun, "I". The verb, dwell, is capitalized here as it is presumed to have a double meaning: the fact of dwelling—as in being inside a bipedal hominid female in copulation, and as well inside the DNA of all of her progeny for all time. This verb, *dwell*, coupled with the subject pronoun, *I*, is the reptile's deliberately chosen assumed name.

TRANSLATED AS: I-Dwell

brought forth abundantly

We encountered the Hebrew word here when it appeared in Verse 20 as "let bring forth abundantly". The word was "𐤉𐤔𐤓𐤑𐤅", and pronounced *ēă·shĭrĕtz·ōō*. It is associated with Strong's H8317. Its simple definition is *to wriggle*. Here the word appears without the prefix, "it", as the word in the text is *shĭrĕtz·ōō* [𐤔𐤓𐤑𐤅|שרצו]. The suffix, *ōōă* [𐤅], means "it"—as a reference to the male phallus.

TRANSLATED AS: wriggles it

the waters

As also previously seen in Verse 20, the exact same Hebrew word appears here. It is *hā·mēm* [𐤄𐤌𐤉𐤌]; and has previously appeared as "the semen". Here, it is semen as the noun form of the verb, *to ejaculate* [ē·jac′·ū·lāt].

TRANSLATED AS: the ejaculate [ē·jac′·ū·lăt]

after their kind

Seen for the first time is the familiar phrase, "after their kind". In contrast to most other Hebrew words here that have been put into English, there *is* a relationship between the traditional phrase and what the Hebrew word tells us. Our word here is *lă·mēn·hām* [𐤋𐤌𐤉𐤍𐤄𐤌|למינהם]. It is Strong's H4327; and it means "*to portion out—i.e. species*". The grammar here is a prefix, 𐤋 (*lămĕd*), meaning, "*in regard to*"; and a suffix, *hām* [-𐤄𐤌], meaning "*them*".

TRANSLATED AS: in regard to portion out them [the spermatozoa for IVF]

and every winged fowl after his kind

and

Our word here, *ōōă·ăt* [𐤅𐤀𐤕|ואת], is as previously explained in this verse. It is Strong's H855—defined as "coulter". It is used here as one of its high-tech synonyms, "*injecting pipette*"—which is a device chiefly consisting of a hollow sharply beveled needle for injecting a sperm cell microscopically into a readied ovum (egg) of the target female of the species. The prefix *ōōă* [𐤅] is "and". Here again, the word is used as a verb in past tense.

TRANSLATED AS: and in-vitro fertilized

every

The word here is *kăl* [𐤊𐤋]. It was explained earlier in this verse. It is the two-letter form of the three-letter word, *kălăl* [𐤊𐤋𐤋]. It is usually associated with Strong's H3605; but it is from H3634—*to complete (to make perfect), the whole—hence, all or every.*

TRANSLATED AS: to make perfect

fowl

The word, "fowl", first seen in Verse 20, is here just *ō·ōōpf* [𐤏𐤅𐤐]. The word is generally associated with Strong's H5775 (*a bird*); but it, per exhaustive treatment, is Strong's H5888/5889—*languid.* The root word is *ōēpf* [𐤏𐤉𐤐]. To be languid is to be exhausted. The word here is one of the biological entities' favored descriptors (as a euphemism) for the act of copulation and its aftermath. As explained in Verse 20, the writer(s) substituted the actual root's middle letter, *yăd* [𐤉], for an *ōōă* [𐤅], so as to indicate that in the context here the verb is in its noun form.

TRANSLATED AS: exhaustion

winged

No wings here. The word, *kănōōpf* [𐤊𐤍𐤐|כנף], means *an edge* or *extremity*. Traditionalists got to "winged fowl", or to "birds", through the idea of the extremities of a bird—its wings[552]. Our word here is another homonym; and its other meaning is *to project laterally*—and, appropriately enough—*to withdraw*[553]. Our translation here takes Dr. Strong's definition in reverse word order; and this translation incorporates the concept of *to withdraw* as it is clearly in context.

Here, the use of the concepts of *exhaustion*, *lateral projection*, and *withdrawal* represent the strange entities' euphemism for copulation-aftermath (*exhaustion*); along with a direct reference to active copulation (*lateral projection*—of the ejaculate from the erect male phallus); and further linked with the post-copulative *withdrawal* of the flaccid phallus.

TRANSLATED AS: lateral projection-and-withdraw [a direct reference to active copulation is "lateral projection" (of the ejaculate from the erect male phallus), and linked with the post-copulative withdrawal of the flaccid phallus—toward perfecting the self-replication of the hybrid species through copulation]

after his kind

The word here is *lă·mēn·hōō* [𐤋𐤌𐤉𐤍𐤄𐤅|למינהו][H4327], *to portion out*. The grammar here is the prefix, 𐤋 (*lămĕd*), *in regard to*; and a suffix, *hōō* [𐤄𐤅-], *him* or *it*.

TRANSLATED AS: in regard to portion out it [their way of expressing intracytoplasmic sperm injection (ICSI) through in-vitro fertilization (IVF) with the spermatozoon of the sperm-donating male] *and God saw that it was good*

and saw
The word, [*ōōă·ē·ra* | 𐤅𐤉𐤓𐤀] [H7200], may be "and saw". Literally, it is "and-it-saw". The root, 𐤓𐤀𐤄, may also be translated as *to see, to exist, to live, to view, to regard,* or *to observe*. Here it will be given as traditionally translated. The pronoun, "it", refers collectively to strange biological entities.

TRANSLATED AS: and it saw

God
The word, *ălăh·ēm* [𐤀𐤋𐤄𐤉𐤌][H430], is commonly, though incorrectly, translated as "God". Here it is treated as the "*strange-biological-entities*" that the beings are.[554]

TRANSLATED AS: strange biological entities

that
The word in the text is *kē* (pronounced "key") [𐤊𐤉]. It is Strong's H3588; and it can act to connect all kinds of causes in a sentence, including the words "for" and "because".

TRANSLATED AS: that

it was good
There's no "it was" on this word in the text. The word, *thōōb* [𐤈𐤅𐤁] [H2896] means "good" in the widest sense. Here it will be given as traditionally translated—in the sense of the practical necessity of the alien's DNA manipulation and genetic engineering.

TRANSLATED AS: good [technical solutions]

A researched translation of the ancient Hebrew Genesis 1:21—
And strange-biological-entities CRISPR manipulated the Elongated Twistings [*a visual description of an elongated DNA molecule*] and in-vitro fertilized to perfect Refresh [*that is, to perfect the ability of the genetically*

engineered hybrid creature to reproduce its own kind through their own copulation]—the Revive [*another euphemism for copulation*]. The reptile I-Dwell wriggles it. [*The Reptilian, I-Dwell, became a sperm donor for its species' IVF project.*] The ejaculate (is) in regard to portioning out them [*the spermatozoa for IVF*]. And in-vitro fertilized to perfect exhaustion, lateral projection, and withdrawal [*a euphemism for copulation-aftermath is "exhaustion"; a direct reference to active copulation is "lateral projection" (of the ejaculate from the erect male phallus), and linked with the post-copulative withdrawal of the flaccid phallus—toward perfecting the self-replication of the hybrid species through copulation*] in regard to the portion it out [*their way of expressing intracytoplasmic sperm injection (ICSI) through in-vitro fertilization (IVF) with the spermatozoon (the fertilizing sperm cell) of the sperm-donor*]. And strange entities saw that (there were) good [*technical solutions*].

Genesis 1:21—*in plain English*

- ☆ The entities report that they cut the hominid DNA to perfect the ability of their hybrid to pass along their modified DNA through their own copulation.
- ☆ An entity, referred to as a reptile and identified by the moniker, "I-Dwell", is a sperm donor for their IVF project.
- ☆ The entities' view their IVF project as a form of successful copulation.
- ☆ Their technical solutions, which they describe as good, go toward the ability of the hybrid species to self-replicate and to pass on the entities' own DNA.

The KJV of Genesis 1:22 (*first phrase*)—
And God blessed them, saying, Be fruitful and multiply,

Ancient Hebrew Anatomic Alphabet writing of that phrase—

𐤅𐤉𐤁𐤓𐤊 𐤀𐤕𐤌 𐤀𐤋𐤄𐤉𐤌 𐤋𐤀𐤌𐤓 𐤐𐤓𐤅 𐤅𐤓𐤁𐤅

An actual translation *with researched explanations below*—
And it is in expertise—(the) I-Complete [*the successful IVF project*]. Strange-biological-entities: toward intending to increase it [*the target species*] and to multiply it by the myriads.

The KJV of Genesis 1:22 (*second phrase*)—
and fill the waters in the seas, and let fowl multiply in the earth.

Ancient Hebrew Anatomic Alphabet writing of that phrase—

𐤅𐤌𐤋𐤀𐤅 𐤀𐤕 𐤄𐤌𐤉𐤌 𐤁𐤉𐤌𐤉𐤌 𐤅𐤄𐤏𐤅𐤐 𐤉𐤓𐤁 𐤁𐤀𐤓𐤑

An actual translation *with researched explanations below*—
And to complete it [*the ovum*]—injection pipetting the spermatozoon among spermatozoa. And the exhaustion [*completed copulation*]—will increase it by the myriads in I-Accomplish.

The Researched Explanations—

and blessed

Even though we have the word "blessed" here, this is not where we encounter the root word for "bless". Inconveniently, the Hebrew word for "bless" is a homonym; and may be, in context, "curse".

The actual Hebrew word here is *ōŏă·ē·bĕ·rĕk* [𐤅𐤉𐤁𐤓𐤊| ויברך]. It is traditionally associated with Strong's H1288, which is defined as, "*to kneel—by implication, to bless* or *to curse*". Let's simply refer, or defer, to the context of what's going on in this ancient account. It is *not* about being blessed *or* being cursed. It is about the entities themselves providing information and detail to the hybrid (or other being) who wrote all of this account down in what we today call *ancient Hebrew*. We must look to where in the word there is another root word that, hopefully, will be in context with what's going on inside of the verse.

Look at the word carefully: *ōōă·ē·bĕ·rĕk* [𐤅𐤉𐤁𐤓𐤊]. If we treat the first three letters as prefixes, (and a Hebrew word can have that many prefixes), then we've got *ōōă* [𐤅] as "and". We've got a *yăd* [𐤉] appearing as "it". There's a letter *bĕt* [𐤁] as "in". The verb "is" is understood in the context of the word. The root word we are left with is "*rĕk*" [𐤓𐤊 (*rĕsh-kăpf*)].

When the Davidson's Lexicon is consulted we find that that *same* word (as "רך") means, among other synonyms, "*tender, delicate, effeminate*"[555]. It's from root "𐤓𐤊𐤊" (*rĕkăk*) [H7401—*soften*]. Here, the word, "expertise", is being used as a synonym for the "softness" of the technique necessary in handling the microscopic instruments as well as the sperm cell and the egg cell for their program of *in-vitro fertilization*.

TRANSLATED AS: and it (is) in expertise

them

Again, the traditional word "them" just doesn't fit the context. The Hebrew word here is *ă·tōōm* [𐤀𐤕𐤌|אתם]. The way it makes sense is for the first letter, *ălăpf* [𐤀], to be the personal pronoun "I"; and for the root word to be "𐤕𐤌𐤌" (*tōōmĕm*) with a dropped final letter, *mĕm* [𐤌]. That root is Strong's H8552—*to complete.* In its context it is another assumed name adapted by a reptile-being.

TRANSLATED AS: I-Complete

God

Covered previously, *ălăh·ēm* [𐤀𐤋𐤄𐤉𐤌] [H430], is traditionally mistranslated as "God". The word is plural.[556]

TRANSLATED AS: strange-biological-entities

saying

First seen in Verse 3 as "said", the word here is *lă·ămĕr* [𐤋𐤀𐤌𐤓]. It is Strong's H559—*used with great latitude*. As examples, we're given: *say, challenge, command,* and *declare.* The root, *ămĕr*, is seen some 5,300 times in the Hebrew Bible[557]. It appears as "*intend*" at Exodus 2:14. The prefix, *lămĕd* [𐤋], is "toward". The verb is given in its gerund, or "-ing" form.

TRANSLATED AS: toward intending

be fruitful

Again, "fruitful", just doesn't fit the context here. The root word for "to bear fruit" is H6509 [𐤐𐤓𐤄 | פרה]. Traditional translators knew that there was a dropped last letter [𐤄] from the root word. The word in the text is *pfār·ōō* [𐤐𐤓𐤅 | פרו]. This space-age translation recognizes that there is a dropped last letter in the root word in the text, which is common. The root word means *to bear fruit (literally or figuratively); to grow, to increase.* The suffix, 𐤅, is "him" or "it". The "it" here refers to the target species—the bipedal hominids—our own distant ancestors.

TRANSLATED AS: to increase it

and multiply

The word in the text is *ōōă·rĕb·ōō* [𐤅𐤓𐤁𐤅|ורבו}. It isn't Strong's H7235 [𐤓𐤁𐤄] (*rĕbĕh*), "*to increase—in whatever respect*"; it's H7231 [𐤓𐤁𐤁] (*rĕbĕb*), "*to multiply* [or increase] *by the myriads*". The prefix, 𐤅, is "and". The suffix, 𐤅, is "it"—the target species.

TRANSLATED AS: and to increase it by the myriads

and fill

Strong's definition of H4390 (*to fill* or *to be full of*) may be used in the widest sense—literally or figuratively. Here the root is "to complete". When the *Brown-Driver-Briggs* lexicon is consulted you will encounter the definition, "*fulfil, accomplish, complete*"[558]. The word here is *ōōă·mĕlă·ōō* [𐤅𐤌𐤋𐤀𐤅|ומלאו] [H4390]. The prefix, 𐤅, is "and"; and suffix, 𐤅, here is "it".

TRANSLATED AS: and to complete it [the ovum (or egg)]

~a Hebrew word untranslated in the KJV~
Our word here, *ăt* [𐤀𐤕|את][H855], has been explained.

TRANSLATED AS: injection pipetting

the waters
As previously seen in Verse 20 and 21, the exact same Hebrew word appears here [Strong's H4325]. It is *hā·mēm* [𐤄𐤌𐤉𐤌]; and has previously appeared as "the semen". Here, it is semen as a single sperm cell, a spermatozoon—the one that fertilizes an egg.

TRANSLATED AS: the spermatozoon

in the seas
We saw "seas" in Verse 10. Here we have the same root word as there and as in *the waters* [Strong's H4325]. The word is *bĕ·ē·mēm* [𐤁𐤉𐤌𐤉𐤌|בימים]. It is still semen—but here the context is the collective noun for the mass of ejaculated sperm cells. The first prefix, 𐤁, is *among*; and the second prefix is, 𐤉, is "it".

TRANSLATED AS: among it spermatozoa

and let fowl
This fowl is not the "*winged fowl*" of Verse 20, but the "*and fowl*" of Verse 21. Our word here is *ōŏă·hā·ō·ōōpf* [𐤅𐤄𐤏𐤅𐤐|והעוף] [H5889—*languid*]. That is, a sense of exhaustion after copulation. The first prefix, 𐤅, is "and"; and the second prefix, 𐤄, is "the".

TRANSLATED AS: and the exhaustion [completed copulation]

multiply
Here we have the same root word just seen as "and multiply". The word in the text is *ēă·rĕb* [𐤉𐤓𐤁]. It is Strong's H7231 [𐤓𐤁𐤁], and is *to multiply* [or increase] *by the myriads*. The prefix, 𐤉, is *it*.

TRANSLATED AS: it will increase by the myriads

in the earth

Last seen in Verse 20, the words "*the earth*" have been previously explained. It is treated here as if the text read, "*bě·ă·rětz·ăh*" {[𐤄]𐤑𐤓𐤀𐤁} [H7521], "*to accomplish*". The root, then, is "𐤄𐤑𐤓" with the assumption of the commonly dropped letter *hāy* [𐤄]. The prefix *bět* [𐤁] is "in". The prefix *alăpf* [𐤀] is "I".

TRANSLATED AS: in I-Accomplish

A researched translation of the ancient Hebrew Genesis 1:22—

And it is in expertise—(the) I-Complete. Strange-biological-entities: toward intending to increase it [*the target species*] and to multiply it by the myriads. And to complete it [*the ovum*]—injection pipetting the spermatozoon among spermatozoa. And the exhaustion [*completed copulation*]—it will increase by the myriads in I-Accomplish.

Genesis 1:22—*in plain English*

- ☆ The entities developed expert laboratory technique.
- ☆ They intended for their hybrid species to multiply rapidly.
- ☆ Their IVF project was successful because the hybrids were able to pass along the entities' DNA through copulation.

Reptilians begin their hybridization project

[Verses 23 through 31]

The KJV of Genesis 1:23—
And the evening and the morning were the fifth day.

Ancient Hebrew Anatomic Alphabet writing of that verse—
𐤅𐤉𐤄𐤉 𐤏𐤓𐤁 𐤅𐤉𐤄𐤉 𐤁𐤒𐤓 𐤉𐤅𐤌 𐤇𐤌𐤉𐤔𐤉

An actual translation *with researched explanations below*—
And it is to intermix and it (is) to research it-and-them [*the ovum (egg cell) is the "it", and the mass of sperm cells is the "them"*]—harnessing my bio-mechanical power [*the power inherent in the biology of the strange entity*].

The Researched Explanations—

and the
The word here is *ōōă·ē·hē* [𐤅𐤉𐤄𐤉][H1961]. It's from the root, "to be". For a review, look back at "Let there be" in Verse 1. The prefix here is 𐤅 ("and"); the second prefix is 𐤉 ("it"). The root word, from the concept of "exists" and "to be", is translated as "is".

TRANSLATED AS: and it is

evening
Yes, the word *ōrĕb* [𐤏𐤓𐤁] is generally given as "evening" [H6153]. Here is given as H6148—in the sense of intermixed mingled seed.

TRANSLATED AS: interbreed

and the
This is the same word as "*and the*" previously explained.

TRANSLATED AS: and it is

morning
The word *bĕqwōōr* [𐤓𐤒𐤁|בקר] can be "morning"; but it can also be *to seek* or *to inquire*[559]. Here the word is treated as a scientific inquiry and seeking out.

TRANSLATED AS: to research

were the
These words do not appear at this place in the ancient text.

day
This word is the same seen twice in Verse 5, once in Verse 8, and once in Verse 19.

TRANSLATED AS: it-and-them [the ovum (egg cell) is the "it", and the mass of sperm cells is the "them"]

fifth
Convenient for the traditional story about a fifth day, the word in the text, *khĕm·ē·shē* [𐤉𐤔𐤉𐤌𐤇|חמישי] is associated with Strong's H2549—*fifth*. H2549 is from Strong's H2568 (root 𐤔𐤌𐤇)—*the numeral, five*. BUT, the actual root is H2571 (root 𐤔𐤌𐤇). That word appears but one time in the first five books of the Bible as "harnessed"[560]. The verb, *to harness*, means, per the eminent 1946 *Webster's Collegiate Dictionary*, "to provide with apparatus so as to secure mechanical power". We can get securing of bio-mechanical power: the original author inserted the letter *yăd* [𐤉] as a heads-up that the meaning of the word was being modified. The suffixed letter *yăd* [𐤉] here is the personal pronoun "my".

TRANSLATED AS: harnessing my bio-mechanical power [the power inherent in the biologic mechanisms of the entity]

A researched translation of the ancient Hebrew Genesis 1:23—
And it is to intermix and it (is) to research it-and-them [*the ovum (egg cell) is the "it", and the mass of sperm cells is the "them"*]—harnessing

my bio-mechanical power [*the power inherent in the biology of the strange reptile-entity*].

Genesis 1:23—*in plain English*

- ☆ An entity reveals that he (or it) intends to use his (its) own bio-mechanical power to enhance the egg and sperm of the target species.

The KJV of Genesis 1:24 (*first phrase*)—
And God said, Let the earth bring forth the living creature

Ancient Hebrew Anatomic Alphabet writing of that phrase—
𐤅𐤉𐤀𐤌𐤓 𐤀𐤋𐤄𐤉𐤌 𐤕𐤅𐤑𐤀 𐤄𐤀𐤓𐤑 𐤍𐤐𐤔 𐤇𐤉𐤄

An actual translation *with researched explanations below*—
And strange-biological-entities said, "!Bring forth the
I-Accomplisher." "Refresh-revive [*euphemisms for copulation*]…

The KJV of Genesis 1:24 (*second phrase*)—
after his kind, cattle, and creeping thing, and beast of the earth after his kind:

Ancient Hebrew Anatomic Alphabet writing of that phrase—
𐤋𐤌𐤉𐤍𐤄 𐤁𐤄𐤌𐤄 𐤅𐤓𐤌𐤔 𐤅𐤇𐤉𐤕𐤅 𐤀𐤓𐤑 𐤋𐤌𐤉𐤍𐤄

An actual translation *with researched explanations below*—
…(is) within semen genetically engineered for loud moaning [*another euphemism for copulating*] since (having been) reptilized." And [*the Reptilian*] lives! (in) it [*the genetically engineered semen*]. "I accomplished concerning genetically engineered semen."

The KJV of Genesis 1:24 (*third phrase*)—
and it was so.

Ancient Hebrew Anatomic Alphabet writing of that phrase—
𐤅𐤉𐤄𐤉 𐤊𐤍

An actual translation *with researched explanations below*—
And it is true.

The Researched Explanations—

and God said
This phrase has been explained in Verses 3, 6, 9, 11, 14, and 20.

TRANSLATED AS: and strange-biological-entities said

let the earth bring forth
—as rearranged in the Hebrew word order,
let bring forth
The Hebrew word behind "bring forth" can be *tōō·ōō·tză* [𐤕𐤅𐤑𐤀| תוצא]. That word is generally cited as Strong's H3318, for which the root is *ēă·tză* [𐤉𐤑𐤀]. It is defined as *to go out*, or *to bring out*—"*in a great variety of applications, literally and figuratively*". Please note that the root word in the text had its first letter substituted—the letter, *ōōă* [𐤅] for the *yăd* [𐤉]. That changes the meaning to just about anything that any translator *needs* the word to mean. The prefix "*tōō*" [𐤕] is "you" or "!". Traditionalists have bequeathed to us the words, "bring forth". We'll employ those exact words here—along with the exclamatory emphatic.

TRANSLATED AS: !bring forth

the earth
The word, *hā·ărĕtz* [𐤄𐤀𐤓𐤑] [H776], is traditionally defined as "ground *or* land" and mistranslated as "earth". Here it is read as "*hā·ă·rĕtz·ăh*" {[𐤄] 𐤄𐤀𐤓𐤑} [H7521], "*to be pleased with* or *accomplish, et cetera*". The prefix *hāy* [𐤄] is the indefinite article, "the". The *ălăpf* [𐤀] is "I". In this instance, the verb, "accomplish", is used by the ancient authors in creative use of the noun form of the moniker, "I-Accomplish". The "I-Accomplisher" is being bought forth, in this narrative, to speak about his (or its) accomplishment.

TRANSLATED AS: the I-Accomplisher

the living creature
—as rearranged in the Hebrew word order,

the creature

Last seen in Verses 20 and 21, the Hebrew word, *nōōpfāsh* [𐤍𐤐𐤔], is associated with Strong's H5315—*to breathe, to breathe upon,* and *to be refreshed.* The word is used here in the present tense. "Refresh" must have been employed as a metaphor for the act of copulation with the target species—us. The hybrids are being engineered to replicate themselves through the act which the alien entities refer to as "refresh"—*aka* "sexual intercourse".

TRANSLATED AS: refresh

living

Seen in Verse 20 and 21 as "that hath life", the word here is the same. It is *khēăh* [𐤇𐤉𐤄][H2421—*to live, to revive,* or, *to be vigorous*]. This translation simply uses the present tense of *to revive*. This is another of their euphemisms for sexual intercourse.

TRANSLATED AS: revive

after his kind

The word here is *lă·mēn·ăh* [𐤋𐤌𐤉𐤍𐤄|למינה][H4325]. The root word is "water"—as *semen*. The prefix, *lămĕd* [𐤋], may be translated in a number of other ways than "*to, toward,* or *in regard to*"[561]. It is used here as "within"—since that is more in context. The suffix, *hāy* [𐤄], denotes *the absolute state* of the root word. In this context the *absolute state* is in having been genetically engineered.

TRANSLATED AS: within semen genetically engineered

cattle

Cattle can appear in the text as, *bĕ·hāmĕăh* [𐤁𐤄𐤌𐤄][H929]—*a dumb beast—cattle.* However, and more consistent with what's going on inside the text here, the word has a prefix, *bĕt* [𐤁]. As a conjunction the word, "for"[562], is consistent within the context of the verse. It has a root, *hāmĕ·ăh* [𐤄𐤌𐤄] [H1993]—*to make a loud sound.* Dr. James Strong also lists synonyms such as *tumult, rage, moan,* or *clamor*. The word choice here is "moan". The

SBE's associate the sounds of moaning with copulation. The phrase "loud moaning" is another of their euphemisms for sexual intercourse.

TRANSLATED AS: for loud moaning [another euphemism for copulating]

and creeping thing

The last time we saw the Hebrew word that appears here was when it appeared in Verse 21 as "that moveth". Here, the word is, *ōōă·rĕmĕsh* [𐤅𐤓𐤌𐤔]. It, again, is H7431—*a reptile*. It is a reptile as well in Davidson's Lexicon[563]. The prefix is *ōōă* [𐤅], is used here as, "since"[564]. The helping verbs, *having been*, are added for clarification. Without doubt, it's highly unusual for us to see a noun such as "reptile" used as a verb—as "reptilized". This seemingly unconventional use creatively expresses the *outcome* of their modification of the hominid's DNA—they "reptilized" it.

TRANSLATED AS: since having been reptilized

and beast

We saw in the word, "cattle", that it was supposed to be a "dumb beast". But it wasn't. Here we have the word "beast" that isn't. Our word in the text is *ōōă·khē·tōō·ōō* [𐤅𐤇𐤉𐤕𐤅|וחיתו][H2416]—*alive, life, raw (flesh)*. Here we have the verb form of life, as, "lives". The prefix is *ōōă* [𐤅], "and". The first suffix is the letter *tōō* [𐤕], an exclamatory emphatic we know as the exclamation point. The second suffix is the letter *ōōă* [𐤅], as "him" or "it". The presence of the Reptilian behind the "I-Accomplish" is understood *in context.*

TRANSLATED AS: and [the Reptilian] lives! (in) it [the genetically engineered semen]

of the earth

The word, *ărĕtz* [𐤀𐤓𐤑] [H776], is traditionally mistranslated as "earth". Here it is read as "*ă·rĕtz·ăh*" {𐤀𐤓𐤑[𐤄]} [H7521], "*to be pleased with* or *accomplish, et cetera*". The *ălăpf* [𐤀] is "I". In this instance, the context of the verb, *accomplish*, is in the past.

TRANSLATED AS: I accomplished

after his kind
As was seen previously in this verse, the word here is *lă·mēn·ăh* [𐤄𐤍𐤉𐤌𐤋|למינה][H4325]. The root word is "water"—as *semen*. The prefix, *lămĕd* [𐤋], may be translated in other ways than "*to, toward,* or *in regard to*"[565]. It is used here as "concerning"—since that is more in context. The suffix, *hāy* [𐤄], denotes *the absolute state* of the root word. In this context the *absolute state* is in having been genetically engineered.

TRANSLATED AS: concerning *genetically engineered* semen

and it was so
This phrase has been seen in Verses 7, 9, 11 and 15.

TRANSLATED AS: and it is true

A researched translation of the ancient Hebrew Genesis 1:24—
And strange-biological-entities said,
"!Bring forth the I-Accomplisher."
"Refresh-revive [*euphemisms for copulation*] is within semen genetically engineered for loud moaning [*another euphemism for copulating*] since having been reptilized."
And [*the Reptilian*] lives in it [*the genetically engineered semen*]!
"I accomplished concerning genetically engineered semen."
And it is true.

Genesis 1:24—*in plain English*

- ☆ In this stylized dialogue a Reptile-entity states that the sex drive is engineered into the hybrid's DNA in its sperm; and is passed on through the hybrid's own sexual procreation.
- ☆ The reptile-being lives inside the DNA of the hybrid's sperm.
- ☆ Their account repeats that it is true.

The KJV of Genesis 1:25 (*first phrase*)—

And God made the beast of the earth after his kind,

Ancient Hebrew Anatomic Alphabet writing of that phrase—

𐤅𐤉𐤏𐤔 𐤀𐤋𐤄𐤉𐤌 𐤀𐤕 𐤇𐤉𐤕 𐤄𐤀𐤓𐤑 𐤋𐤌𐤉𐤍𐤄

An actual translation *with researched explanations below*—
And strange-biological-entities made in-vitro fertilization bring about life! "The I-Accomplish concerns genetically engineered semen."

The KJV of Genesis 1:25 (*second phrase*)—
and cattle after their kind, and every thing that creepeth upon the earth after his kind:

Ancient Hebrew Anatomic Alphabet writing of that phrase—

𐤅𐤀𐤕 𐤄𐤁𐤄𐤌𐤄 𐤋𐤌𐤉𐤍𐤄 𐤅𐤀𐤕 𐤊𐤋 𐤓𐤌𐤔 𐤄𐤀𐤃𐤌𐤄
𐤋𐤌𐤉𐤍𐤄𐤅

An actual translation *with researched explanations below*—
"And in-vitro fertilization (is just the same as) the in-loud-moaning [*copulation*] as it concerns genetically engineered semen which (has been) in-vitro fertilized to perfect′ Reptilization (of) the genetically engineered I-Blood [*the hybridized hominid*] in regard to portion out it [*intracytoplasmic sperm injection (ICSI) through in-vitro fertilization (IVF) with the spermatozoon of the sperm-donating male*]."

The KJV of Genesis 1:25 (*third phrase*)—
and God saw that it was good.

Ancient Hebrew Anatomic Alphabet writing of that phrase—

𐤅𐤉𐤓𐤀 𐤀𐤋𐤄𐤉𐤌 𐤊𐤉 𐤈𐤅𐤁

An actual translation *with researched explanations below*—
And strange-biological-entities saw that (they had) good [*technical solutions*].

The Researched Explanations—

and made
The Hebrew word in the text is *ōōă·ē·ōsh* [WOZY|ויעש][H6213]. For that number, Dr. Strong gives us a laundry list of words across a broad spectrum of definitions. Strictly speaking, the root is "to do" or "to make". The root word is "𐤄WO" with a "dropped" last letter, *hāy* [𐤄]. The prefix here is *ōōă* [Y], "and"; the second prefix is *yăd* [Z], "it".

TRANSLATED AS: and it made

God
The word, *ălăh·ēm* [𐤌Z𐤄𐤋𐤀][H430], commonly translated "God", is a plural word. In context, it has nothing at all to do with any *uberGod*. It is treated here variously as "entities", "strange entities", "biological entities", "aliens", and as a variant of Extra-Terrestrial Biological Entities. Any of these terms are in context.

TRANSLATED AS: strange-biological-entities

the
As frequently seen here previously, the word, *ăt* [X𐤀][H855] is a "coulter" in the KJV at I Samuel 13:20. A high tech synonym for "coulter" is an "injecting pipette": the process of using a sharply beveled injecting pipette to microscopically inject a sperm cell into an egg cell. The word here is used as a noun form of IVF.

TRANSLATED AS: in-vitro fertilization

beast

Previously encountered as, "and its beasts", the word here doesn't have *and* or *its*. The word is *khēt* [𐤇𐤉𐤕|חית] [H2416—*alive, life*]. The words, "bring about", are understood *in context.*

TRANSLATED AS: bring about life!

of the earth

Last seen in Verse 24, the word, *hā·ărětz* [𐤄𐤀𐤓𐤑] [H776], is mistranslated as "earth". It is meant to be read as "*hā·ă·rětz·ăh*" {[𐤄]𐤑𐤓𐤀𐤄} [H7521], "*to be pleased with* or *accomplish*". The prefix *hāy* [𐤄] is the indefinite article, "the". The *ălăpf* [𐤀] is "I".

TRANSLATED AS: the I-Accomplish

after his kind

Last seen in Verse 24, the word here is the exact same. The word is *lă·mēn·ăh* [𐤋𐤌𐤉𐤍𐤄|למינה]. The suffix, *hāy* [𐤄], denotes *the absolute state* of the root word. The word's root, "semen", has been genetically engineered by the entities.

TRANSLATED AS: in regard to genetically engineered semen

and

The Hebrew word here, *ōōă·ăt* [𐤅𐤀𐤕][H855] is a "coulter"—exactly as previously explained. The word has a prefix, 𐤅, which means "and".

TRANSLATED AS: and in-vitro fertilization

cattle

We saw "*bě·hāměăh*" (*in loud moaning*) in Verse 24 because the root, *hāměăh* [𐤄𐤌𐤄][H1993], can be *to make a loud sound.* The word, *hā·bě·hāměăh* [𐤄𐤁𐤄𐤌𐤄], is what's in the text here. The prefix *hāy* [𐤄] is the article, "the". The prefix *bět* [𐤁] is "in".

TRANSLATED AS: the in-loud-moaning

after their kind

We saw this (above) as "after his kind". The Hebrew word here is the same word, *lă·mēn·ăh* [𐤋𐤌𐤉𐤍𐤄], as previously explained; except that here the prefix, *lamed* [𐤋] is being translated as "as concerns"[566].

TRANSLATED AS: as concerns genetically engineered semen

and

Seen again as "and", the word, *ōōă·ăt* [𐤅𐤀𐤕][H855] acts as a high tech "coulter"—as previously explained. The prefix, 𐤅, is being treated here as "which"[567]. Because the action in the sentence has largely already happened, the helping verbs "has been" are added. The noun, fertilization, needs to be a verb—in past tense.

TRANSLATED AS: which (has been) in-vitro fertilized

every thing

Last seen in Verse 21 as "every", the word here is *kăl* [𐤊𐤋]. It is the two-letter abbreviated form of the three-letter word, *kălăl* [𐤊𐤋𐤋]. It is usually associated with Strong's H3605; but it is from H3634—*to complete (to make perfect), the whole—hence, all or every*. Here, "to make perfect" is being used as a verb.

TRANSLATED AS: to perfect′

that creepeth

The pure root appearing here is simply *rĕmĕsh* [𐤓𐤌𐤔][H7431]—*a reptile.* The root is singular and has no prefix, no suffix, nor an inserted letter. Many words in Hebrew may act as a noun or as a verb—depending on their context in a sentence. The preceeding word, *kăl*, is the verb, "to perfect′". The word that follows is what the word, "reptile", *as an adjective*, will modify.

TRANSLATED AS: reptilization

upon the earth

The Hebrew word seen before as "earth" is a different word than has previously appeared. Here, it is *hā·ă·dăm·ăh* [𐤄𐤀𐤃𐤌𐤄|האדמה]. It is not "earth" (Strong's Number H127). Our root here is *dăm* [𐤃𐤌|דם]—*blood*[568] [H1818]. The word's first prefix *hāy* [𐤄] is the indefinite article, "the". The second prefix *ălăpf* [𐤀] is "I"; and the suffix, *hāy* [𐤄], denotes *the absolute state* of the root word: that of having been genetically engineered.

No drum roll is offered by the ancient text for the introduction "ă·dăm". Yes, that word sure looks like "Adam". There is no one named "Adam". That is just a "workhorse" word—the Reptilians own cryptic *bottom-line* description of the successful outcome of their interbreeding research and development program regarding the planet's ancient resident mammalian hominids.

TRANSLATED AS: (of) the genetically engineered I-Blood [the hybridized hominid]

after his kind

So far in this verse we have seen "after their kind" and "after his kind". In both instances the same Hebrew word was behind each—𐤋𐤌𐤉𐤍𐤄 | למינה (*lă·mēn·ăh*). The word here, though, appears twice in Verse 12 and once in Verse 21—as *lă·mēn·hōō* [𐤋𐤌𐤉𐤍𐤄𐤅|למינהו][H4327], *to portion out.* The grammar here is the prefix, 𐤋 (*lămĕd*), *in regard to*; and a suffix, *hōō* [𐤄𐤅-], *it.*

TRANSLATED AS: in regard to portion out it [intracytoplasmic sperm injection (ICSI) through in-vitro fertilization (IVF) with the spermatozoon of the sperm-donating male]

and God saw that it was good

and saw

TRANSLATED AS: and saw

God
The explanation of the Hebrew word here is the same as previously seen in this verse.

TRANSLATED AS: strange-biological-entities

that
The word in the text is *kē* (pronounced "key") [𐤉𐤊]. It is Strong's H3588; and it can act to connect all kinds of causes in a sentence, including the words "for" and "because".

TRANSLATED AS: that

it was good
There is no "it was" on this word in the text. The word, *thōōb* [𐤁𐤅𐤈] [H2896] means "good" in the widest sense. Here it will be given as traditionally translated—in the sense of the practical necessity of the aliens' DNA manipulation and genetic engineering.

TRANSLATED AS: good [technical solutions]

A researched translation of the ancient Hebrew Genesis 1:25—
And strange-biological-entities made in-vitro fertilization bring about life! "The I-Accomplish concerns genetically engineered semen. And in-vitro fertilization (is just the same as) the in-loud-moaning [*copulation*] as it concerns genetically engineered semen which (has been) in-vitro fertilized to perfect′ Reptilization (of) the genetically engineered I-Blood [*the hybridized hominid*] in regard to portion out it [*intracytoplasmic sperm injection (ICSI) through in-vitro fertilization (IVF) with the spermatozoon of the sperm-donating male*]."
And strange-biological-entities saw that (they had) good [*technical solutions*].

Genesis 1:25—*in plain English*

- ☆ The Reptile-entities document continued success using IVF.
- ☆ They note that the I-Accomplish Project extends to genetically engineering the sperm of the male of the target species.
- ☆ For the Reptile-beings, the process of in-vitro fertilization is just a laboratory metaphor for sexual copulation so that their Reptilized genetically engineered semen will be genetically passed on by the hybrid-beings through their own copulation.
- ☆ IVF was used to perfect the genetic engineering of the hybrid's own spermatozoa in its own semen.
- ☆ The entities recognized that they had good technical solutions.

The KJV of Genesis 1:26 (*first phrase*)—
And God said, Let us make man in our image, after our likeness:

Ancient Hebrew Anatomic Alphabet writing of that phrase—
𐤅𐤉𐤀𐤌𐤓 𐤀𐤋𐤄𐤉𐤌 𐤍𐤏𐤔𐤄 𐤀𐤃𐤌 𐤁𐤑𐤋𐤌𐤍𐤅
𐤊𐤃𐤌𐤅𐤕𐤍𐤅

An actual translation *with researched explanations below*—
And strange-biological-entities declared, "Ourselves accomplish (the) I-Blood [*the hybrid*] in our likeness in regard to blood as-related-to us;

The KJV of Genesis 1:26 (*second phrase*)—
and let them have dominion over the fish of the sea,

Ancient Hebrew Anatomic Alphabet writing of that phrase—
𐤅𐤉𐤓𐤃𐤅 𐤁𐤃𐤂𐤕 𐤄𐤉𐤌

An actual translation *with researched explanations below*—
and subjugate him in spawning the semen,

The KJV of Genesis 1:26 (*third phrase*)—
and over the fowl of the air, and over the cattle, and over the earth,

Ancient Hebrew Anatomic Alphabet writing of that phrase—
𐤅𐤁𐤏𐤅𐤐 𐤄𐤔𐤌𐤉𐤌 𐤅𐤁𐤁𐤄𐤌𐤄 𐤅𐤁𐤊𐤋 𐤄𐤀𐤓𐤑

An actual translation *with researched explanations below*—
and in exhaustion [*a post-copulative descriptor*]—The-Amazements; also through in-loud-moaning [*a euphemism for active copulation*]. And in perfecting the I-Accomplish;

The KJV of Genesis 1:26 (*fourth phrase*)—
and over every creeping thing that creepeth upon the earth.

Ancient Hebrew Anatomic Alphabet writing of that phrase—

An actual translation *with researched explanations below*—
and in perfecting the Reptilian—Reptilian yoke [*a descriptor for the phosphate-deoxyribose "yoke" holding the DNA double helix structure together*]—the I-Accomplish."

The Researched Explanations—

and God said
This phrase has been explained in Verses 3, 6, 9, 11, 14, 20, and 24.

TRANSLATED AS: and strange-biological-entities declared

let us make
We first saw "made" in Verse 16 as "made ready". We saw "made" in Verse 25 as "made". Here, the same word could be used; but in its context in this verse, another word will be used—since this is a word used *"in the broadest sense and widest application"*. Our word is *nōō·ōshăh* [𐤍𐤏𐤔𐤄][H6213]. It is translated in the KJV as "accomplish" in the Book of First Kings 5:9. We will follow suit. Here, the prefix *nōō* [𐤍], is reflexive—that give us "ourselves".

TRANSLATED AS: ourselves accomplish

man
The word in the ancient text is *ădăm* [𐤀𐤃𐤌 |מדא][H119—*to show blood in the face*]. Strong's H120 is "*rosy, red, ruddy, a human being—an individual or the species*". *Rosy, red, and ruddy* each refer to visibly increased blood flow in the face. Blood is at the heart of these definitions. The word for "blood" is *dăm* [𐤃𐤌][H1818—*blood*]. Dr. Strong tells us that H1818 is from the root, *dămĕm* [𐤃𐤌𐤌], which means *to be silent* or *to be astonished*. Here, the word in the text will be treated as "ă·dăm"; where *dăm* is

"blood" and the prefix, *ălăpf* [𐤀] is the pronoun, "I". That treatment may be unconventional; but the actual account is also. Additionally, treating *ă·dăm* as "I-Blood" will exactly fit in with the context of the phrases to follow.

TRANSLATED AS: I-Blood

in our image

Spoiler alert—the translation of the Hebrew word here is going to be "likeness". It may be wondered why *that* word—when *that* word in English is traditionally used in the phrase that follows. Follow-up spoiler alert—the next phrase is *about* "likeness"—through *blood.*

The word here is *bĕ·tzălăm·nōō* [𐤅𐤍𐤌𐤋𐤑𐤁|בצלמנו]. It is H6754—*a phantom, illusion, resemblance, idol,* or *image*. The word, "image", is from the Latin, *imitari*—referring to an imitation or to a *likeness*. That's the definition used here. The prefix, *bĕt* [𐤁], means "in"; and the suffix, *nōō* [𐤅𐤍-] means "our" (or "us").

TRANSLATED AS: in our likeness

after our likeness

Per the spoiler alert, the root word here is *dăm* [H1818] as *blood* [𐤌𐤃]. The complete word in the text is *kă·dăm·ōōt·nōō*. In Hebrew it is, "𐤅𐤍𐤕𐤅𐤌𐤃𐤊" [כדמותנו]. The prefix is the letter *kăpf* [𐤊]—*like, as,* or *according to*. The first suffix is *ōōt* [𐤕𐤅] means *as-related-to*. The second suffix is *nōō* [𐤅𐤍-]. Here, it means *us*.

TRANSLATED AS: according to blood as-related-to us

and let them have dominion

The meaning of the suffix of the Hebrew word here presents a real problem for this traditional phrase—as the suffix *ōō* [𐤅] means "him", "it", and occasionally "her" (not "them"). The word in the text is *ōōă·ērĕd·ōō* [𐤅𐤃𐤓𐤉𐤅|וירדו]. Closely related in meaning is Strong's H7287 [*rĕdăh* | 𐤄𐤃𐤓]—*to tread down* or *to subjugate*. The root we can see in the text is *ēărĕd* [𐤉𐤓𐤃][H3381], whose meaning is similar—*to descend* or *to subdue*. To subdue *is* to subjugate. The prefix *ōōă* [𐤅] means "and".

TRANSLATED AS: and subjugate it [the hybrid-being species]

over the fish

There are more problems here for the traditional fake narrative owing to the Hebrew word's actual definition. The word in the text is *bĕ·dăg·ĭt* [𐤁𐤃𐤂𐤕|בדגת]. The traditionally assigned Strong's Number, H1710 [𐤃𐤂𐤄 (*dăgĭăh*)], is given as "fish"—but H1711 (also *dăgĭăh*) is given as "*to move rapidly*", and "*to spawn*". The *bĕt* [𐤁] is "in". The *tōō* [𐤕] suffix can mean "you" (or "your") or "!".

TRANSLATED AS: in spawning!

of the sea

Seen before quite a number of times, the Hebrew word *mēm* [𐤌𐤉𐤌][H4325] is traditionally "water". It can refer also to *urine* or *semen*—so does the word, "*ēm*" [𐤉𐤌]. Examples of "*ēm*" as "sea" may be found one other place in Genesis (14:3), four places in Exodus, seven places in Numbers, and six places in Deuteronomy. The word in the text is *hā·ēm* [𐤄𐤉𐤌|הים].

TRANSLATED AS: the semen

and over the fowl

Fowl were first seen in Verse 20. The word in the text here is *ōōă·bĕ·ō·ōōpf* [𐤅𐤁𐤏𐤅𐤐|ובעוף]. It is associated with Strong's H5775. *However*, that word is a homonym. Its other meaning is "to faint" [H5774]. We can see this word used in that sense in several places in the Hebrew Bible, such as in each of the Books of Samuel. Isn't it true that in the aftermath of sexual relations there is, or can be, a sense of exhaustion, or of feeling *simply spent*? The first prefix, *ōōă* [𐤅], means "and". The second prefix, *bĕt* [𐤁], is "in".

TRANSLATED AS: and in exhaustion [after copulation]

of the air

The Hebrew word here was first seen in Verse 1 as *hā·shĭm·ēm*— "of the heavens". The heavy definitional lifting here is the root, Strong's H8074 [שמם]—*to stun, to devastate, to be astonished,* or *an amazement.* The word here is *hā·shĭm·ēm* [השמים]. The prefix is *hāy* [ה]—*the*; and the suffix is *"-ēm"* [ים-]—a pluralizer.

TRANSLATED AS: the amazements

and over the cattle

We saw *cattle* in Verses 24 and 25. There, the Hebrew word was *bĕ·hāmĕăh* [בהמה][H929]—*a dumb beast—cattle.* It was treated in both verses as "loud moaning". Our word in the text, *ōōă·bĕ·bĕhāmĕăh* [ובבהמה|ובבהמה], is another word with three prefixes. The prefix, *ōōă* [ו], means "and". The second prefix, (the first letter *bĕt* [ב]) takes on the meaning, "through". The third prefix, (the second letter *bĕt,* ב) is "in".

TRANSLATED AS: and through in-loud-moaning [another euphemism for active copulation]

and over

Seen in Verses 21 and 25 as "every", the word here is *ōōă·bĕ·kăl* [ובכל], from the root, *kălăl* [H3634]—*to make perfect.*

TRANSLATED AS: and in perfecting

the earth

We have the word "accomplish" again, but by a different route than through *ōshăh* [H6213], seen at the beginning of this verse. The word, *hā·ărĕtz* [הארץ] [H776], is meant to be read as *"hā·ă·rĕtz·ăh"* {[ה]הארץ} [H7521], *"to be pleased with* or *accomplish, et cetera*". The prefix *hāy* [ה] is the indefinite article, "the". The *ălăpf* [א] is "I".

TRANSLATED AS: the I-Accomplish

and over every

Seen in Verses 21 and 25 as "every", the word here is *ōōă·bĕ·kăl* [𐤅𐤁𐤊𐤋], from the root, *kălăl* [H3634]—*to make perfect.*

TRANSLATED AS: and in perfecting

creeping thing

The first time we encountered these *creeping things* was under the rock of "that moveth" in Verse 21. It was defined as "reptile", and translated as "Reptile". In Verse 24 we saw *the creeping thing*. In Verse 25—*that creepeth.* Here the word is *hā·rĕmĕsh* [𐤄𐤓𐤌𐤔|הרמש] [H7430—*a reptile*]. The prefix is the letter *hāy* [𐤄] as "the". Here, the word is treated as a collective proper noun.

TRANSLATED AS: the reptile ***as*** the Reptilian—

that creepeth

Appearing in Verse 25 as simply *rĕmĕsh* [𐤓𐤌𐤔][H7431—*a reptile*], it appears here just as in the previous word—*hā·rĕmĕsh* [𐤄𐤓𐤌𐤔].

TRANSLATED AS: reptile ***as*** the Reptilian

upon

First encountered in Verse 2, we also saw this word in Verses 15, 17, and twice in Verse 20—as "yoke". The word, *ōl* [𐤏𐤋], is H5923; and is the original text-writer's chosen description of the *fastening framework* of the phosphate-deoxyribose "*yoke*" fastening the nucleotides of the DNA molecular structure.

TRANSLATED AS: yoke

the earth

Last seen in Verse 25, the word, *hā·ărĕtz* [𐤄𐤀𐤓𐤑] [H776], is not "earth" in this context. Read as "*hā·ă·rĕtz·ăh*" [𐤄𐤀𐤓𐤑][𐤄] [H7521], "*to be pleased with* or *accomplish*". The prefix *hāy* [𐤄] is the indefinite article, "the". The *ălăpf* [𐤀] is "I".

TRANSLATED AS: the I-Accomplish

A researched translation of the ancient Hebrew Genesis 1:26—
And strange-biological-entities declared, "Ourselves accomplish (the) I-Blood [*the hybrid*] in our likeness in regard to blood as related to us. And subjugate it [*the hybrid species*] in spawning semen, and in exhaustion [*a post-copulative descriptor*]—The-Amazements; also through in-loud-moaning [*a euphemism for active copulation*]. And in perfecting the I-Accomplish; and in perfecting the Reptilian—Reptilian yoke [*a descriptor for the phosphate-deoxyribose "yoke" holding the DNA double helix structure together*]—the I-Accomplish."

Genesis 1:26—*in plain English*

- ☆ The Reptile beings declared that they would engineer a hybrid resembling them in likeness by blood.
- ☆ They understood they could subjugate their hybrid species by intensifying their sex drive.
- ☆ By binding hominid and Reptilian DNA-segments the alien Reptilians DNA-engineered their hybrid species—referred to as *the I-Accomplish.*

The KJV of Genesis 1:27 (*first phrase*)—
So God created man in his own image,

Ancient Hebrew Anatomic Alphabet writing of that phrase—

ויברא אלהים את האדם בצלמו

An actual translation *with researched explanations below*—
And strange-biological-entities cut—CRISPR-manipulating the I-Blood [*the hybrid*] in its likeness [*the entities' own likeness*].

The KJV of Genesis 1:27 (*second phrase*)—
in the image of God created he him;

Ancient Hebrew Anatomic Alphabet writing of that phrase—

בצלם אלהים ברא אתו

An actual translation *with researched explanations below*—
For likeness [*of themselves*] strange-biological-entities, as visually discerned [*under microscopy*], CRISPR manipulated it [*the DNA of the target species*].

The KJV of Genesis 1:27 (*third phrase*)—
male and female created he them.

Ancient Hebrew Anatomic Alphabet writing of that phrase—

זכר ונקבה ברא אתם

An actual translation *with researched explanations below*—
"Mark and puncture [*with the bevel of the injecting pipette*], as visually discerned [*under microscopy*]: injection pipette them [*the prepared ova (eggs) of the female of the target species—the bipedal hominids*]."

The Researched Explanations—

so created

Sure, the word "so" could be spun from the Hebrew prefix 𐤅 (*ōōă*). So can the conjunction, "but". Just plain "and" is the preferred translated word here. The word in the text is *ōōă·ē·bĕră* [𐤅𐤉𐤁𐤓𐤀|ויברא]. As much as one may like the word "created' to go here, the actual context of this sentence requires the word "cut". The second prefix, *yăd* [𐤉], is "it"—as a reference to the subject of the sentence—those *strange entities*.

TRANSLATED AS: and it cut

God

This word has been explained multiple times previously.

TRANSLATED AS: strange-biological-entities

~a Hebrew word untranslated in the KJV~

The untranslated word in the text here is, "*ăt*" [𐤀𐤕]. Per any standard Hebrew Dictionary of the Old Testament, it can be found as Strong's H855—defined as "coulter". We can find a *coulter* in KJV at First Samuel 13:20 and 21. A coulter cuts through soil.

Some new high technology must be reintroduced here—as this hi-tech technique is a synonym of *coulter*. CAS-9, or Cas9, stands for "CRISPR associated protein 9". It is a RNA-guided DNA endonuclease enzyme associated with the CRISPR (Clustered Regularly Interspaced Short Palindromic Repeats) technique—a hi-tech tool of genetic engineers. A CAS-9 "cleaver" cuts DNA like scissors to make precision changes. Nevertheless, the entire technique is still a process of CRISPR manipulation.

TRANSLATED AS: CRISPR-manipulating

man

The word in the ancient text is *hā·ădăm* [𐤄𐤀𐤃𐤌|האדם][H119—*to show blood in the face*]. Strong's H120 is "*rosy, red, ruddy, a human being—an individual or the species*". Blood is at the heart of these definitions. The word for "blood" is *dăm* [𐤃𐤌][H1818—*blood*]. Dr. Strong tells us that

H1818 is from the root, *dăměm* [𐤃𐤌𐤌], which means *to be silent* or *to be astonished*. Here, the word in the text will be treated as "*ă·dăm*"; where *dăm* is "blood" and the prefix, *ălăpf* [𐤀] is the pronoun, "I". The prefix, *hāy* [𐤄] is "the". The translation of this word may appear to be unconventional; but it is exact translation and is in exact context.

TRANSLATED AS: the I-Blood [the hybrid]

in his own image

Previously, we saw a variant of the word in Verse 26, as *bĕ·tză·lăm·nōō* [𐤁𐤑𐤋𐤌𐤍𐤅][H6754– *to shade, a phantom, illusion, resemblance, idol, image, vain shew*]. There, the traditional language was "in *our* image"; here, it is "in his own image". The only element changed on the word here is the Hebrew suffix for "his"—or "its". The word here is *bĕ·tzălăm·ōō* [𐤁𐤑𐤋𐤌𐤅|בצלמו]. The prefix, *bĕt* [𐤁], is "in". The suffix, *ōōă* [𐤅] is "its".

TRANSLATED AS: in its likeness [the E.T. entities' own likeness]

in the image

Here, there is no "the" prefix on the Hebrew word. The word appearing here is *bĕ·tzălăm* [𐤁𐤑𐤋𐤌]. Here, the prefix, *bĕt* [𐤁], means "for"—in the sense of *to obtain for their purposes.*

TRANSLATED AS: for likeness [of themselves]

of God

English translators supply the "of". The subject word has been deliberately mistranslated as "God". After all, the ancient text *is* about the strange-biological-entities' interventions with our bipedal hominid ancestors.

TRANSLATED AS: strange-biological-entities

created

The word in the text here sure looks like a *pure root—bĕră* [𐤁𐤓𐤀] [H1254]. The word's main definitions are *to create* and *to cut down*. But this word's context is less about cutting, which has already been mentioned by the text's authors, than it is about *how* they are going to cut—that is, DNA-manipulate via CAS-9. The *how* here has to do with *how* they are visualizing the cuts to be made. What is being visualized is happening using high-power microscopes—just as it would be by genetic scientists today.

What must be done is to revisualize this Hebrew word as having had its final letter [a *hāy*— 𐤄|ה] dropped either by the author or by a subsequent editor. Now we read, *bě·răăh* [𐤁𐤓𐤀𐤄|בראה]. That exact word is used at the KJV Isaiah 28:7 where it was translated as "in vision". It is associated with Strong's Number 7803 ("vision") or H7200—*to see (literally or figuratively)*.

Now we have a prefix, *bět*, treated in this instance as "as". The root-word, "𐤓𐤀𐤄" is being translated as "visually discerned"; since that word may mean (among other definitions), "vision" *and* "discern". The method of discernment is in brackets.

TRANSLATED AS: as visually discerned [under microscopy]

he him

The word in the text is here *mis*translated as "he him". The word here is, "*ăt·ōō*" [𐤀𐤕𐤅|אתו]. Here, in context, is the same new hi-tech just encountered. CAS-9, or Cas9. A hi-tech tool of genetic engineers, CAS-9 is a RNA-guided DNA endonuclease enzyme associated with CRISPR (Clustered Regularly Interspaced Short Palindromic Repeats). A CAS-9 "cleaver" cuts DNA like scissors for precision changes to DNA. The suffix, 𐤅, is "it".

TRANSLATED AS: CRISPR CAS-9 manipulated it [the DNA of the target species]

male

The Hebrew word here, *zăkăr* [𐤆𐤊𐤓][H2142 – 2145], means *to mark, to remember,* or *male*. The function of *to mark* comes from *remembering* something. Here, the function of *to mark* is purely practical—that is, to identify where on the surface of the ovum (egg) to puncture it with the sharp bevel of an injecting pipette.

TRANSLATED AS: mark

and female

The definition of the Hebrew word here could be the poster-child for the psychopathology of linking *puncture with violence* to the female of the species. The ancient word here is *ōōă·nōō·qwōōb·ăh* [𐤅𐤍𐤒𐤁𐤄|ונקבה]. Though it is associated with Strong's H5347 [𐤍𐤒𐤁𐤄 (*nōō·qwōōb·ăh*)], the actual root is *nōō·qwōōb* [H5344 | 𐤍𐤒𐤁|נקב]—*to puncture or perforate with more-or-less violence, to bore, pierce, with holes, strike through*); *the sexual form—female, woman.* The root, *nōō·qwōōb* [𐤍𐤒𐤁] never appears in the Hebrew Bible[569]. The word's prefix, 𐤅 (*ōōă*), is "and". The word's suffix, 𐤄 (*hāy*), denotes the *absolute state* of its root.

We may take that to mean that the strange-biological-entities have marked, with absolute precision, where the sharp beveled tip of their injecting pipette will puncture the ovum of the target female specimen from among the planet's population of bipedal hominids. Yes, i*n-vitro fertilization* is what is happening here. What's being described is a DNA manipulation event through which an alien species of reptilian hominids mix their DNA with that of our own mammalian hominid ancestors.

TRANSLATED AS: and absolute state (of) puncture [of the ovum with the bevel of the injecting pipette]

created

The word in the text here is a *pure root—bĕră* [𐤁𐤓𐤀|ברא][H1254—*to create, to cut down*]. That, of course, is what we are supposed to see. But the context here, as just laid out by the scriptural authors themselves, is that the surface of the genetically engineered ovum has been marked for precision puncture by their injecting pipette to be in-vitro fertilized. The stark concept of "cut" simply does not seamlessly fit in here; nor does any variation of "create". The word here is to be visualized and treated just the same as previously discerned.

TRANSLATED AS: as visually discerned [under microscopy]

he them

Our Hebrew word here, "*ăt·ōōm*" [𐤀𐤕𐤌], was last seen twice in Verse 26 as "and". The word, here, is a referrence to the injecting pipette used in IVF. The traditional word "them" is the correct personal pronoun, as the three-letter word's suffix, 𐤌, means "they", "their", or "them".

TRANSLATED AS: injection pipette them [the prepared ova (eggs) of the female of the target species—the bipedal hominids]

A researched translation of the ancient Hebrew Genesis 1:27—

And strange-biological-entities cut—CRISPR-manipulating the I-Blood [*the hybrid*] in its likeness [*the entities' own likeness*]. For likeness [*of themselves*] strange-biological-entities, as visually discerned [*under microscopy*], CRISPR manipulated it [*the DNA of the target species*]. Mark and puncture [*with the bevel of the injecting pipette*], as visually discerned [*under microscopy*]: injection pipette them [*the prepared ova (eggs) of the female of the target species—the bipedal hominids—our ancestors*].

Genesis 1:27—in plain English

- ☆ The Reptile-entities used their version of the CRISPR CAS-9 cleaver to cut the hominid DNA in their own likeness.
- ☆ They marked the puncture point on the hominid female egg to exactly place their injecting pipette.

The KJV of Genesis 1:28 (*first phrase*)—
And God blessed them, and God said unto them,

Ancient Hebrew Anatomic Alphabet writing of that phrase—
𐤅𐤉𐤁𐤓𐤊 𐤀𐤕𐤌 𐤀𐤋𐤄𐤉𐤌 𐤅𐤉𐤀𐤌𐤓 𐤋𐤄𐤌 𐤀𐤋𐤄𐤉𐤌

An actual translation *with researched explanations below*—
And in delicate expertise strange-biological-entities injection pipetted them [*a DNA-manipulated sperm cell into the DNA-manipulated female hominid egg*]. And it [*the strange-biological-entities*] said in regard to animal sounds [*those the bipedal hominids made*], "(They sound like) strange-biological-entities".

The KJV of Genesis 1:28 (*second phrase*)—
Be fruitful, and multiply, and replenish the earth, and subdue it:

Ancient Hebrew Anatomic Alphabet writing of that phrase—
𐤐𐤓𐤅 𐤅𐤓𐤁𐤅 𐤅𐤌𐤋𐤀𐤅 𐤀𐤕 𐤄𐤀𐤓𐤑 𐤅𐤊𐤁𐤔𐤄

An actual translation *with researched explanations below*—
"Increase it [*the target species*], and increase it by the myriads; and complete it: in-vitro fertilizing the I-Accomplish. And absolute subjugation:

The KJV of Genesis 1:28 (*third phrase*)—
and have dominion over the fish of the sea,

Ancient Hebrew Anatomic Alphabet writing of that phrase—
𐤅𐤓𐤃𐤅 𐤁𐤃𐤂𐤕 𐤄𐤉𐤌

An actual translation *with researched explanations below*—
and subjugate it inside space craft! (of the) seas,

The KJV of Genesis 1:28 (*fourth phrase*)—
and over the fowl of the air,

Ancient Hebrew Anatomic Alphabet writing of that phrase—

𐤅𐤁𐤏𐤅𐤐 𐤄𐤔𐤌𐤉𐤌

An actual translation *with researched explanations below*—
and in flight—The Amazements;

The KJV of Genesis 1:28 (*fifth phrase*)—
and over every living thing that moveth upon the earth.

Ancient Hebrew Anatomic Alphabet writing of that phrase—

𐤅𐤁𐤊𐤋 𐤇𐤉𐤄 𐤄𐤓𐤌𐤔𐤕 𐤏𐤋 𐤄𐤀𐤓𐤑

An actual translation *with researched explanations below*—
and in perfecting Revive [*one of their euphemisms for copulation*]—the Reptilian! yoke: the I-Accomplish."

The Researched Explanations—

and God blessed

No "god", nor even "God", blessed anything or any thing in the actual Hebrew text. Yes, the prefix, 𐤅 (*ōōă* aka "waw", "wav", or "vav"), is our word "and"; but that letter is just the first of this word's three prefixes *before* we get to the word's root. This interesting word is *ōōă·ē·bĕ·rĕk* [𐤅𐤉𐤁𐤓𐤊|ויברך]. Traditionally associated with Strong's H1228, Dr. Strong informs us that word means, "*to kneel—by implication, to bless* or *to curse*". Sure enough, there are places in the Hebrew biblical text where the context gives us either "*to bless*" or "*to curse*". This is not one of those places.

Since the verse's context doesn't indicate any blessing, we must analyze the word for information in each of the letters. First, if the definition of the word's root, "*bĕ·rĕk*" [𐤁𐤓𐤊], is "to kneel", then there really isn't any implication to bless or to curse. There is a word for "to kneel". It is H7812, *shĭkhăh* [𐤔𐤇𐤄|שחה]; and appears two times[570] in the Bible: Genesis 24:11, where camels are to kneel down; and Psalms 95:6, where people are kneeling down.

So let's look at the word's first three letters—its first three prefixes. We have seen each one of these letter-prefixes already. The "𐤅" as "and" we already know. The "𐤉" (*yăd*) is "it". The "𐤁" (*bět*) is "in". Our own English language will supply the "is". So now we have, "and it (is) in".

We are left with two letters, *rěsh* and *kăpf* [𐤓𐤊]. When Davidson's *Analytical Hebrew and Chaldee Lexicon* is consulted, we learn that the word, "𐤓𐤊" ["רך"] means "*tender, delicate, effeminate*"[571]. It is from the roots of H7397 (*softness*) and H7401 (*to soften*)[572]. *This* word is used, in the context of *tender* or *softness* in three places in the Hebrew biblical text[573]. Here, we will combine the concepts of *delicate* and *softness* for our translation. In other words, the Reptilian entities' injection pipetting called for delicate skill in technique.

The word "expertise" may be used as a synonym of the "softness" of technique necessary in handling the microscopic instruments as well as for manipulation of the sperm cell and the egg cell for their program of *in-vitro fertilization*.

Now, for *blessing purists*, the word "blessed" could be the word in translation here; but we would still have the same translated outcome—that of the Reptilian entities' injection pipetting DNA-manipulated sperm cells into the eggs of our female hominid ancestor.

TRANSLATED AS: and it (is) in delicate expertise

God

The word, *ălăh·ēm* [𐤀𐤋𐤄𐤉𐤌] [H430], has been previously explained. The Reptile biological beings are not from this planet.

TRANSLATED AS: strange-biological-entities

them

We have seen the Hebrew word here, *ăt* ["𐤀𐤕"], multiple times. Here it appears, *in context*, as an injecting pipette. The letter *měm* [𐤌] is "*them*" is the suffix of the word, *ăt·ōōm* [𐤀𐤕𐤌].

TRANSLATED AS: injection pipetted them [a DNA-manipulated sperm cell into the hominid egg] *and God said unto them*

The word order in this phrase is *and-said unto them God.* We have seen *and-said* before—the first time in Verse 3—where it was (and again is), *ōōă·ē·ămĕr* [𐤅𐤉𐤀𐤌𐤓][H559], is "and-it-said".

unto them

These two words are a different kettle of fish. Yes, the word *lă·hām* [𐤋𐤄𐤌|להם] can be *unto them* or *to them.* But our word, in context has the prefix, 𐤋, meaning *in regard to*. The root word is *hāmăh* [𐤄𐤌𐤄][H1993] with a dropped final letter, 𐤄. If we consult Davidson's *The Analytical Hebrew and Chaldee Lexicon* we read about "*a humming noise—as of the sounds of certain animals—to growl, to howl*"[574]. Inside of this word, the aliens (called *reptile*, or *remesh* in the ancient text) hear the bipedal hominids speaking. The word that follows in the text is what the Remesh-beings thought what our ancestors sounded like.

TRANSLATED AS: in regard to animal sounds [those the hominids made]

God

As previously explained, the beings [אלהים] self-identify as *reptilies*.

TRANSLATED AS: strange-biological-entities

be fruitful

Here's a word that's pretty straightforward: *pfār·ōō* [𐤐𐤓𐤅|פרו] [H6509]. Its root, "פרה", had its final letter, ה, dropped by its authors or by a subsequent editor. Its definition is *to be fruitful, to grow,* or *to increase*. The suffix, ōō [𐤅] is "it".

TRANSLATED AS: increase it

and multiply

Where something will multiply it will increase. No exception here. The word here is *ōōă·rĕb·ōō* [𐤅𐤓𐤁𐤅|ורבו][H7231]. The root is *rĕbĕ*b [𐤓𐤁𐤁]—with a dropped final letter, 𐤁. It means *to increase by the myriads*. The prefix, *ōōă* [𐤅], is *and*. The suffix, 𐤅, is "it".

TRANSLATED AS: and increase by the myriads it [the target species] *and replenish*

Here again we have the letter *ōōă* [𐤅] as both prefix and as a suffix. The context is that our suffix, *ōōă* [𐤅], is "it". The word is *ōōā·mělă·ōō* [𐤅𐤀𐤋𐤌𐤅|ומלאו][H4390]—*to fill* or *to complete.*

TRANSLATED AS: and complete it

~a Hebrew word untranslated in the KJV~

The word here in the text, is, *ăt* [𐤕𐤀|את][H855]. It has been thoroughly explained previously.

TRANSLATED AS: in-vitro fertilizing

the earth

Last seen in Verse 26, the word, *hā·ărětz* [𐤑𐤓𐤀𐤄][H776], is traditionally defined as "ground or land" and mistranslated as "earth". It is to be read as, "*hā·ă·rětz·ăh*" {[𐤄]𐤑𐤓𐤀𐤄} [H7521], "to be pleased with or accomplish". The word's first prefix *hāy* [𐤄] is the indefinite article, "the". The second prefix, *ălăpf* [𐤀], is "I".

TRANSLATED AS: the I-Accomplish

and subdue it

The word "subdue" could be left alone; but standard definitions of the root word here [*kăběsh* (𐤔𐤁𐤊)][H3533] give us a stronger and more fitting translation. Strong's defines this root as *to tread down, disregard, conquer, subjugate,* or, *violate*. Our word here is *ōōă·kăběsh·ăh* [𐤄𐤔𐤁𐤊𐤅|וכבשה]. The prefix, *ōōă* [𐤅], is "and". The word's suffix, 𐤄 (*hāy*), denotes the *absolute state* of its root—the meaning of which should be perfectly obvious.

TRANSLATED AS: and [the absolute state of] subjugation

and have dominion

To subdue is to subjugate. To subjugate is to have dominion; and the Hebrew word here is a synonym of the word just considered. Here, the word is *ōōă·rĕd·ōō* [𐤅𐤓𐤃𐤅|וירדו][H7287]—*to tread down; to subjugate*. The prefix, *ōōă* [𐤅], is *and*. Our suffix, 𐤅, in proper context, is "it".

TRANSLATED AS: and subjugate it [the target species]

over the fish

To solve a word puzzle about how *the fish* is to become an *under-sea-worthy space craft* we must have a frank discussion about *fish*. We must admit that "over the fish" simply is not in context anywhere in this first chapter of the first book of the Bible. Also, how many of us can actually believe that the famous Jonah, of three-days-in-the-belly-of-a-whale fame was *actually* in the belly of a whale (or a fish) doing whatever he did for three days?

When we look at what was happening in the Bible's Book of Jonah regarding his being in the "fish"—in Jonah 2:1, Jonah says he was swallowed by a "great fish"—*dăg gĭdōōl* [𐤃𐤂 𐤂𐤃𐤅𐤋]. Note here that the word, "great" is *gĭdōōl* |𐤂𐤃𐤅𐤋. Its root word is *gĭdăl* |𐤂𐤃𐤋. Here, there is an inserted letter, *ōōă* [𐤅], which changes the meaning to whatever the writer had in mind when he wrote. Most of us have heard the story where he's in a whale—not a "great fish". We may handily translate the word, *gĭdōōl*, to something like our modern *hybridized* word, *ginormous* [gigantic combined with enormous]. The text also relates that for three days and nights he was in the "belly" of said *ginormous* "fish".

In the Hebrew text we read two variations of the word for "belly" of the fish (or whale)—*but* the actual definition is neither *belly* nor *stomach.* It is "interior". Both are from the same root word. The first word is *bĕ·mō·ē* [𐤁𐤌𐤏𐤉][root, 𐤌𐤏𐤄] [H4579 —*in its interior*]. The second is *mĕ·mō·ē* [𐤌𐤌𐤏𐤉] [H4579—*from its interior*]. So now, we have a *ginormous interior*.

The narrative continues with an apt description of, say, a space ship descending into the depths of an ocean. We read about his being in "the heart of the seas and the current surrounded me" amid "breakers and waves" passing over him. The "depth" closed around him; and he went "to the base of the mountains". When the being, "It-Exists" [𐤉𐤄𐤅𐤄|יהוה](*ēă·hōōăh*)] spoke to the under-sea-going craft, it "vomited" [𐤒𐤀𐤄 (*qwă·ăh*) him out. Actually, spewed him out— onto "dry land" [𐤄𐤉𐤁𐤔𐤄 (*hā·ēbĕsh·ăh*) H3006—*the dry*]. So, after three days, Jonah was forcefully ejected from the under-sea-going craft onto "the dry"—presumably dry land.

There are accounts of UFO's descending into the ocean or into bodies of water—such as Lake Titicaca. [See the video at https://www.youtube.com/watch?v=zHvRwNIhMvs]. There are also reports of unidentified submergible objects at Guadalcanal[575].

With all that out of the way, the word in the Hebrew text here is *bĕ·dăg·ĭt* "𐤁𐤃𐤂𐤕" [בדגת][H1710 | 𐤃𐤂—*fish*]. Since the hero of the Book of Jonah was in the interior of a great something, the presumption is that it was neither fish nor whale. Since the Genesis narrative is all about the SBE/aliens' intervention, it's no stretch at all to treat *dăg* as the entities' space craft of some kind. The prefix, *bĕt* [𐤁], is "in". The suffix, *tōō* [𐤕], also completely in context, is our exclamation point.

TRANSLATED AS: in[side] space craft!

of the sea
Previously encountered as a variation of "waters", the word has been treated in this chapter as another biblical euphemism, "semen". *However*, in the context of *this* verse, the Hebrew word in the text, *hā·ēm* [𐤄𐤉𐤌], is exactly as traditionally rendered.

TRANSLATED AS: (of) the sea

and over the fowl
The word in the text here is *ōōă·bĕ·ō·ōōpf* [𐤅𐤁𐤏𐤅𐤐|ובעוף] H5774—*to cover...with wings...to fly*. Again, *fowl*, just as *fish*, are not in context. The root, *ō·ōōpf* [𐤏𐤅𐤐], appears 27 times in the biblical text[576]; and it appears in context as "fly" in the Book of Job 5:7 [*as the sparks fly upward*][577]. The verb, *fly*, may also be a noun, "flight". The prefix, *ōōă* [𐤅], is "and". The prefix, *bĕt* [𐤁], is "in".

TRANSLATED AS: and in flight

of the air

The Hebrew word here was first seen in Verse 1 and last seen in Verse 26, as *hā·shĭm·ēm*—given in the KJV as "of the heavens". The definition is the root, Strong's H8074 [𐤔𐤌𐤌]—*an amazement*. The word here is *hā·shĭm·ēm* [𐤄𐤔𐤌𐤉𐤌]. The prefix is *hāy* [𐤄]—*the*; and the suffix is "-*ēm*" [-𐤉𐤌]. It makes a word plural.

TRANSLATED AS: the amazements

and over every

All, any, because, every, though, what, where, and *who* are among the several specialties on the definition menu of Strong's H3605. The Hebrew word-basis of that Strong's number is H3634—*to complete, to make perfect, the whole—hence, all or every*. Our word in the text here is *ōōă·bĕ·kăl* [𐤅𐤁𐤊𐤋|ובכל]. Its root is "𐤊𐤋𐤋" with a dropped final letter, *lămĕd* [𐤋]. The prefix, *ōōă* [𐤅], is "and"; the prefix, *bĕt* [𐤁], is "in".

TRANSLATED AS: and in perfecting

living thing

The Hebrew word is *khēăh* [𐤇𐤉𐤄][H2421—*to live; to revive*].

TRANSLATED AS: Revive [one of their euphemisms for copulation]

that moveth

Seen here exactly as it appeared in Verse 21, and as a slight variation of the way it was seen in Verses 24 and 26, is the word, *hā·rĕmĕsh·ĭt* [𐤄𐤓𐤌𐤔𐤕|הרמשת]. It is Strong's H7431—"*a reptile*". The suffix, 𐤕, is a mark of exclamation.

TRANSLATED AS: the reptile! **as** the Reptilian!

upon

First encountered in Verse 2, we also saw this word in Verses 15, 17, twice in Verse 20, and again in Verse 26—as "yoke". The word, *ōl* [𐤏𐤋], usually cited as H5927. It is actually H5923. It is the original text-writer's chosen description of the *fastening framework* of the phosphate-deoxyribose "*yoke*" of the nucleotides of DNA.

TRANSLATED AS: yoke

the earth

Last seen in earlier in this verse, the word, *hā·ărĕtz* [𐤄𐤀𐤓𐤑] [H776], is usually defined as "*ground, land* or *earth*". Read the word as, "*hā·ă·rĕtz·ăh*" {𐤄𐤀𐤓𐤑[𐤄]} [H7521], "*to be pleased with* or *accomplish, et cetera*". Its root, "𐤓𐤑𐤄", has a dropped final letter, *hāy* [𐤄]. The prefix *hāy* [𐤄] is "the". The second prefix, *ălăpf,* [𐤀] is "I".

TRANSLATED AS: the I-Accomplish

A researched translation of the ancient Hebrew Genesis 1:28—

And in delicate expertise strange-biological-entities injection pipetted them [*DNA-manipulated sperm cells into DNA-manipulated female hominid egg cells*]. And it [*the strange-biological-entities*] said in regard to animal sounds [*those the bipedal hominids made*], "(They sound like) strange-biological-entities. Increase it [*the target species*] and increase it by the myriads; and complete it: in-vitro fertilizing the I-Accomplish. And absolute subjugation: and subjugate it inside space!craft of the seas, and in flight—The Amazements; and in perfecting Revive [*a euphemism for copulation*] the Reptilian! yoke: the I-Accomplish."

Genesis 1:28—in plain English

- ☆ The Reptilian entities expertly inject DNA-manipulated hominid sperm cells into female hominid egg cells.
- ☆ They hear the speech sounds of the bipedal hominids— whom they described as strange-biological-entities.
- ☆ The hybrids' numbers were to be dramatically increased.
- ☆ The Reptilian entities intend absolute subjugation of their hybrid species from inside seaworthy flying spacecraft.
- ☆ The hybrids' own DNA-segments have been DNA-manipulated to be hyper-sexualized—which they describe as *the Reptilian! yoke*. To them, that is a signficant accomplishment.

The KJV of Genesis 1:29 (*first phrase*)—
And God said, Behold, I have given you every herb

Ancient Hebrew Anatomic Alphabet writing of that phrase—
𐤅𐤉𐤀𐤌𐤓 𐤀𐤋𐤄𐤉𐤌 𐤄𐤍𐤄 𐤍𐤕𐤕𐤉 𐤋𐤊𐤌 𐤀𐤕 𐤊𐤋 𐤏𐤔𐤁

An actual translation *with researched explanations below*—
And strange-biological-entities declared, “Consider this: I have given you my concerning-exhaustion [*genetically engineered drive to copulate*] in-vitro fertilized to perfect′ green

The KJV of Genesis 1:29 (*second phrase*)—
bearing seed, which is upon the face of all the earth,

Ancient Hebrew Anatomic Alphabet writing of that phrase—
𐤆𐤓𐤏 𐤆𐤓𐤏 𐤀𐤔𐤓 𐤏𐤋 𐤐𐤍𐤉 𐤊𐤋 𐤄𐤀𐤓𐤑

An actual translation *with researched explanations below*—
disseminated spermatozoa (of) I-Dwell—yoking my presence to perfect′ the I-Accomplish;

The KJV of Genesis 1:29 (*third phrase*)—
and every tree which is the fruit of a tree yielding seed;

Ancient Hebrew Anatomic Alphabet writing of that phrase—
𐤅𐤀𐤕 𐤊𐤋 𐤄𐤏𐤑 𐤀𐤔𐤓 𐤁𐤅 𐤐𐤓𐤉 𐤏𐤑 𐤆𐤓𐤏 𐤆𐤓𐤏

An actual translation *with researched explanations below*—
and in-vitro fertilized to properly complete the fabrication [*hybridized sperm inside a hybridized egg*] which in it grows. My fabrication [*the mature hybrid being*] will disseminate spermatozoa

The KJV of Genesis 1:29 (*fourth phrase*)—
to you it shall be for meat.

Ancient Hebrew Anatomic Alphabet writing of that phrase—
𐤋𐤊𐤌 𐤉𐤄𐤉𐤄 𐤋𐤀𐤊𐤋𐤄

An actual translation *with researched explanations below*—
in regard to exhaustion [*copulation*]. It is in regard to I-Complete."

The Researched Explanations—

and God said—

and said
Although this phrase was explained in Verses 3, 6, 9, 11, 14, 20, 24 and 26, the word here is going to be handled a bit differently. The word, again, is *ōōă·ē·ămĕr* [𐤅𐤉𐤀𐤌𐤓][H559]–*a primary root used with great latitude*. The latitude we are going to take is limited to using the word "declared" instead of "said". As we have seen multiple times before, the prefix *ōōă* [𐤅] means "and". The prefix *yăd* [𐤉] may mean "he" or "it". Here, the pronoun, "it", refers to the strange entities *as a collective noun*.

TRANSLATED AS: and it declared

God
As previously explained, the word in the text is *ălăh·ēm* [𐤀𐤋𐤄𐤉𐤌] [H430]. It is traditionally mistranslated. The word "strange-biological-entities" is what is in context here—unless you want "God" to be the DNA-manipulating and subjugating bad-guy.

TRANSLATED AS: strange-biological-entities

behold
If we were to look at each of the 500-or-so places in the Hebrew biblical text where the word *hānōōăh* [𐤄𐤍𐤄][H2007, H2008, *and* H2009] appears[578],

we would see that the traditionally translated words range from "*lo*" and "*behold*" to "*therein, these, those*", to "*here, this way*", and "*thus far*"[579]. The common conceptual thread here is of a stylized literary request for the reader to take something into consideration. That's how "*hānōōăh*" is treated.

TRANSLATED AS: consider this

I have given

This interesting word gives us a root with a dropped final letter and two suffixes. It is *nōōt·tē* [𐤍𐤕𐤕𐤉|נתתי][H5414]— *to give, to put, to make—with a great latitude of application*. The root is "𐤍𐤕𐤍". The "I" is understood in context. The first suffix *tōō* [𐤕] is "you". The second suffix *yăd* [𐤉] is "my".

TRANSLATED AS: (I) have given you my

you

The sighting of this Hebrew word-construct, *lă·kăm* [𐤋𐤊𐤌|לכם], is its first appearance in the ancient biblical text. In the KJV Bible, as well as practically every English-language edition, it is treated as the word, "you". However, when ancient Hebrew text-writers wanted to express the concept of "you" they generally used the word, "𐤀𐤕𐤄"|"אתה". [Where "modern Hebrew" is taught, that word is pronounced "ătăh". Look up Strong's H859 and you'll see "*you*"[580].] The use of those two letters, "𐤀𐤕", here in this context, has no relationship to the two-letter word, 𐤀𐤕, seen throughout this foundational text.

Here, the word is treated the way it was intended to be from the moment it was written—as a "contraction" of the prefix, *lămĕd* [𐤋], *concerning*; and the root, *kămăh* [𐤊𐤌𐤄] [H3642]—*to pine after* or *to long for*[581]. As we have seen in plenty of other instances, the final *hāy* [𐤄] has been dropped from the word in the ancient text.

In Psalm 63:1, King David uses the same word here, *kămăh* [𐤊𐤌𐤄|כמה], to describe himself feeling "faint" in the wilderness[582]. "Faint" and "exhausted" are synonyms. The noun form of *exhausted* is used by the Reptile entities as another of their many euphemisms for copulation.

TRANSLATED AS: concerning exhaustion [another euphemism of the Reptile entities for copulation]

~a Hebrew word untranslated in the KJV~
Our word here, *ăt* [𐤀𐤕 |"את"][H855], has been explained. Injection pipetting is expressed here as IVF as a verb.

TRANSLATED AS: in-vitro fertilized

every
Last seen in Verse 21 as "every" and in Verse 25 as "every thing", the word here is *kăl* [𐤊𐤋]. It is the two-letter contraction of the three-letter word, *kălăl* [𐤊𐤋𐤋]. It is usually associated with Strong's H3605; but it is H3634—*to complete (to make perfect)*. Here it is expressed as the infinitive of the verb.

TRANSLATED AS: to perfect′

herb
Seen in Verses 11 and 12 as, our word here is the same. It is *ōshĭb* [𐤏𐤔𐤁|עשב] [H6212]. The word means *to glisten* or *to be green*.

TRANSLATED AS: green

bearing seed
The mini-mystery of "bearing seed" is solved when we simply look up the Strong's numbers associated with the two words in the text: "𐤆𐤓𐤏 𐤆𐤓𐤏" (*zărō zărō*) [זרע זרע]. The first word is H2232—*to disseminate*. The second is H2233—*seed*[583]. It should be translated as the technical word for human seed—spermatozoa.

TRANSLATED AS: disseminated spermatozoa

which
This word has been explained earlier. We encountered the Reptile-being, "I-Dwell", in Verse 21. The word, *ăshĭr* [𐤀𐤔𐤓], is to be read as *ă·shĭrăh* [𐤀𐤔𐤓𐤄]. The root, *shĭrăh*, is translated as "dwelleth" in the King James

Bible in the Book of Daniel 2:22. The prefix, *ălăpf* [𐤀], is the first person singular pronoun, "I".

TRANSLATED AS: I-Dwell

is upon

First encountered in Verse 2, we saw this word in Verses 15 and 17, twice in Verse 20, and again in Verses 26 and 28—as "yoke". The word, *ōl* [𐤏𐤋], is H5923. It is the original text-writer's chosen description of the *fastening framework* of the phosphate-deoxyribose "*yoke*" of the nucleotides of the DNA molecule. Here the word is treated as a verb.

TRANSLATED AS: yoking

the face

The last time we saw this Hebrew word was in Verse 2—where it was cast in a role as "face". We saw it again in Verse 20 as "the open". It is the exact same word here, *pfān·ē* [𐤐𐤍𐤉]. It is traditionally cited as H6440 ("face"); *but*—that word's root, *pfānăh* |𐤐𐤍𐤄, also means "presence"[584]. The suffix, *yăd* [𐤉], is "my".

TRANSLATED AS: my presence

of all

We just saw the ancient word that appears here. It is *kăl* [𐤊𐤋]—the two-letter contraction of the three-letter word, *kălăl* [𐤊𐤋𐤋]. It is generally associated with Strong's H3605. Here it is H3634—*to complete (to make perfect)*, as the verb, to perfect′.

TRANSLATED AS: to perfect′

the earth

First seen in Verse 1, and as the last word of Verse 28, the word here is *hā·ărĕtz* [𐤄𐤀𐤓𐤑][H776]. It is a key, central, fundamental, and foundational concept (or *brag*) of the Reptile-beings. As explained, the word is traditionally defined as *ground* or *land*. It is *mis*translated. "Earth" isn't the context.

Our word here is read as “*hā·ă·rĕtz·ăh*” [𐤄]𐤑𐤓𐤀𐤄][H7521], “*to be pleased with, accomplish*”. The prefix *hāy* [𐤄] is “the”. The prefix *ălăpf* [𐤀] is “I”.

TRANSLATED AS: the I-Accomplish

and

Our word here, *ōōă·ăt* [𐤕𐤀𐤅|“ואת”][H855], has already been explained.

TRANSLATED AS: and in-vitro fertilization

every

Up to this point, each appearance of the word here, [*kăl* [𐤋𐤊], has been translated as “to make perfect”. Here, the word, *kăl,* is associated with Strong’s H3605, which is from H3634, “𐤋𐤋𐤊” (*kălăl*). It means *to complete (to make perfect)*. Our word here had it last letter, 𐤋, dropped by the original writer. Although the translation, “to make perfect”, could be used here, “to *properly* complete” is more in context with what is going on in this verse.

TRANSLATED AS: to properly complete

tree

The word in the text is *hā·ōtz* [𐤑𐤏𐤄|העץ]. When we consult the eminent Davidson Lexicon, the first definition of *ōtz* [𐤑𐤏] is “to close” and is linked to “the eyes” [Proverbs 16:30 is cited[585]]. A problem remains: the verb, “to close”, is no more in context here than a tree is.

Since *ōtz* [𐤑𐤏] is from the root, *ōtzăh* [𐤄𐤑𐤏][H6097], and the word in our text here has its own last letter dropped, we must look to another Hebrew word that appropriately fits the context. There is such a word, *ōtzăb* [𐤁𐤑𐤏] [H6087]—*to carve, i.e. to fabricate or fashion (in a bad sense)*[586]. As it turns out, *ōtzăb* [H6087], is a synonym of the first and second words of this chapter—*bĕra* [H1254], which also can mean *to form* or *to fashion*[587]. Just as the original text drops the last letter of the root the same practice will be followed here.

Here, “the fabrication”, refers to Reptilian entities’ over-time experimentation in their laboratories perfecting a species of self-replicating hybridized bipedal hominids.

TRANSLATED AS: the fabrication

which
The traditional translation of *ăshĭr* [𐤀𐤔𐤓] [H834] is “which”. That word is in context here.

TRANSLATED AS: which

is the
We’ve seen this Hebrew word before—not as “is the” but as “is in itself” in Verse 11. The Hebrew word is *bōō* [𐤁𐤅|בו]. There is no Strong’s number for it. It is a word with one a prefix, *bĕt* [𐤁], “in”, and one suffix, *ōōă* [𐤅], “it”.

TRANSLATED AS: in it

fruit
Again, “fruit” doesn’t fit the context here. We saw the word “fruit” in Verses 11 and 12, both in the context of “increase”, as *pfăr·ē* [𐤐𐤓𐤉|פרי]. The word in the text is the same. It is the root word itself with a commonly dropped last letter. The root word means *to bear fruit (literally or figuratively), to grow* or *to increase*[588]. The context here, however, is not about increase—it’s about growth. There’s a fabricated sperm cell inside a fabricated egg which grows into a mature hybrid which then has the ability to reproduce itself with its own kind—others of the opposite sex. The word choice is simply the present tense of *grow*. The word has a suffix, 𐤉—“my”.

TRANSLATED AS: grows my

of a tree
Many Hebrew root-words may act as a noun *or* as a verb. In this reappearance of *ōtz* [𐤏𐤑|עץ][H6087] the context is the same. The *fabrication* is the DNA-manipulated spermatozoon (sperm cell) injected into the female hominid ovum (egg) through the entities’ program of *in-vitro fertilization* with an injecting pipette.

TRANSLATED AS: fabrication

yielding seed

As you may already suspect, “yielding seed” is from the exact same Hebrew words, *zărō zărō*, as “bearing seed”. Spelled the ancient way (as well as in “modern”), the words are: 𐤆𐤓𐤏 𐤆𐤓𐤏 |זרע זרע. The word *yielding* [𐤆𐤓𐤏|זרע] is H2232—*to disseminate* (here as *future tense*). The word *seed* [𐤆𐤓𐤏|זרע] is H2233—*seed*[589]. Here, the translation is the technical word for human seed. The auxiliary (or “helping”) verb, “will”, is utilized here.

TRANSLATED AS: will disseminate spermatozoa

to you

Again, as may be suspected (or expected), the Hebrew word here for “to you” is the exact same word as we had a good long look at when considering the previous appearance of “you”. Our word here is *lă·kăm* [𐤋𐤊𐤌]. Its root-word is *kămăh* [𐤊𐤌𐤄] [H3642]—*to pine after* or *to long for*. Here we have yet another dropped final letter from the root-word in the text. In Psalm 63:1, King David uses the same word, *kămăh* [𐤊𐤌𐤄] to express what *The Interlinear Bible* puts as, “my soul faints for you”[590]. Since “faints” is in context of the Judean wilderness—King David is thirsty and exhausted. We use a synonym of the verb *kămăh*: *to be exhausted*—though used as a noun.

The concept of *exhaustion* represents another euphemism that the entities use—particularly for the aftermath of copulation. The prefix, *lămĕd* [𐤋], is *in regard to*.

TRANSLATED AS: in regard to exhaustion [a euphemism used by the Reptile-entities for copulative aftermath]

it shall be

Here the word in the text is *ēă·hēăh* [𐤉𐤄𐤉𐤄|יהיה][H1961]. It is from the root word, “*to be*”. No dropped letters in this root. The word’s grammar is simple. The prefix, *yăd* [𐤉], is “it”. The words “to be” may be expressed in English as “is”.

TRANSLATED AS: it is

for meat

To be "for meat" is to have something to eat. That, however, is not in context here. An examination of the word in the text shows it to be *lă·ăkăl·ăh* [𐤋𐤀𐤊𐤋𐤄|לאכלה]. Here's the inevitable *however*: the words *meat*, *food*, and *eat* are nowhere in sight of the actual context of the entire verse and chapter.

We must look for another easily spotted root word that *is* in context. Such a word just *pops out* when we shift our vision to see the word with its letters rearranged: *lă·ă·kălăh.*

The root, *kălăh* | 𐤊𐤋𐤄, is Strong's H3617, and means *to finish,* or, *to be complete*. The word's first prefix *lămĕd* [𐤋] is *in regard to*. Its second prefix, *ălăpf* [𐤀], is "I".

TRANSLATED AS: in regard to I-Complete

A researched translation of the ancient Hebrew Genesis 1:29—
And strange-biological-entities declared, "Consider this: I have given you my concerning-exhaustion [*genetically engineered drive to copulate*] in-vitro fertilized to perfect′ green disseminated spermatozoa (of) I-Dwell—yoking my presence to perfect′ the I-Accomplish; and in-vitro fertilized to properly complete the fabrication [*hybridized sperm inside a hybridized egg*] which in it grows. My fabrication [*the mature hybrid being*] will disseminate spermatozoa in regard to exhaustion [*copulation*]. It is in regard to I-Complete."

Genesis 1:29—in plain English

- ☆ The entities consider that the hybrid species has been given, via IVF, the ability to pass along perfect Reptilian DNA.
- ☆ The perfected Reptilian DNA represents them in each future procreated member of the hybrid species.
- ☆ The perfected passing-along of DNA is The I-Accomplish.

☆ Through IVF, the DNA-modified sperm and egg are fabricated to pass along the Reptilian DNA through the newly fabricated hybrids' sexual activity.

☆ The entire wrapped-up technical aspect of in-vitro fertilization of their DNA modifications to the hominids' sperm and egg are referred to as I-Complete.

The KJV of Genesis 1:30 (*first phrase*)—
And to every beast of the earth, and to every fowl of the air,

Ancient Hebrew Anatomic Alphabet writing of that phrase—
ולכל חית הארץ ולכל עוף השמים

An actual translation *with researched explanations below*—
"And in regard to complete alive!—the I-Accomplish. And in regard to complete exhaustion [*copulation*]—The-Amazements.

The KJV of Genesis 1:30 (*second phrase*)—
and to every thing that creepeth upon the earth,

Ancient Hebrew Anatomic Alphabet writing of that phrase—
ולכל רומש על הארץ

An actual translation *with researched explanations below*—
And in regard to complete Reptilian yoke—the I-Accomplish.

The KJV of Genesis 1:30 (*third phrase*)—
wherein there is life, I have given every green herb for meat:

Ancient Hebrew Anatomic Alphabet writing of that phrase—
אשר בו נפש חיה את כל ירק עשב לאכלה

An actual translation *with researched explanations below*—
I-Dwell in her. Refresh. Revive. (An) injecting pipette completes:
it spit green in regard to I-Complete.

The KJV of Genesis 1:30 (*fourth phrase*)—
and it was so.

Ancient Hebrew Anatomic Alphabet writing of that phrase—
ויהי כן

An actual translation *with researched explanations below*—
And it is true."

The Researched Explanations—

and to every
We encountered this root word back in Verse 28 when we looked at "*of all*". We saw *kăl* [𐤊𐤋]—the two-letter contraction of the three-letter word, *kălăl* [𐤊𐤋𐤋]. Generally associated with Strong's H3605, it is H3634—*to complete (to make perfect), the whole—hence, all or every*. The definition "to make perfect" fits the context of Verse 28. "To complete" appears to better fit the context throughout this verse. Our word here, *ōōă·lă·kăl* [𐤅𐤋𐤊𐤋], has two prefixes we have seen often before. The first, the letter *ōōă* [𐤅], is "*and*"; and the second, *lăměd* [𐤋], as "*in regard to*".

TRANSLATED AS: and in regard to complete

beast
Last seen in Verse 25, the word is *khēt* [𐤇𐤉𐤕][H2421—*alive, life, raw (flesh)*]. Here, in this verse, the first two letters of the root 𐤇𐤉𐤄 are used with a 𐤕 suffix—which is an exclamatory emphatic. In English, our exclamatory emphatic is an exclamation point(!)

TRANSLATED AS: alive!

of the earth
First seen in Verse 1, and as the last word of Verse 28, and in Verse 29, the word here is *hā·ărětz* [𐤄𐤀𐤓𐤑][H776]. It is a foundational concept of these strange-biological-entities. The word is simply misrepresented as "earth". Our word here is read as "*hā·ă·rětz·ăh*" [𐤄]𐤄𐤀𐤓𐤑][H7521], with a dropped final letter, *hay* [𐤄]. It means "*to be pleased with, accomplish*". The prefix *hāy* [𐤄] is "the"; and the *ălăpf* [𐤀] is the pronoun, "I".

TRANSLATED AS: the I-Accomplish

and to every

We encountered the root word here three words previous. The word here is the exact same word, *ōōă·lă·kăl* [𐤅𐤋𐤊𐤋].

TRANSLATED AS: and in regard to complete

fowl

This root word, *ō·ōōpf* [𐤏𐤅𐤐][H5889/5889], has appeared in this chapter as *flight* and as *faint*. We first saw this word in Verse 20—where a full explanation was given. The context here is "copulation". Nothing is in flight here. "Exhaustion" is one of the strange-biological-entities' *code-words*, or euphemisms, for copulation. In Verse 28 we have the word *kămăh* [𐤊𐤌𐤄] [H3642] as a synonym of this euphemism.

TRANSLATED AS: exhaustion [after copulation]

of the air

The Hebrew word here was first seen in Verse 1 and last seen in Verse 28, as *hā·shĭm·ēm*— "of the air". The definition is the root, Strong's H8074 [𐤔𐤌𐤌]—*to stun, to devastate, to be astonished,* or *an amazement*. The word here is *hā·shĭm·ēm* [𐤄𐤔𐤌𐤉𐤌]. The prefix is *hāy* [𐤄]—*the*; and the suffix is *"-ēm"* [-𐤉𐤌]—a pluralizer.

TRANSLATED AS: the amazements

and to every thing

We encountered exact same word here as the first word of this verse. The word here is *ōōă·lă·kăl* [𐤅𐤋𐤊𐤋].

TRANSLATED AS: and in regard to complete

that creepeth

This sixth appearance of a *creeping creeper* creeping or moving is its final appearance in this first chapter of Genesis. Each time previously, Strong's H7431 (*a reptile*), appeared as *rĕmĕsh* [𐤓𐤌𐤔]. It appeared by itself in Verse 25. It appeared as 𐤄𐤓𐤌𐤔𐤕 in Verses 21 and 28. It appeared as 𐤅𐤓𐤌𐤔

in Verse 24; and as 𐤄𐤓𐤌𐤔 in Verse 26. Here we have the root with the insertion-letter, *ōōă* [𐤅], as *rōōmĕsh* [𐤓𐤅𐤌𐤔]. An inserted letter, (such as a 𐤅 or a 𐤆), is put into a word's root to alter its meaning. The context here determines that the word, as a collective noun, is in its possessive form. The word, Remeshian, would be its *transliteration.* The word, Reptilian, is its exact translation.

TRANSLATED AS: Reptilian

upon

Seen as recently in Verse 29 as *upon* and *every*, the word in the text is still *ōl* [𐤏𐤋][Strong's H5923]. It is the ancient text-writer's word for the *fastening framework* of the phosphate-deoxyribose "*yoke*" of the nucleotides of the DNA molecule.

TRANSLATED AS: yoke

the earth

The Hebrew word here has been thoroughly explained multiple times—as recently as a few words previous. The word here is *hā·ărĕtz* [𐤄𐤀𐤓𐤑] H776]—read as "*hā·ă·rĕtz·ăh*" [𐤄]𐤄𐤀𐤓𐤑] [H7521]. It means "*to be pleased with, accomplish*". The prefix *hāy* [𐤄] is "the"; and the *ălăpf* [𐤀] is "I".

TRANSLATED AS: the I-Accomplish

wherein

The English word here is definitely on the laundry-list of relative pronouns and adjectives of words associated with the Hebrew word, *ăshĭr* [𐤀𐤔𐤓]—which is associated with Strong's H834. We encountered the Reptilian, "I-Dwell", in Verse 21, as the result of reading *ăshĭr* [𐤀𐤔𐤓] as *ă·shĭrăh* [𐤀𐤔𐤓𐤄]. That root, *shĭrăh,* is translated as "dwelleth" in the King James Bible in the Book of Daniel 2:22. The prefix, *ălăpf* [𐤀], is the first person singular pronoun, "I". The verb, dwell, has a double meaning: the fact of dwelling, as portions of his DNA, in the hominid hybrids' genome, and literally dwelling inside a hominid female while copulating.

TRANSLATED AS: I-Dwell

there is

Razor sharp readers will recall the Hebrew word, *bōō* [𐤅𐤁|בו], in Verse 11 as "*is in itself*". Those words, as well as "*there is*" are strictly for the convenience of language experts who just aren't that much into allowing the Hebrew *just to say what it says.*

This word won't be found in any Strong's dictionary of Hebrew. Why? It is made of a prefix, *bĕt* [𐤁], (meaning "*in*") superglued to a suffix, *ōōă* [𐤅], which may be *he* (or *him*), *she* (or *her*), or *it*. Owing to what's going on in the verse here, the translated pronoun of choice is "*her*". In an explanation of the root, "𐤅𐤀𐤁" (*băōō*), by Davidson[591], it can mean *to have intercourse with* or *to have connection with a woman*. Theological and academic experts take note: that's the context.

TRANSLATED AS: in her

life

There is more going on behind this four-letter English word than meets the eye at first (*or second*) blush. We encountered, back in Verse 20, this Hebrew word—*nōōpfāsh* [𐤔𐤐𐤍], which was the star of the English word, "*creature*". As it turned out there, and turns out here as well, we're talking about Strong's H5315—*to breathe, to breathe upon,* and *to be refreshed.* The word here is present tense. Note: The word "refresh" is another of their euphemisms for active copulation as well as to the feelings of euphoric refreshment associated with orgiastic copulation.

TRANSLATED AS: refresh

~a Hebrew word untranslated in the KJV~

We saw the Hebrew word that goes here in the ancient text back in Verse 20 as "*that hath life*". The word in the text here is *khēăh* [𐤄𐤉𐤇|חיה]

[H2421]—*to live, to revive,* or, *to be vigorous*. We may expect "*life*" when we've got IVF and copulation as the verse's contexts.

The preferred translated word comes from among the word's definitions. This translation presumes that the word selection here more accurately characterizes the Reptilian hominid entities' reaction to the orgasm reflex during copulation.

TRANSLATED AS: revive

I have given
The Hebrew word that could express these English words simply is not in the ancient text here.

~a Hebrew word untranslated in the KJV~
The *ăt* [𐤀𐤕|"תא"][H855], has been explained multiple times here.

TRANSLATED AS: injecting pipette

every
The two-letter Hebrew word here is *kăl* [𐤊𐤋]. We saw its root in the explanation of the first word of this verse— *kălăl* [𐤊𐤋𐤋]. The word, *kălăl,* is associated with Strong's H3634—*to complete (to make perfect), the whole—hence, all or every*. Our translation has *to complete* in the present tense.

TRANSLATED AS: completes

green

Any reader would be entirely correct in thinking that we've seen this word before. We have. It's the translated word from the word "herb" earlier in the text. "Herb" is wrenched from the Hebrew word, *ōshĭb* [𐤏𐤔𐤁], back in Verses 11, 12, and 29. It's Strong's H6212—*to glisten* or *to be green*. As may be quickly guessed, that is *not* the word in the text here.

The word here is *ĕă·rĕqw* [𐤉𐤓𐤒|ירק]. In Bibles which associate Strong's numbers with words, H3418 is the one for this word[592]. When you look up that number you'll find the wiggly way traditionalists distance themselves from H3417. If you look up Strong's H3418, you will read that it is *"from 3417 (in the sense of acuity of color)"*. You will then see: *"pallor"*, *"yellowish green of young and sickly vegetation"*, *"grass"*, and *"green thing"*. Well, there's their "green". Please—*not so fast.*

When you look one entry back—to H3417 [יָרַק]—you'll see two definitions: *to spit*; and you'll also see "but". That Strong's number is only represented three times in the King James Bible—twice as *spit.* The other time it appears right along beside "spit" in the Book of Numbers 12:14 *in the context of someone spitting.*

You know by now that in this ancient biblical text there are root words with dropped last letters all over the place. This place is no exception. If you look up Strong's H7556 you'll find our actual root word here for *to spit.* It is *rĕqwōōqw* [𐤓𐤒𐤒 | רקק]. Knowing that's our actual root word here we can now properly translate the word in the text, *ĕă·rĕqw* [𐤉𐤓𐤒].

Our root is *rĕqwōōqw* [𐤓𐤒𐤒] with a dropped final letter, *qwōōpf* [𐤒]. The prefix letter here is, *yăd* [𐤉], a third-person singular pronoun, *he* or *it*—rarely *she*. Here, it is "it".

TRANSLATED AS: it spit

herb

From the reference to our previous treatment of *ōshĭb* [𐤏𐤔𐤁] [H6212], the word means *to glisten* or *to be green*. Note: "green" is supposedly conveyed through association with the color of herbs.

TRANSLATED AS: green

for meat

The word here is the exact same as the last word of Verse 29's "for meat". It is *lă·ă·kălăh* [𐤋𐤀𐤊𐤋𐤄]—from H3617, *to be complete.*

TRANSLATED AS: in regard to I-Complete

and it was so

The two ancient words here are *ōōă·ē·hē kăn* [𐤅𐤉𐤄𐤉 𐤊𐤍]. They are associated with H1961 and H3651. The prefix, *ōōă* [𐤅], is "and"; the *yăd* [𐤉] is the *second* prefix, “it”; and the root fragment, *hē* [𐤄𐤉], is “is”. The second word, *kăn* [𐤊𐤍] can mean “so”; but it also can mean “thus” and “true”.

TRANSLATED AS: and it is true

A researched translation of the ancient Hebrew Genesis 1:30—
“And in regard to complete alive!—
the I-Accomplish.
And in regard to complete exhaustion [*copulation aftermath*]—
The-Amazements.
And in regard to complete Reptilian yoke—
The I-Accomplish.
I-Dwell in her. Refresh. Revive.
(An) injecting pipette completes: it spit green in regard to
I-Complete.
And it is true.”

Genesis 1:30—in plain English

- ☆ The Reptilian entities refer to The I-Accomplish as being completely alive as it transmits their DNA-segments.
- ☆ They refer to completed copulation as The-Amazements.
- ☆ The Reptilian called *I-Dwell* refers to being inside of a female hominid.
- ☆ The Reptilian is refreshed and revived as a result of having been inside of her.
- ☆ He says that their injecting pipette “spit” green. He says that completes the I-Complete.
- ☆ The account states that what they are relating is true.

The KJV of Genesis 1:31 (*first phrase*)—
And God saw every thing that he had made,

Ancient Hebrew Anatomic Alphabet writing of that phrase—
𐤅𐤉𐤓𐤀 𐤀𐤋𐤄𐤉𐤌 𐤀𐤕 𐤊𐤋 𐤀𐤔𐤓 𐤏𐤔𐤄

An actual translation *with researched explanations below*—
And strange-biological-entities saw (an) injecting pipette completes: I-Dwell prepared.

The KJV of Genesis 1:31 (*second phrase*)—
and, behold, it was very good.

Ancient Hebrew Anatomic Alphabet writing of that phrase—
𐤅𐤄𐤍𐤄 𐤈𐤅𐤁 𐤌𐤀𐤃

An actual translation *with researched explanations below*—
And consider this—good intermixing [*a DNA-manipulated sperm cell into a DNA-manipulated female hominid egg cell*].

The KJV of Genesis 1:31 (*third phrase*)—
And the evening and the morning were the sixth day.

Ancient Hebrew Anatomic Alphabet writing of that phrase—
𐤅𐤉𐤄𐤉 𐤏𐤓𐤁 𐤅𐤉𐤄𐤉 𐤁𐤒𐤓 𐤉𐤅𐤌 𐤄𐤔𐤔𐤉

An actual translation *with researched explanations below*—
And it is to interbreed and it is to research it-and-them [*the ovum (egg cell) is the "it", and the mass of sperm cells is the "them"*]—the white stuff [*a mass of human semen*].

The Researched Explanations—

and saw

TRANSLATED AS: and saw

God
As previously explained, the word in the text is *ălăh·ēm*. The wording "strange-biological-entities", or variants, is used here.

TRANSLATED AS: strange-biological-entities

~a Hebrew word untranslated in the KJV~
The *ăt* [𐤀𐤕|את][H855], has been explained in detail.

TRANSLATED AS: injecting pipette

every thing
Last seen in the preceding verse as "every", the two-letter Hebrew word here is *kăl* [𐤊𐤋]. The root word is *kălăl* [𐤊𐤋𐤋]—Strong's H3634—*to complete (to make perfect)*. Present tense is used here.

TRANSLATED AS: completes

that
This English word here is definitely on the laundry-list of relative pronouns and adjectives of words associated with the Hebrew word, *ăshĭr* [𐤀𐤔𐤓|אשר] [Strong's H834]. We encountered the Reptilian being, "I-Dwell", in Verse 21, as the result of reading *ăshĭr* [𐤀𐤔𐤓] as *ă·shĭrăh* [𐤀𐤔𐤓𐤄]. That root, *shĭrăh*, is translated as "dwelleth" in the King James Bible in the Book of Daniel 2:22. The prefix, *ălăpf* [𐤀], is the first person singular pronoun, "I".

TRANSLATED AS: I-Dwell

he had made
The reader might be impressed by a complete listing of all the words used in the KJV for the word, *ōshăh* [𐤏𐤔𐤄|עשה] [H6213]. Strong's gives us a long list of words across a spectrum of definitions. Strictly speaking, the root is "to do" or "to make". Included in the KJV for the word, *ōshăh*, are:

did, perform, occupied, committed, deal, offer, work, observe, and *prepared.* Our preferred word is found in the Book of Exodus[593]. Note: there is no "he" prefix on the word here. The translation is in past tense, just as it is in that King James Version Bible verse.

TRANSLATED AS: prepared

and behold
The *heavy lifting* word here, *hānōōăh* [𐤄𐤍𐤄][H2007, H2008, *and* H2009], was explained early on in Verse 29. The word was translated as "consider this". Here, the word has an "and" prefixed to it, as, *ōōă·hānōōăh* [𐤅𐤄𐤍𐤄|והנה].

TRANSLATED AS: and consider this

it was
The Hebrew word that could express these words is not in the ancient text here.

good
The word, *thōōb* [𐤈𐤅𐤁|טוב][H2896] means "good" in the widest sense. Here it will be given as traditionally translated—in the sense of the practical necessity of the SBE's DNA manipulation and genetic engineering.

TRANSLATED AS: good [as in good technical solutions]

very

When Strong's H3966 is consulted, even before we get to the business of what the word means, we are informed that the word, "meh·ode" ["מאד"], is *from the same as H181*[594]. Only then are we offered *vehemence* and *vehemently*, followed by other contenders—including *diligently, exceedingly, greatly,* and *very.*

When we look up H181 ["ood"|"אוד"], we find a verb phrase, *to rake together*[595]. But then we're offered a noun, *a poker (for turning or gathering embers)* as an example.

How do we resolve the gulf between *very* and *raking together*? That is done by reading the word here in the text as *mĕ·ăd* [𐤃𐤀𐤌 |מאד]. The letter *mĕm* [𐤌] is a utility determinative; and *ăd* [𐤃𐤀] is our root word [𐤃𐤅𐤀] with its middle letter, 𐤅, dropped. What, then, *is* the utility of raking together? Its utility is intermixture—raking together (intermixing) a DNA-manipulated sperm cell into a DNA-manipulated female hominid egg cell. That's the operational definition of *in-vitro fertilization* using an injecting pipette.

The use of the word *mĕ·ăd* is going to be a synonym of a word coming up in the text—*ōrĕb* [𐤁𐤓𐤏]—*to intermix*, (that is, to interbreed). It is also part of the intended internal word-play.

TRANSLATED AS: intermixing [a DNA-manipulated sperm cell into a DNA-manipulated female hominid egg cell]

and the

The word here is *ōōă·ē·hē* [𐤉𐤄𐤉𐤅][H1961] from the root, "to be". The prefix here is *ōōă* [𐤅], "and"; the second prefix is *yăd* [𐤉], "it".

TRANSLATED AS: and it is

evening

Yes, the word *ōrĕb* [𐤁𐤓𐤏] is generally given as "evening" [H6153]. Here is given as H6148—*braid* and *intermix*—in the sense of mingled seed. The previous word, "*mĕ·ăd* |" 𐤃𐤀𐤌" is a synonym—as word play by the ancient writers. Here means to "interbreed".

TRANSLATED AS: interbreed

and the

The word here is the same as appeared two words ago: *ōōă·ē·hē* [𐤉𐤄𐤉𐤅]. The prefix is "and". This is the same word as "*and the*" previously explained.

TRANSLATED AS: and it is

morning
Yes, the word *bĕqwōōr* [𐤓𐤒𐤁|בקר] can be "morning". That's Strong's Number H1242; but the eminent authority, Dr. Strong, tells us that H1242 is derived from H1239 [𐤓𐤒𐤁], which is *to break forth, to search, to seek out.* H1240 is *to seek* or *to inquire* in all five places in the text. Strong's H1241 is *cattle, herds, oxen,* and *bullocks.* The definition, "seek out", is being treated as *to research.*

TRANSLATED AS: to research

were the
These words do not appear at this place in the ancient text.

day
This word is the same seen twice in Verse 5, once in Verse 8, once in Verse 19, and once in Verse 23.

TRANSLATED AS: it-and-them [the ovum (egg cell) is the "it", and the mass of sperm cells is the "them"]

sixth

Yes, the concept of "sixth" in the ancient text generally appears as *shĭshē* [𐤉𐤔𐤔]. That's Strong's H8345; and derived (so we're informed) from H8337 [𐤔𐤔|*shĭsh*], which is "six". *But*, if you look back one entry, to H8336 (*same spelling*), you'll see "*bleached stuff—white linen or marble*"[596]. White stuff such as bleached linen (or, more rarely, white marble) appears some 42 times in the Hebrew Bible[597]. Another translation problem is that the word, "sixth", isn't the context here. What *is* in context here is whiteish hominid semen which contains a mass of spermatozoa.

Our word here is *hā·shĭsh·ē* [𐤉𐤔𐤔𐤄|השׁשׁי][H8336]—*bleached stuff.* The prefix here is *hāy* [𐤄], *the.* The suffix is *yăd* [𐤉]—which can make a word plural—as it stands for the contraction of the common plural suffix, "𐤌𐤉-" (-ēm)[598]. The root is, "white stuff"—as is the color of *bleached linen.*

TRANSLATED AS: the white stuff [a mass of hominid semen]

A researched translation of the ancient Hebrew Genesis 1:31—
And strange-biological-entities saw (that an) injecting pipette completes: I-Dwell prepared. And consider this—good intermixing [*a DNA-manipulated sperm cell into a DNA-manipulated female hominid egg cell*]. And it is to interbreed; and it is to research it-and-them [*the ovum (egg cell) is the "it", and the mass of sperm cells is the "them"*]—the white stuff [*a mass of hominid semen*].

Genesis 1:31—in plain English

- ☆ The Reptilian called *I-Dwell* completed the IVF project.
- ☆ The beings refer to their interbreeding project as being good.
- ☆ They repeat that their intention is to interbreed and to research the relationship between the solitary egg and the mass of spermatozoa which encounters it.

The conclusions of the hybridization project
[Chapter 2, Verses 1, 2 *and* 3]

The KJV of Genesis 2:1 (*first phrase*)—
Thus the heavens and the earth were finished,

Ancient Hebrew Anatomic Alphabet writing of that phrase—
𐤅𐤉𐤊𐤋𐤅 𐤄𐤔𐤌𐤉𐤌 𐤅𐤄𐤀𐤓𐤑

An actual translation *with researched explanations below*—
And it [*the Reptilian, I-Dwell*] completed it [*the DNA-manipulated hybrid*]: The Amazements and the I-Accomplish;

The KJV of Genesis 2:1 (*second phrase*)—
and all the host of them

Ancient Hebrew Anatomic Alphabet writing of that phrase—
𐤅𐤊𐤋 𐤑𐤁𐤀𐤌

An actual translation *with researched explanations below*—
and completed their reptilian-hominid hybrid slave-mass.

The Researched Explanations—

thus...were finished

The KJV phrase here requires reformatting. The first Hebrew word in this verse incorporates both the idea of "thus" and the idea of "finished". The word here is *ōōă·ē·kăl·ōō* [𐤅𐤉𐤊𐤋𐤅|ויכלו][H3615 or H3617]—*to be finished; a completion.*

This root word was encountered in Verse 30 as, "*lă·ă·kălăh*|𐤋𐤀𐤊𐤋𐤄", translated as, "in regard to I-Complete". Thus, we can see there the complete root word (𐤊𐤋𐤄).

The first prefix on our word in the text is *ōōă* [𐤅], "and". The second prefix is *yăd* [𐤉], *it*—which we take as the text's own references to the

Reptilian, "I-Dwell". The root word, as can be readily seen, had its last letter [𐤄] dropped. The suffix is also the letter, *ōōă* [𐤅], which can be "him" or "it". This translation could handle either pronoun; but the choice is "it"—as a reference to the DNA-manipulated hybrid—our ancestor of our own deep past.

TRANSLATED AS: and it [the Reptilian scientist, I-Dwell] completed it [the DNA-manipulated hybrid]

the heavens

The last time we saw this very same Hebrew word was in Verse 28 where had the starring role in "of the air". We first saw this word in Verse 1 and again in Verse 26, as *hā·shĭm·ēm,* where it was "of the heavens". The definition of Strong's H8074 [𐤔𐤌𐤌] is *to stun, to devastate, to be astonished,* or *an amazement*. Our word here is *hā·shĭm·ēm* [𐤄𐤔𐤌𐤉𐤌]. The prefix is *hāy* [𐤄]—*the*; and the suffix is *"-ēm"* [𐤉𐤌-], which makes the word plural.

TRANSLATED AS: the amazements

and the earth

Last sighted in Verse 30, this word has been explained previously. Our word here is read as *"ōōă·hā·ă·rĕtz·ăh"* [𐤄]𐤅𐤄𐤀𐤓𐤑| [ה]והארצ][H7521], with a dropped final letter, *hay* [𐤄]. It means *"to be pleased with, accomplish"*. The first prefix *ōōă* [𐤅] is "and". The second is *hāy* [𐤄], as "the". The third prefix, *ălăpf* [𐤀], is "I".

TRANSLATED AS: and the I-Accomplish

and all

The Hebrew root word here is the same as the first word of this verse. The word here is *ōōă·kăl* [𐤅𐤊𐤋][H3634—root, 𐤊𐤋𐤋—*to complete (to make perfect] properly, the whole—hence, all or every*. The prefix, *ōōă* [𐤅], is *and.*

TRANSLATED AS: and completed

the host of them

There is no "the" here on this Hebrew word—*tzăbăm* [𐤑𐤁𐤀𐤌|צבאם]. In English, the root, *tzăbă*, usually becomes "host"—as in "the host of heaven". This word is associated with Strong's H6633 [𐤑𐤁𐤀 (*tzăbă*)]; and means, *to mass (an army or servants).* Note: to be a servant is to be a slave. If we look at H6632 we find the root, *tzăb* (𐤑𐤁). What's interesting about this root? Other than meaning, "*to establish*", it means "*also a species of lizard [as an order of reptile]*"[599]. For this translation, the meaning of *tzăb*| 𐤑𐤁 is overlaid on the meaning of *tzăbă*| 𐤑𐤁𐤀. The suffix, *mĕm* [𐤌] is *their* or *them.*

TRANSLATED AS: their reptilian-hominid hybrid slave-mass

A researched translation of the ancient Hebrew Genesis 2:1—

And it [*the Reptilian, I-Dwell*]-completed it [*the DNA-manipulated hybrid*]: The Amazements and the I-Accomplish; and completed their reptilian-hominid hybrid slave-mass.

Genesis 2:1—in plain English

- ☆ The Reptilian scientist named *I-Dwell* completed their DNA-manipulated hybrid projects.
- ☆ The Reptilians referred to their hybridization projects as The Amazements and The I-Accomplish.
- ☆ *I-Dwell* also contributed to their completion of the DNA-manipulated reptilian-hominid hybridized slave-beings.

The KJV of Genesis 2:2 (*first phrase*)—
And on the seventh day God ended

Ancient Hebrew Anatomic Alphabet writing of that phrase—
𐤅𐤉𐤊𐤋 𐤀𐤋𐤄𐤉𐤌 𐤁𐤉𐤅𐤌 𐤄𐤔𐤁𐤉𐤏𐤉

An actual translation *with researched explanations below*—
And it [*the Reptilian, I-Dwell*] completed (the) strange-biological-entities' in-it-[*the hominid egg cell*]-and-them [*hominid sperm cells*]: The-Completions.

The KJV of Genesis 2:2 (*second phrase*)—
his work which he had made;

Ancient Hebrew Anatomic Alphabet writing of that phrase—
𐤌𐤋𐤀𐤊𐤕𐤅 𐤀𐤔𐤓 𐤏𐤔𐤄

An actual translation *with researched explanations below*—
From in-regard-to I-break-it-in-pieces [*the Twisting Spiral, aka the DNA molecular structure*]—I-Dwell [*CRISPR CAS-9*] cut;

The KJV of Genesis 2:2 (*third phrase*)—
and he rested on the seventh day

Ancient Hebrew Anatomic Alphabet writing of that phrase—
𐤅𐤉𐤔𐤁𐤕 𐤁𐤉𐤅𐤌 𐤄𐤔𐤁𐤉𐤏𐤉

An actual translation *with researched explanations below*—
and it [*the Twisting Spiral—aka the DNA molecular structure*] broken into pieces in it-and-them [*the ovum (egg cell) is the "it", and the mass of sperm cells is the "them"*]: The-Completions.

The KJV of Genesis 2:2 (*fourth phrase*)—
from all his work which he had made.

Ancient Hebrew Anatomic Alphabet writing of that phrase—
𐤌𐤊𐤋 𐤌𐤋𐤀𐤊𐤕𐤅 𐤀𐤔𐤓 𐤏𐤔𐤄

An actual translation *with researched explanations below*—
Completion: From in-regard-to I-break-it-in-pieces [*the Twisting Spiral—the DNA molecular structure*]: I-Dwell [*CRISPR CAS-9*] cut.

The Researched Explanations—

and on the seventh day God ended
—as rearranged in the Hebrew word order,
and ended God day on the seventh

and ended
The word here is virtually the same as the first word of Gen 2:1, but without the *ōōă* [𐤅] suffix. The root is *kălăl*| 𐤊𐤋𐤋. It is Strong's H3634—*to complete, to make perfect.* The ancient word here is *ōōă·ē·kăl* [𐤅𐤉𐤊𐤋]. The first prefix on our word in the text is *ōōă* [𐤅], *and.* The second prefix is *yăd* [𐤉], *it.*

TRANSLATED AS: and it [*the Reptilianian, I-Dwell*] completed

God
The word, *ălăh·ēm* [𐤀𐤋𐤄𐤉𐤌][H430], commonly translated "God". Here it is translated as "*strange-biological-entities*", though it could just as readily be translated as "aliens", or any strange variation.

TRANSLATED AS: strange-biological-entities

day
We have seen this word many times before—twice in Verse 5, once in Verse 8, once in Verse 19, once in Verse 23, and once in Verse 31. The context isn't

about any “day”. It is all about the Reptilians’ DNA-manipulative interventions which became the DNA-altered foundation of our own species[600-603]. Here, the word in the text is actually *bĕ·ē·ōō·m* [𐤁𐤉𐤅𐤌|ביום].

This word is particularly interesting. Its letters are not constructed around a “root word”. This word, as constructed, is a word-metaphor for the Reptilians’ hybridization program. Why? The word itself is a hybrid. It is made of four separate and readily identifiable grammatic elements—each previously used in the Reptilian’s ancient text and strategically and creatively combined to communicate exactly what they are doing here.

The word has a prefix, *bĕt* [𐤁], which may denote the following prepositions: *in, among, against, with, by, through, for,* and *because of*[604]. Its second letter generally appears as the prefix, *yăd* [𐤉]. It is a common prefix which denotes the third person singular subject pronoun “he” or “it” (sometimes “she”). Here, the prefix-letter means “it”[605].

In the context of the entirety of the entities’ *executive summary* (*Genesis One*) the “it” here refers to the ovum—the solitary egg of their laboratory homind female readied for conceptive penetration by one sperm cell among a roiling mass of sperm cells swimming toward the solitary egg cell—as visualized under electron microscopy.

The word’s third letter, *ōōă* [“wav”][𐤉|ו], is that of another common prefix—the conjunction “and”. (The sighting of the prefix “and” as a third prefix will be rarer than a hen’s tooth in traditional Hebrew grammar books.) Here, the entities are teaching *us* how their language functions. This translation has not presumed to tell the authors of the ancient text how their language is to function.

The word’s fourth and final letter, *mĕm* [𐤌|ם], is a common suffix which represents the third person plural object pronoun “them”[606]. The “them” refers to the mass of sperm cells surrounding the solitary ovum awaiting conceptive penetration by the fastest strongest swimmingest sperm cell.

TRANSLATED AS: in it [the hominid egg cell] and them [hominid sperm cells] *on the seventh*

Since the cardinal number "seventh" is not in context here we can afford to ignore the Strong's number associated with it. That number, though, is H7637—*seventh.* The nut of the actual word here, *hā·shĭb·ē·ō·ē* [𐤄𐤔𐤁𐤉𐤏𐤉|השביעי], is not that difficult to crack. The root word is *shĭbō* |𐤔𐤁𐤏. That word is a very busy homonym, as it has *seven* Strong's numbers associated with it[607].

Here's what will be found on the word's definition menu: *to fill to satisfaction, satisfaction, copiousness, to be complete, satiated, to swear,* and, *the cardinal number seven.* The most apt Strong's number for our word here is H7650—*to be complete*[608].

The grammar of the word is: prefix, 𐤄, as "the". The root, *shĭbō* [𐤔𐤁𐤏], has an inserted letter, 𐤉, which changes or alters the meaning. Here it is changed from a verb infinitive, *to complete*, into a noun, *completion.* It has a suffix, 𐤉, which can be the personal pronoun designator for *me* or *my.* Alternatively, it can make a word plural[609].

TRANSLATED AS: The-Completions

his work

The word in the text here is going to be a considerably tougher nut to crack. The word itself is a complex compound word, *mĕ·lă·ă·kăt·ōō.* In the ancient text it is "𐤌𐤋𐤀𐤊𐤕𐤅". It is spelled, *mĕm-lămĕd-ălăpf-kăpf-tōō-ōōă* [מלאכתו].

The KJV translation guys got their word, "work", from the root word, *mĕlă* [𐤌𐤋𐤀|מלא]. That root is associated with Strong's H4399—*(manner of) work*; as well as with H4390—*to fill.* The idea of "work" comes from the idea of *to fill* your hands with food. They got their word, "his", from the third person singular object pronoun suffix, *ōōă* [𐤅]. That treatment, however, left them with a nagging question: *What about the two letters* "𐤊𐤕" [*kăpf-tōō*|כת]? Their solution was to just blow them off.

This historic translation does not blow off letters: each letter is accounted for and explained. Each letter acts as an *information-unit*; and this translation does not want to miss any information any letter brings to a word.

As with many other word-puzzles (or puzzling words) in this verse the role of intrepid word-detective must be taken up. We must go where no word detection has gone before. So we must look for a root word, the first two letters of which are 𐤊𐤕 (*kăpf-tōō*)("כת"), and from which we may presume a final letter has been dropped. The word that fits that description which *is* in context is H3807 (כתת) [𐤊𐤕𐤕] (spelled *kăpf-tōō-tōō* and pronounced *kă·tōōt)—bruise, violently strike, beat to pieces,* or *break in pieces*[610].

Now the story that word's letters are telling us can begin to be told. We *could* use the KJV word, "work", and combine it with *break in pieces*. However, the first three letters of this word tell a much more interesting, *and accurate*, story. Let's allow each letter to give us its information so that the whole story of this word may be finally told—in its proper, and textually truthful, context.

We want to visualize the letters as *information-units*. The word in the ancient text is *mĕ·lă·ă·kăt·ōō* [𐤌𐤋𐤀𐤊𐤕𐤅]. Let's break it down: *mĕ* [𐤌] · *lă* [𐤋] · *ă* [𐤀] · *kăt* [𐤊𐤕] · *ōō* [𐤅].

Here, we only have one root word, *kă·tōōt* [𐤊𐤕𐤕][H3807]—*break in pieces*. The final letter *tōō* [𐤕] has been dropped by the original writer (or by a subsequent editor). That leaves three prefixes. We've seen each one of them before; and the suffix as well. The *mĕm* [𐤌] appears here as "from". The *lămĕd* [𐤋] appears here as "in regard to". The *ălăpf* [𐤀] appears here as the personal pronoun "I". The suffix, *ōōă* [𐤅], appears here as "it".

We have some consistent concepts here. One of them is DNA manipulation—*breaking DNA in pieces*. The "I" here is *I-Dwell*, the named and identified *Reptilian* scientist.

TRANSLATED AS: from in-regard-to I-break-in-pieces-it [the Twisting Spiral—aka the DNA molecular structure]

which

This English word, *which*, is definitely on the laundry-list of words associated with the Hebrew word, *ăshĭr* [𐤀𐤔𐤓][Strong's H834]. We encountered the Remesh (Reptilian) alien being, "I-Dwell", in Verse 21, as the result of reading *ăshĭr* [𐤀𐤔𐤓] as *ă·shĭrăh* [𐤀𐤔𐤓𐤄]. That root, *shĭrăh,* is translated as "dwelleth" in the King James Bible in the Book of Daniel 2:22. The prefix, *ălăpf* [𐤀], is the first person singular pronoun, "I".

TRANSLATED AS: I-Dwell

he had made

The verbs "to do" or "to make" are first out of the gate of Strong's H6213; but this word is like silly putty in the hands of translators, as it is used "*in the broadest sense and widest application*". It is that spirit that the word here—*ōshăh* [ᴲWO]—is translated (in context) as "cut". There is no prefix to indicate a personal pronoun. Nothing suggests that the word is meant to be in the past tense, (such an inserted letter Z or Y).

TRANSLATED AS: cut

and he rested on the seventh day
in actual word order, *and he rested day on the seventh*

and he rested

The word in the ancient text here is *ōōă·ē·shĭb·ĕt* [X9WZY|וישבת]. The *presumed* root word is X9W [שבת]. It is traditionally associated with Strong's H7673—*to repose* or *to rest*. Our word could be "rest" or "rested"—*if* it were in context. It's not.

As you may have already figured, some other root word must be considered. It must have as its first two letters, *shĭn* [W] and *bĕt* [9]. The word must fit the context. Another root word which can be easily located in any Strong's Hebrew Dictionary is the word *shĭbĕb* [99W|שבב]. That word is associated with H7616—*to break up; broken in pieces*[611].

So: our root here is *shĭbĕb*. Our word in the text is *ōōă·ē·shĭb·ĕt* [X9WZY |וישבת]. The first prefix is *ōōă* [Y], "and". The second prefix is *yăd* [Z], "it". The suffix, *tōō* [X], is an exclamatory emphatic—our exclamation point.

Here we have a synonym of the root word just considered: *kă·tōōt* [XXℽ][H3807]—*break in pieces*. The root word of choice is *shĭbĕb* [99W] [H7616]—*to break up; broken in pieces*. The appearance of this word is yet another instance and demonstration of the cohesive internal consistency of this ancient text—as well as the accuracy of this translation.

TRANSLATED AS: and it [the Twisting Spiral—aka the DNA molecular structure] broken into pieces!

day
This word was explained in the first phrase of this verse. Here the prefix, *bet*, is treated as "in".

TRANSLATED AS: in it-and-them [the ovum (egg cell) is the "it", and the mass of sperm cells is the "them"]

on the seventh
The word here is the same word as the previous "on the seventh".

TRANSLATED AS: The-Completions

from all
While we have seen the root word here, *kăl* [𐤋𐤋𐤊] [H3634 *to complete (to make perfect)*], we haven't seen it as it appears here—as *mĕ·kăl* [𐤋𐤊𐤌]. The prefix *mĕm* [𐤌] is a *utility determinative*. The utility of the verb, "to complete", is the noun, "completion".

We have just seen, in the form of the word traditionally offered up as "seventh", *hā·shĭb·ē·ō·ē* [𐤉𐤏𐤉𐤁𐤔𐤄], the root, "𐤏𐤁𐤔" (*shĭbō*) with an inserted letter, 𐤉 (*yăd*), which changes the meaning of the word from the verb, *to complete*, to its noun form, *completion*. The total effect is to lead us to the Reptilians' all-important concept of "completion"—by way of two different word-making routes—as if to reinforce that very concept by way of cleaver word-construction used in deliberate repetition.

TRANSLATED AS: completion

his work
This tough nut to crack was fully explained earlier in this verse.

TRANSLATED AS: from in-regard-to I-break-in-pieces-it [the Twisting Spiral—the DNA molecular structure]

which
This word was explained earlier in this verse. We encountered the Reptilian alien being, "I-Dwell", in Verse 21. We read *ăshĭr* [𐤓𐤔𐤀], the word in the text, as *ă·shĭrăh* [𐤄𐤓𐤔𐤀]. The root, *shĭrăh*, is translated as "dwelleth" in

the KJV Book of Daniel 2:22. The prefix, *ălăpf* [𐤀], is the first person singular pronoun, "I".

TRANSLATED AS: I-Dwell

he had made
This word was explained earlier in this verse. It is the exact same word, *ōshăh* [𐤏𐤔𐤄]—is translated (in context) as "cut". That may be done as this Hebrew word is used "*in the broadest sense and widest application*". Note: this word is the root only.

TRANSLATED AS: cut

A researched translation of the ancient Hebrew Genesis 2:2—
And it [*the Reptilian, I-Dwell*] completed (the) strange-biological-entities' in-it-[*inside the hominid egg cell*]-and-them [*hominid sperm cells*]: The-Completions. From in regard to I-break-it-in-pieces [*the Twisting Spiral, aka the DNA molecular structure*]—I-Dwell [*CRISPR CAS-9*] cut; and it [*the Twisting Spiral—aka the DNA molecular structure*] broken into pieces in it-and-them [*the ovum (egg cell) is the "it", and the mass of sperm cells is the "them"*]—The-Completions. Completion: From in regard to I-break-it-in-pieces [*the Twisting Spiral*]: I-Dwell cut.

Genesis 2:2—in plain English

- ☆ The Reptilians repeat that the one called *I-Dwell* completed their hybridization project—now termed The-Completions.
- ☆ The one called *I-Dwell* relates that he, himself, cut the hominid's *Twisting Spiral* (DNA) into pieces.
- ☆ *I-Dwell* considers himself to be inside DNA of the hybrid's egg cells as well as inside the DNA of its sperm cells.
- ☆ The Reptilian scientist, *I-Dwell*, refers to that project by the name they give it—The Completions.
- ☆ *I-Dwell* repeats that he completed the project, as he uses his personal identifier as the verse's punchline, *I-Dwell cut*.

The KJV of Genesis 2:3 (*first phrase*)—
And God blessed the seventh day,

Ancient Hebrew Anatomic Alphabet writing of that phrase—
𐤅𐤉𐤁𐤓𐤊 𐤀𐤋𐤄𐤉𐤌 𐤀𐤕 𐤉𐤅𐤌 𐤄𐤔𐤁𐤉𐤏𐤉

An actual translation *with researched explanations below*—
And strange-biological-entities expertly in-vitro fertilized it-and-them [*the egg cell is "it", and the mass of sperm cells is "them"*]: The-Completions.

The KJV of Genesis 2:3 (*second phrase*)—
and sanctified it: because that in it he had rested

Ancient Hebrew Anatomic Alphabet writing of that phrase—
𐤅𐤉𐤒𐤃𐤔 𐤀𐤕𐤅 𐤊𐤉 𐤁𐤅 𐤔𐤁𐤕

An actual translation *with researched explanations below*—
And it [*strange-biological-entity lab staff*] prepared its [*I-Dwell's*] injecting pipette because in it [*the hominid sperm cell*] had been broken apart [*having been DNA-manipulated*]!

The KJV of Genesis 2:3 (*third phrase*)—
from all his work which God created and made.

Ancient Hebrew Anatomic Alphabet writing of that phrase—
𐤌𐤊𐤋 𐤌𐤋𐤀𐤊𐤕𐤅 𐤀𐤔𐤓 𐤁𐤓𐤀 𐤀𐤋𐤄𐤉𐤌 𐤋𐤏𐤔𐤅𐤕

An actual translation *with researched explanations below*—
"Completion (is) from in-regard-to I-break-it-in-pieces [*to insert some Reptilian DNA segments into the DNA of the hominid species*]. I-Dwell." Cutting-entities attend to cutting-matters.

The Researched Explanations—

—as rearranged in the Hebrew word order,
and blessed God day the seventh

and blessed

The Hebrew word here is *ōōă·ē·bĕ·rĕk* [𐤊𐤓𐤁𐤉𐤅|ויברך]. It is traditionally associated with Strong's H1288, which is defined as, "*to kneel—by implication, to bless* or *to curse*". The translation problem is that there's no kneeling, blessing, or cursing here.

But we know that already. We saw this word as the first word in Verse 22; and it is fully explained there. The context in that verse was of the strange-biological-entities intending to increase the target species (that is, *us*) by the myriads—initially by way of in-vitro fertilization using an injecting pipette to insert a DNA-modified sperm cell into the ovum of our female hominid ancestor.

The first three letters are prefixes, and a Hebrew word can have one, two, or three prefixes. We've got *ōōă* [𐤅] as *and*, a *yăd* [𐤉] appearing as *it*; and the letter *bĕt* [𐤁] as *by*. The verb "is" is understood in the context of the word. The root word we are left with is "𐤊𐤓" [*rĕsh-kăpf*], which is from root "𐤄𐤊𐤓" [H7397—*softness*] and/or root "𐤊𐤊𐤓" [H7401—*soften*]. The word, "expertly", is being used as a synonym for the "softness" of technique necessary in handling the microscopic instruments as well as the sperm cell and the egg cell for their program of IVF.

TRANSLATED AS: and it [*the entities*] expertly

God

Although *ălăh·ēm* [𐤌𐤉𐤄𐤋𐤀][H430] has been covered many times previously, it bears repeating that "God" is not in context. A final note on the matter: This word is "אלהים" in the synagogue. It is not "Elohim" in this translation. That word is proprietary to Judaism. One *could* call them "alah" beings, as the word is in the plural. We will get "full disclosure" as to the true nature of the word's root, "ălăh", when Genesis Two is unleashed upon the world.

TRANSLATED AS: strange-biological-entities

~a Hebrew word untranslated in the KJV~
The word, *ăt* [𐤀𐤕|את][H855], has been explained multiple times. Here, the high-tech coulter of the injecting pipette is better expressed as IVF.

TRANSLATED AS: in-vitro fertilized

day
The word [𐤉𐤅𐤌|יום] is the same seen twice in Verse 5, once in Verse 8, once in Verse 19, once in Verse 23, and twice in the 2:2 Verse. The 𐤉 is "it". The 𐤅 is "and". The 𐤌 is "them".

TRANSLATED AS: it-and-them [the egg cell is "it", and the mass of sperm cells is "them"]

the seventh
We saw this word at the beginning of the last verse. The word here is *hā·shĭb·ē·ō·ē* [𐤄𐤔𐤁𐤉𐤏𐤉|השביעי]. The root word is *shĭbō* |𐤔𐤁𐤏, a homonym—as it has *seven* Strong's numbers. The most apt Strong's number for our word here is H7650—*to be complete*. The grammar of the word is: prefix, 𐤄, as "the". The root, "𐤔𐤁𐤏", has an inserted letter, 𐤉, which changes or alters the meaning. Here it is changed from a verb, *complete*, into a noun, *completion*. It has a suffix, 𐤉, which can make a word plural—where the final letter, *mĕm* [𐤌], of the common Hebrew pluralizer suffix (𐤉𐤌-) has been dropped.

TRANSLATED AS: The-Completions

and sanctified it
The majority of the times the Hebrew root word here is used in the Bible it is "sanctified" or "hallowed". The root, *qwōōdăsh* [𐤒𐤃𐤔|קדש][H6942], is "*to be clean—ceremonially or morally*"[612].

Our root, though most often "sanctified"[613], is "proclaim" at Second Kings 10:20; and "dedicated" at Second Kings 12:18. It is "bid" at Zephaniah 1:7. It is "prepare" in Jeremiah in the five places it appears; as well as at Joel 3:9 and Micah 3:5.

Our word here is *ōōă·ē·qwōōdăsh* [W𐤃𐤒ZY|ויקדש]. You may have already noticed the word's first prefix, the letter *ōōă* [Y], is "and". The second prefix, the letter *yăd* [Z], is the pronoun "it". We will use "prepare" as the translation of the root word here.

It may be interesting to note that our root word here is *also* Strong's H6945—*a (quasi) sacred person; a devotee (by prostitution) to licentious idolatry*. It is translated as "unclean" in the Bible's Book of Job 36:14.

TRANSLATED AS: and it prepared

~a Hebrew word untranslated in the KJV~
The word is a variation of a word seen often here. It is a variation of the word, *ăt* [X𐤀][H855]; and has already been explained.
Our word here is *ăt·ōō* [YX𐤀|אתו]. The suffix *ōōă* [Y] is "its".

TRANSLATED AS: its injecting pipette

because
We last saw this somewhat versatile Hebrew word in Verse 25 as "that". The word there, and here, is *kē* (pronounced "key") [Z𐤊]. It is Strong's H3588; and it can act to connect all kinds of causes in a sentence, including the words "for" and "because".

TRANSLATED AS: because

that in it

We have seen the Hebrew word here appear in Verse 11 as "*is in itself*" and in Verse 20 as "*there is*". At the center of these three variations is the two-letter word, *bōō* [Y𐤁|בו].This word may not be found in your dictionary of Biblical Hebrew because it consists of a prefix *bĕt* [𐤁] (*in*) attached to a suffix, *ōōă* [Y], which can be *he* (or *him*) or *it* (rarely *she* or *her*). Owing to what's going on in the verse, the pronoun of choice is "*it*".

The root, *băōō,* [Y𐤀𐤁], is explained by Davidson[614], as meaning *to have intercourse with* or *to have connection with a woman*. However, the context here is not of sexual intercourse but of IVF; and likewise, the connection with a woman does not have to do with sexual intercourse, but as the recipient of the Reptilian-modified sperm cell into the woman's egg cell to be surgically reinserted into the woman. That's the context here.

TRANSLATED AS: in it [the hominid sperm cell]

he had rested
We saw the phrase, "and he rested", in the previous verse. There, the ancient word was *ōōă·ē·shĭb·ĕt* [X9WZY|וישבת]. At this place in the text we have the word *shĭbĕt* [X9W]. As was the case in the previous use of the word our root here is *shĭbĕb* [H7616—*to break up; broken in pieces.* The KJV translators put the word in past tense with the helping verb, *had.* So will this translation. The word has no prefix; only the suffix, *tōō* [X]. It is an exclamatory emphatic—our exclamation point.

TRANSLATED AS: is broken into pieces! ***as*** had been broken apart [having been DNA-manipulated]!

from all
We saw this same word in the previous verse: *mĕ·kăl* [L ϡ M]. The root word is *kăl* [LLϡ][H3634 *to complete (to make perfect*]. The prefix *mĕm* [M] is a utility determinative. The utility of the verb, "to complete", is the noun, "completion".

TRANSLATED AS: completion

his work

This tough nut to crack was fully explained in the previous verse. This word is a complex compound word: *mĕ·lă·ă·kăt·ōō* |YXϡ≮LM|אכתו מל]. The root word is H3807 (כתת) [XXϡ] (spelled *kăpf-tōō-tōō* and pronounced *kă·tōōt*). It means *to bruise, violently strike, beat to pieces,* or *break in pieces*[615].

The total effect is to lead us to one of the Reptilians' all-important concepts—*breaking into pieces*—by way of two different word-making routes—as if to reinforce that very concept by way of cleaver word-construction used in deliberate repetition.

TRANSLATED AS: from in-regard-to I-break-in-pieces-it [to insert some Reptilian DNA segments into the DNA of the hominid species]

which

This word has been explained earlier. It is from the same root as the word, *shĭrăh*, above. We encountered the Remesh alien being, “I-Dwell”, in Verse 21. We read *ăshĭr* [𐤀𐤔𐤓] as *ă·shĭrăh* [𐤀𐤔𐤓𐤄]. The root, *shĭrăh*, is translated as “dwelleth” in the King James Bible in the Book of Daniel 2:22. The prefix, *ălăpf* [𐤀], is the first person singular pronoun, “I”.

TRANSLATED AS: I-Dwell

created

The word here is the same word “created” as from the first verse of Genesis One: *bĕră* [𐤁𐤓𐤀][H1254]. It can be “create”, “fashion”, or “form” It can also be “*cut up*” or “*carved out*”. Here it is treated in its present participle form.

TRANSLATED AS: cutting

God

The word, *ălăh·ēm* [𐤀𐤋𐤄𐤉𐤌][H430], is traditionally translated “God”. “God” is not in context. Strange Reptilian aliens are.

TRANSLATED AS: strange-biological-entities

and made

This root of the Hebrew word here was explained in the previous verse. It is *ōshăh* [𐤏𐤔𐤄]—translated as “cut”. Our word here is *lă·ōsh·ōōt* [𐤋𐤏𐤔𐤅𐤕|לעשות] [H6213]. The *lămĕd* (𐤋) here is being tweaked from *in-regard-to* to *attend to*. The root, “𐤏𐤔𐤄”, had its letter *hāy* [𐤄] dropped by the original writer. The suffix, *ōōt* [𐤅𐤕], can pluralize a word *or* can mean “*as related to*”. More simply put, it is translated here as, “*matters*”. Although “and made” may be about hybrids being made, it is more about designer cutting of DNA in a program of genetically engineering a hybridized being.

TRANSLATED AS: attend to cutting matters

A researched translation of the ancient Hebrew Genesis 2:3—

And strange-biological-entities expertly in-vitro fertilized it-and-them [*the egg cell is "it", and the mass of sperm cells is "them"*]: The-Completions. And it [*strange-biological-entity lab staff*] prepared its [*I-Dwell's*] injecting pipette because in it [*the hominid sperm cell*] had been broken apart [*having been DNA-manipulated*]!

"Completion (is) from in-regard-to I-break-it-in-pieces [*to insert some Reptilian DNA segments into the DNA of the hominid species*]. I-Dwell." Cutting-entities attend to cutting-matters.

Genesis 2:3—in plain English

☆ They reassert their expertise regarding their IVF technique—which they again refer to as The-Completions.

☆ They again recount that IVF was successful.

☆ They again refer to The-Completions as the result of cutting apart the hominid DNA.

☆ The Reptilian entity called *I-Dwell* causes his name to be attached to the entirety of the project.

☆ The Genesis document ends with its cold direct conclusion: Cutting-entities attend to cutting-matters.

Afterword

What may now be seen from the totality of what has been disclosed by ancient Reptilians themselves in this opening chapter of the first book of the Hebrew scriptural text is that it is all only about the hybridization project—the chief enterprise of the Reptilian biological entities.

This present volume represents a proclamation of emancipation from the informational and scriptural tyranny of the clerics of each of the religions that flows from out of the "Biblical Hebrew" and Greek Genesis fabrication. The clerics have had two-plus millennia to let humanity know what this foundational ancient scripture actually says. To cite a scriptural anecdote, they have been weighed—and are found wanting. Now that this ancient account is *back* in the world, the age of the Abrahamic tradition, based as it is on the Genesis Greek and "modern" Hebrew language laundering operation, has reached its expiration date.

Let's be frank: humanity has been kept illiterate; kept unable to read or to write the language of the foundational scriptural text that has formed the bedrock of Western civilization. This present volume has sought, in one swoop, to be the remedy . . . even if it has made any now-literate readers sick to the stomach and/or sick at heart. What should make us really sick, on the other hand, is in knowing that the priestcraft of clerics of all stripes has kept believers of all stripes in the thralldom of *pay, pray, and obey*.

The next volume of this series will permit anyone with interest and patience to read exactly how the particular and peculiar conjuring act—of mere words—has hidden these Reptilians and their own true historical account from curious and prying eyes for well over two millennia. All that information already exists in the form of extensive written research behind each word in Genesis chapters 2 and 3. That necessary sequel will lay out those chapters for all to see, inspect, or to debunk. The essential difficulty in debunking or disproving even the present volume is that what has been laid out here *is* what is in the ancient text.

Objections . . . with Responses

There will be objections to this translation. Several are presented.

- ☆ What makes you an authority on translating Hebrew?

Response: I have offered a full translation of Genesis 1, have shown where defintions of the words have come from (or how they were derived), and have shown how each of the verses fit together as a consistent and continuous narrative. I have spent a dozen years studying how this ancient text is structured and how its own words reveal their own plain meanings.

- ☆ How do you justify something that goes against what has been accepted by everyone for thousands of years?

Response: By having offered a translation that is consistent with the actual root words as well as with the grammar of the original text; and by clearly showing how traditionally translated words simply cannot be viable translations of Hebrew words in the ancient text.

- ☆ How can I, as a reader, check to see if what you are translating is true?

Response: Simply look up each of the root words to see that the definitions used here are the same as those you look up. Alternatively, you could just look up words that are of particular interest to you; or just look up one word in 10—that would end up being only about a dozen and half words.

☆ How do I know what you are translating is the truth? I'm just an average person, and I don't have time to check behind you.

Response: In this translation you have the actual definitions of words and the grammar that contributes meaning to the words. Do the explanations here of each word from the scriptural text make sense? Does the story as a whole fit together to make as much (or more) sense as the traditional story? There's your truth.

You now have the true workings of ancient documentation of extraterrestrial Reptilian encounters with our own primate ancestors in our remote past. If you would, please share how you are affected by this revelation.

react@albertepottsauthor.com

Endnotes

Chapter 1

1. Shemuel Ahituv, *Echoes from the Past—Hebrew and Cognate Inscriptions from the Biblical Period* (translator and academic editor, Anson F. Rainey) (Jerusalem: Carta, 2008).
2. Isaac Taylor, *The Alphabet: An Account of the Origin and Development of Letters, Volume 2* (London: Kegan Paul, Trench & Company, 1883), 236, https://books.google.com/books/about/The_Alphabet.html?id=v0I5AQAAMAAJ (accessed December 2009).
3. D.N. Freedman and K.A. Mathews, *The Paleo-Hebrew Leviticus Scroll* (11QpaleoLev), with contributions by R.S. Hanson (Alexandria, Virginia: American Schools of Oriental Research, 1985).
4. Sir Lancelot C.L. Brenton, ed., *The Septuagint with Apocrypha: Greek and English* (Peabody, Mass.: Hendrickson Publishers, 2003), i.

Chapter 2

5. M.H. Abrams, ed., *The Norton anthology of English literature* (New York: W.W. Norton, 1968), 73.
6. "Two Stone Tablets," Lanier Theological Library, https:www.laniertheologicallibrary.org/two-stone-tablets/ (accessed July 2020).
7. J.P. Green, Sr., ed., *The Interlinear Bible—Hebrew-Greek-English,* 4 volume edition (Mulberry, Ind.: Sovereign Grace Publishers, 1985).
8. Rud. Kittel, ed., *Biblia Hebraica* (Stuttgart, Germany: Württembergische Bibelanstalt, 1937).
9. Brenton, *The Septuagint with Apocrypha: Greek and English.*

10. Albert E. Potts, *The Latest and Best Bible Translation—Yours! An Introduction to Easy Step-by-Step Translating What the Bible Really Says* (Denver, Colo.: Outskirts Press, 2014).

11. James Strong, *Strong's Exhaustive Concordance of the Bible* [*supplemental section*, "A concise dictionary of the words in the Hebrew Bible"] (Iowa Falls, Iowa: World Bible Publishers: 1980) 22 (Number 855).

Chapter 3

12. Ibid, 156 (Number 8064).

13. Ibid (Number 8047).

14. Ibid (Number 8074).

15. Ibid.

16. Ibid, 22 (Number 853).

17. Ibid (Number 855).

18. Ibid, 20 (Number 776).

19. Ibid, 146 (Number 7521).

20. Genesis 1:2 (KJV).

21. Strong, *Strong's Exhaustive Concordance of the Bible,* 23 (Number 922).

22. Ibid.

23. Ibid, 116 (Number 5927).

24. Ibid (Number 5923– *a yoke*).

25. "RNA Splicing", DNA Learning Center, https://dnalc.org/resources/3d/rna-splicing.html (accessed July 2020).

26. Genesis 1:1 (KJV).

27. Davar4 Scripture Study Tool, www.davar3.net (accessed July 2020).

28. Deut. 32:11 (KJV).

29. Benjamin Davidson, *The Analytical Hebrew and Chaldee Lexicon* (Peabody, MA: Hendrickson Publishers, 1981), 681.

30. Strong, *Strong's Exhaustive Concordance of the Bible,* 143 (Number 7363).

31. E.A. Wallis Budge, *First Steps in Egyptian Hieroglyphics—A Book for Beginners* (Mineloa, NY: Dover Publications, 2003) 11.

32. Strong, *Strong's Exhaustive Concordance of the Bible,* 86 (Number 4325).

33. Genesis 1:3 (KJV).

34. Strong, *Strong's Exhaustive Concordance of the Bible,* 11 (Number 216).
35. Ibid, 68 (Number 3384).
36. "in-vitro fertilization", The Free Dictionary, https://medical-dictionary.thefreedictionary.com/in+vitro+fertilization, (accessed July 2020).
37. "Intracytoplasmic Sperm Injection," The Free Dictionary, https://www.myvmc.com/treatments/intracytoplasmic-sperm-injection-icsi/, (accessed July 2020).
38. Genesis 1:5 (KJV).
39. Davar4 Scripture Study Tool, www.davar3.net, (King James Version Bible – *search* H3117 [יוֹם]). It appears 2,287 times in 1,931 verses. It is given as "the foundation" at Exodus 9:18, as "…such as hath not been in Egypt since the foundation thereof even until now."
40. Rud. Kittel, ed., *Biblia Hebraica,* 91 [Note: from BH, the words for "the day the foundation", *as,* (הַיּוֹם הִוָּסְדָה) [Sh'mot (שמות) 9:18].
41. Strong, *Strong's Exhaustive Concordance of the Bible,* 79 (Number 3915).
42. Ibid, 78 (Number 3883).
43. Ibid, 79 (Number 3924).
44. Green, *The Interlinear Bible—Hebrew-Greek-English,* Vol. 1, 1 (Genesis 1:6).
45. Davidson, *The Analytical Hebrew and Chaldee Lexicon,* 692 [רקע].
46. Ibid, 692.
47. "Semen Analysis: All you ever wanted to know about Sperm and Infertility", Malpani Infertility Clinic, https://www.drmalpani.com/knowledge-center/articles/sperm, (accessed July 2020).
48. Ibid.
49. Genesis 1:6 (KJV).
50. Strong, *Strong's Exhaustive Concordance of the Bible,* 23 (Number 914).
51. "Sperm Separation to Improve IVF Success Rate," Melbourne School of Engineering, http://ingenium.eng.unimelb.edu.au/2018/06/04/sperm-separation-to-improve-ivf-success-rate/, (accessed July 2020).
52. Genesis 1:6 (KJV).
53. Strong, *Strong's Exhaustive Concordance of the Bible,* 86 (Number 4325).
54. Ibid.
55. Song of Sol. 4:15, 5:12, and 8:7, (KJV).
56. Strong, *Strong's Exhaustive Concordance of the Bible,* 86 (Number 4325).

57. Song of Sol. 4:15 (KJV).
58. Strong, *Strong's Exhaustive Concordance of the Bible,* 91 (Number 4599).
59. Ibid, 50 (Number 2416), 86 (Number 4325).
60. Ibid, 77 (Number 3836), 89 (Number 4478), 102 (Number 5140).
61. Ibid, 102 (Number 5140).
62. Ibid, 89 (Number 4478).
63. Ibid, 77 (Number 3836).
64. Song of Sol. 5:12 (KJV).
65. Strong, *Strong's Exhaustive Concordance of the Bible,* 65 (Number 3196), 115 (Number 5869).
66. Ibid 18 (Number 650), 86 (Number 4325).
67. Ibid 51 (Number 2459), 69 (Number 3427), 87 (Number 4390), 143 (Number 7364).
68. Song of Sol. 8:7 (KJV).
69. Strong, *Strong's Exhaustive Concordance of the Bible,* 9 (Number 157), 65 (Number 3201), 71 (Number 3515), 76 (Number 3808), 86 (Number 4325), 140 (Number 7232).
70. Ibid.
71. Ibid, 101 (Number 5102), 152 (Number 7858).
72. Genesis 1:7 (KJV).
73. Strong, *Strong's Exhaustive Concordance of the Bible,* 22 [Number 834 (אֲשֶׁר) *–a primary relative pronoun of every gender and number*].
74. *Ibid,* 160 [Number 8271 (שְׁרֵא) *–free, unravel, reside, dwell*].
75. Green, *The Interlinear Bible—Hebrew-Greek-English,* 4 volume edition, 3:2050 (Dan. 5:12).
76. Rud. Kittel, ed., *Biblia Hebraica,* 1 (מִתַּחַת) [Bereshit (בראשית) 1:7].
77. Strong, *Strong's Exhaustive Concordance of the Bible,* 164 (Number 8480, תַּחַת).
78. Ibid (Number 8478).
79. Davar, Davar4 Scripture Study Tool, www.davar3.net.
80. Strong, *Strong's Exhaustive Concordance of the Bible,* 164 (Number 8480, תַּחַת – *Tahath*).
81. Davar, Davar4 Scripture Study Tool, www.davar3.net. (King James Version Bible – Num. 33:26, 33:27, 1 Chron. 6:24, 6:37, 7:20, 7:20).

82. Strong, *Strong's Exhaustive Concordance of the Bible,* 164 (Number 8480, תַּחַת – *Tahath*).
83. Genesis 1:7 (KJV).
84. Rud. Kittel, ed., *Biblia Hebraica* , 1 (וַיְהִי) [Bereshit (בראשית) 1:7].
85. Strong, *Strong's Exhaustive Concordance of the Bible,* 42 (Number 1961).
86. Ibid, 74 (Number 3651).
87. Genesis 1:8 (KJV).
88. Strong, *Strong's Exhaustive Concordance of the Bible,* 120 (Number 6153).
89. Ibid (Number 6154).
90. Ibid.
91. Genesis 1:8 (KJV).
92. Strong, *Strong's Exhaustive Concordance of the Bible,* 29 (Number 1239).
93. Genesis 1:9 (KJV).
94. Biblia Hebraica, op cit., 1 (וְתֵרָאֶה) [Bereshit (בראשית) 1:9].
95. Thomas O. Lambdin, *Introduction to Biblical Hebrew* (New York: Charles Scribner's Sons, 1971) 40.
96. Strong, *Strong's Exhaustive Concordance of the Bible,* 160 (Number 7200).
97. Ibid.
98. Ibid, 61 (Number 3004).
99. Ibid (Number 3001).
100. Davar, Davar4 Scripture Study Tool, (King James Version Bible – *search H3001*).
101. Genesis 1:10 (KJV).
102. Ibid.
103. Strong, *Strong's Exhaustive Concordance of the Bible,* 86 (Number 4325).
104. Ibid, 135 (Number 6960).
105. Rud. Kittel, ed., *Biblia Hebraica,* 1 (יַמִּים) [Bereshit (בראשית) 1:10].
106. "Spermatazoon", The Free Dictionary, https://medical-dictionary.thefreedictionary.com/spermatozoon, (accessed July 2020).
107. Genesis 1:10 (KJV).
108. Strong, *Strong's Exhaustive Concordance of the Bible,* 59 (Number 2896), 72 (Number 3588), 160 (Number 7200).
109. Genesis 1:11 (KJV).

110. Rud. Kittel, ed., *Biblia Hebraica,* 1. (תַּדְשֵׁא) [Bereshit (בראשית) 1:11].

111. Strong, *Strong's Exhaustive Concordance of the Bible,* 40 (Number 1876).

112. Ibid.

113. Rud. Kittel, ed., *Biblia Hebraica,* 1. (עֵשֶׂב) [Bereshit (בראשית) 1:11].

114. Strong, *Strong's Exhaustive Concordance of the Bible,* 122 (Number 6212).

115. Rud. Kittel, ed., *Biblia Hebraica,* 1 (מזריע – as adapted) [Bereshit (בראשית) 1:11].

116. Strong, *Strong's Exhaustive Concordance of the Bible,* 47 (Number 2232).

117. Genesis 1:11 (KJV).

118. Strong, *Strong's Exhaustive Concordance of the Bible,* 47 (Number 2233).

119. Ibid, 74 (Number 3651).

120. Davidson, *The Analytical Hebrew and Chaldee Lexicon.*

121. Ibid, 463 [מְאֹרֹת].

122. Ibid, 14 [אור].

123. Ibid, 48 [ארר]; Strong op cit., 14 (Number 422).

124. Strong, *Strong's Exhaustive Concordance of the Bible,* 146 (Number 7554).

125. Proverbs 3:33 (KJV).

126. Genesis 1:11 (KJV).

127. Strong, *Strong's Exhaustive Concordance of the Bible,* 78 (Number 3924), 79 (Number 3915—from the same as Number 3883).

128. Genesis 1:11 (KJV).

129. Rud. Kittel, ed., *Biblia Hebraica,* 1. (וּלְמוֹעֲדִים) [Bereshit (בראשית) 1:14].

130. Strong, *Strong's Exhaustive Concordance of the Bible,* 66 (Number 3259), 83 (Number 4150).

131. "How DNA Works", How Stuff Works, https://science.howstuffworks.com/life/cellularmicroscipic/dna3.htm, (accessed July 2020).

132. Green, *The Interlinear Bible—Hebrew-Greek-English,* 4 volume edition.

133. Rud. Kittel, ed., *Biblia Hebraica,* 1. (וְשָׁנִים) [Bereshit (בראשית) 1:14].

134. Strong, *Strong's Exhaustive Concordance of the Bible,* 157 (Number 8141).

135. Ibid (Number 8139).

136. Ibid (Number 8138).

137. "What is CRISPR-Cas9", Your Genome, https://www.yourgenome.org/facts/what-is-crispr-cas9, (accessed July 2020).

138. Rud. Kittel, ed., *Biblia Hebraica,* 1. (את) [Bereshit (בראשית) 1:16].

139. Strong, *Strong's Exhaustive Concordance of the Bible,* 22 (Number 855).

140. Rud. Kittel, ed., *Biblia Hebraica,* 1. (הַגְּדֹלִים) [Bereshit (בראשית) 1:16].

141. Strong, *Strong's Exhaustive Concordance of the Bible,* 32 (Number 1419), 33 (Number 1431).

142. https://medlineplus.gov/genetics/understanding/basics/dna/, (accessed October 2020).

143. As adapted from the Biblia Hebraica, הַגְּדֹלִים ("the twists") and לַיְלָה ("twisting spiral").

144. Genesis 1:16 (KJV).

145. Rud. Kittel, ed., *Biblia Hebraica,* 1. Note: הַגָּדֹל ("the twist", *as adapted from Strong's H1431*) [Bereshit (בראשית) 1:16].

146. Genesis 1:16 (KJV).

147. Rud. Kittel, ed., *Biblia Hebraica,* 1. (וְאֶת־הַמָּאוֹר הַקָּטֹן לְמֶמְשֶׁלֶת הַלַּיְלָה) [Bereshit (בראשית) 1:16].

148. Ibid, 1.

149. Strong, *Strong's Exhaustive Concordance of the Bible,* 136 (Number 6996).

150. Davar, Davar4 Scripture Study Tool (King James Version Bible – *search H6996*).

151. Rud. Kittel, ed., *Biblia Hebraica,* 1. (קָטֹן) [Bereshit (בראשית) 1:16].

152. Strong, *Strong's Exhaustive Concordance of the Bible* , 135 (Number 6962).

153. Rud. Kittel, ed., *Biblia Hebraica,* 1. (לְמֶמְשֶׁלֶת) [Bereshit (בראשית) 1:16].

154. Ibid.

155. Strong, *Strong's Exhaustive Concordance of the Bible*, 89 (Number 4475).

156. Ibid, 97 (Numbers 4910, 4911, 4912, 4914, & 4915).

157. Ibid (Number 4911).

158. Ibid.

159. Rud. Kittel, ed., *Biblia Hebraica,* 1. (וְאֵת) [Bereshit (בראשית) 1:16].

160. Strong, *Strong's Exhaustive Concordance of the Bible*, 22 (Number 855).

161. Genesis 1:16 (KJV).

162. Rud. Kittel, ed., *Biblia Hebraica,* 1. (הַכּוֹכָבִים) [Bereshit (בראשית) 1:16].

163. Note: The apparent root word of Strong's H3556 (כּוֹכָב) should logically be "ככב". Dr. Strong, however, gives it as H3522 (כבון) or as H3554 *in the sense of blazing* (כוה).

164. Note: The presence of the letter [ו] in the word "כוכב".
165. Davar, Davar4 Scripture Study Tool (Biblia Hebraica – *search* "ככב").
166. Ibid (Biblia Hebraica – *search* "כוכב").
167. Ibid (Biblia Hebraica – *search* "כוכב"): Numbers 24:17 & Amos 5:26.
168. Strong, *Strong's Exhaustive Concordance of the Bible*, 72 (Number 3552).
169. Note: Observe the presence of the [ו] in the word "כוכב".
170. Genesis 1:17 (KJV).
171. Rud. Kittel, ed., *Biblia Hebraica,* 1. (וַיִּתֵּן) [Bereshit (בראשית) 1:17].
172. Strong, *Strong's Exhaustive Concordance of the Bible*, 107 [(נָתַן) *–to give (used with great latitude)*].
173. Ibid.
174. Ibid, 165 [תַּן – *probably meaning to elongate*].
175. Ibid.
176. Latin Dictionary, http://www.online-latindictionary.com, (accessed July 2020).
177. "What Is Teratozoospermia?" https://www.invitra.com/en/teratospermia/, (accessed July 2020).
178. Webster's Collegiate Dictionary, 5th Ed. (Springfield, MA: G.&C. Merriam Company, Publishers, 1941) 1029.
179. "Egg Fertilization," Ovation Fertility, https://www.austinivf.com/embryology/egg-fertilization/, (accessed July 2020).
180. Genesis 1:17 (KJV).
181. Robert Yawanathan Denis (ed.), *The Torah in Ancient Hebrew* (New York: Israelite Network, 2000) [p. 𐤂 (3) – (𐤋𐤄𐤀𐤉𐤓).
182. Rud. Kittel, ed., *Biblia Hebraica,* 1. (לְהָאִיר) [Bereshit (בראשית) 1:17].
183. Strong, Strong, *Strong's Exhaustive Concordance of the Bible,* 11 [Number 216 (אור) – there transliterated as *ore*)].
184. Rud. Kittel, ed., *Biblia Hebraica,* 1. (לְהאִיר) [Bereshit (בראשית) 1:17].
185. Note: the letter [ו] has been swapped in the text for the letter [י].
186. Genesis 1:17 (KJV).
187. Rud. Kittel, ed., *Biblia Hebraica,* 1. (עַל) [Bereshit (בראשית) 1:17].
188. Strong, *Strong's Exhaustive Concordance of the Bible,* 116 (Number 5923– *a yoke*).

189. “RNA Splicing”, Cold Springs Harbor Laboratory, https://dnalc.org/resources/3d/rna-splicing.html, (accessed July 2020).

190. Strong, *Strong's Exhaustive Concordance of the Bible,* 97 (Number 4911).

191. Note: The [Biblical] Hebrew word for the words, “the day” in Verse 18 is “ביום”—*b'ēōōm*. Also note that there is no “root word” in this word. It is constructed of four different elements of Hebrew grammar. Here's how the word is to be dissected and translated. The first letter (ב), a common prefix, means “in.” The second letter (י), also a common prefix, means “it.” The third letter (ו), also a common prefix, means “and”. The fourth letter (ם), a common suffix, means “them”. The full translation is “in-it-and-them,” This translation has the added benefit of being in exact context. The words “the day” are not in context.

192. Strong, *Strong's Exhaustive Concordance of the Bible,* 78 (Number 3883), 79 (Number 3915), 79 (Number 3924).

193. Genesis 1:18 (KJV).

194. Rud. Kittel, ed., *Biblia Hebraica,* 1. (וּלֲהַבְדִּיל) [Bereshit (בראשית) 1:18].

195. Note: The translation breakdown of “וּלֲהַבְדִּיל.” The first letter, a first prefix [ו] means *and.* The second letter, a second prefix [ל] means *in regard to.* The third letter, a third prefix [ה] means *the.* The *root word* [בְּדִיל] has an inserted letter [י] which modifies the meaning of the root—from “separated, divided, *or* distinguished” [Strong's H914] to *differentiation.*

196. Rud. Kittel, ed., *Biblia Hebraica,* 1. (בֵּין) [Bereshit (בראשית) 1:18].

197. Strong, *Strong's Exhaustive Concordance of the Bible,* 24 (Number 995– *to separate mentally or to distinguish*).

198. Rud. Kittel, ed., *Biblia Hebraica,* 1. (הַחֹשֶׁךְ) [Bereshit (בראשית) 1:18].

199. Strong, *Strong's Exhaustive Concordance of the Bible,* 58 (Number 2821– *to be dark (as withholding light)*).

200. Genesis 1:19 (KJV).

201. Rud. Kittel, ed., *Biblia Hebraica,* 2. (רְבִיעִי) [Bereshit (בראשית) 1:19].

202. Strong, *Strong's Exhaustive Concordance of the Bible,* 141 (Number 7243 – *from* H7251) (Number 7251—*identified with* 7250 *through the idea of sprawling “at all fours”*) (Number 7250– *to squat or lie flat out, i.e. (speculative) in copulation: let gender, lie down*).

203. Ibid, 141 (Number 7243).

204. Ibid, 141 (Number 7250).

205. Note: The word, "rĕbō," is the transliteration of the letters, *rĕsh, bĕt,* and *ōyēn.* The Biblical Hebrew transliteration, per Strong [Number 7250] is "*raw-bah*'".
206. Davar, Davar4 Scripture Study (King James Version Bible – *search Strong's* 7250). Results from the KJV Bible: Lev. 18:23, 19:19, and 20:16.
207. Note: The Biblical Hebrew word is "רְבִיעִי". The *root word* is "רְבַע". The letter inserted into the root in the original text is [י].
208. Davidson, *The Analytical Hebrew and Chaldee Lexicon,* 12 [*Section III.–Suffixes to the Noun in the Singular*].
209. Genesis 1:20 (KJV).
210. Strong, *Strong's Exhaustive Concordance of the Bible,* 86 (Number 4325).
211. Rud. Kittel, ed., *Biblia Hebraica,* 2. (יִשְׁרְצוּ) [Bereshit (בראשית) 1:20].
212. Ibid.
213. Rud. Kittel, ed., *Biblia Hebraica,* 2. (הַמַּיִם) [Bereshit (בראשית) 1:20].
214. Note: The are multiple examples of the prefix form of the first person singular subject pronoun, *he, she,* or *it* in the biblical text itself. A good example is the famous phrase, "and it was so". The word for "and it was" is "וַיְהִי". The first letter [ו] is the first prefix, "and". The second letter [י] is the word's second prefix, "it". [The abbreviated two letters (הי) of a three-letter root (H1961 – היה) represents the word, "is".] The word *so* is a separate word, "כֵן".
215. Davidson, *The Analytical Hebrew and Chaldee Lexicon,* 12 [*Section III.–Suffixes to the Noun in the Singular*].
216. Strong, *Strong's Exhaustive Concordance of the Bible,* 161 (Number 8317– *to wriggle, i.e. by implication to swarm or abound:—breed (bring forth, increase) abundantly*).
217. Ibid, 86 (Number 4325– *noun; water; figuratively juice; by euphemism urine, semen:—piss, wasting, water*).
218. Genesis 1:20 (KJV).
219. Strong, *Strong's Exhaustive Concordance of the Bible,* 161 (Number 8317– *to wriggle*).
220. Ibid, 105 (Number 5314 (נֶפֶשׁ)–*to breathe; figuratively refreshed*).
221. Genesis 1:20 (KJV).
222. Rud. Kittel, ed., *Biblia Hebraica,* 2. (חַיָּה) [Bereshit (בראשית) 1:20].
223. Strong, *Strong's Exhaustive Concordance of the Bible,* 50 (Number 2421).
224. Genesis 1:20 (KJV).

225. Strong, Strong, *Strong's Exhaustive Concordance of the Bible,* 133 [Number 6833 (צפור) – *a little bird (as hopping)*].

226. Rud. Kittel, ed., *Biblia Hebraica,* 2. (וְעוֹף) [Bereshit (בראשית) 1:20].

227. Strong, *Strong's Exhaustive Concordance of the Bible,* 114 [Number 5775 (עוף) – *from* 5774; *a bird*].

228. Ibid, 113 [Number 5774 (עוף) – *to cover (with wings or obscurity); hence (as denominated from 5775) to fly; also (by implication of dimness) to faint (from the darkness of swooning):—brandish, be (wax) faint, flee away, fly away, shine forth, weary*].

229. Davidson, *The Analytical Hebrew and Chaldee Lexicon.*

230. Rud. Kittel, ed., *Biblia Hebraica,* 2. ("עוף") from (וְעוֹף) [Bereshit (בראשית) 1:20].

231. Strong, *Strong's Exhaustive Concordance of the Bible,*113 [Number 5774 (עוף)].

232. Ibid, 116 [Number 5888 (עיף); Number 5889 (עיף)].

233. Ibid.

234. Genesis 1:21 (KJV).

235. Rud. Kittel, ed., *Biblia Hebraica,* 2. (הַתַּנִּינִם) [Bereshit (בראשית) 1:21].

236. Davidson, Davidson, *The Analytical Hebrew and Chaldee Lexicon,* 766, [תנן – *Root not used; to which is ascribed the sense of stretching out, extending.*]

237. Note: the two common *inserted letters* are [ו] and [י]; the letter [י] is inserted into the root "תנן" of the word "הַתַּנִּינִם".

238. Davidson, *The Analytical Hebrew and Chaldee Lexicon,* 13 [*Section V. Suffixes attached...*]. The example of the letter [ם] as a suffixed third person plural object pronoun is given in the table in column (b); "בם" translated as "in [ב] them [ם]".

239. Strong, *Strong's Exhaustive Concordance of the Bible,* 165 [Number 8577 (תנין) *–from the same as* 8565; *a marine or land monster, i.e. sea-serpent or jackal:—dragon, sea monster, serpent, whale*].

240. Ibid, 165 [Number 8565 (תן) *–from an unused root probably meaning to elongate*].

241. Ibid.

242. Davidson, *The Analytical Hebrew and Chaldee Lexicon,* 766, [תנן – *Root not used; to which is ascribed the sense of stretching out, extending*].

243. Rud. Kittel, ed., *Biblia Hebraica,* 2. (הַגְּדֹלִים) [Bereshit (בראשית) 1:21].

244. Strong, *Strong's Exhaustive Concordance of the Bible,* 32 [Number 1419 (גדול) *–from* 1431; *great (in any sense)*]. Note: The complete word in the Biblia Hebraica text is "הַגְּד֫לִים".

245. Ibid, 33 [Number 1431 (גדל) *–to twist (compare to* 1434*)*].

246. Ibid [Number 1434 (גדל) *–from* 1431 *in the sense of twisting*].

247. Thomas O. Lambdin, *Introduction to Biblical Hebrew,* 9.

248. Genesis 1:21(KJV).

249. Rud. Kittel, ed., *Biblia Hebraica,* 2. (כָּל) [Bereshit (בראשית) 1:21].

250. Strong, *Strong's Exhaustive Concordance of the Bible,* 73 [Number 3605 (כל) *–from* 3634; *the whole, all, any, every*].

251. Ibid [Number 3634 (כלל) *–to complete:—(make) perfect*].

252. Rud. Kittel, ed., *Biblia Hebraica,* 2. (הַחַיָּה) [Bereshit (בראשית) 1:21].

253. Genesis 1:21 (KJV).

254. Note: From the Biblia Hebraica, the word translated, "that moveth" is, "הָר֫מֶשֶׂת". That word, transliterated into the ancient Hebrew writing is, "𐤄𐤓𐤌𐤔𐤕".

255. Strong, *Strong's Exhaustive Concordance of the Bible,* 144 [Number 7430 (רמש) *–to glide swiftly, i.e. to crawl or move with short steps; by analogy to swarm:—creep, move*].

256. Ibid [Number 7431 (רֶמֶשׂ) *–from* 7430; *a reptile or any other rapidly moving animal:—that creepeth, creeping (moving) thing*].

257. Ibid.

258. Genesis 1:21 (KJV).

259. Rud. Kittel, ed., *Biblia Hebraica,* 2. (אֲשֶׁר) [Bereshit (בראשית) 1:21].

260. Strong, *Strong's Exhaustive Concordance of the Bible,* 22 [Number 834 (אֲשֶׁר)*—a primary relative pronoun of every gender and number*].

261. Note: from the Biblia Hebraica, the word translated, "which" is, "אֲשֶׁר". That word, transliterated into the ancient Hebrew writing is, "𐤀𐤔𐤓".

262. Davidson, *The Analytical Hebrew and Chaldee Lexicon*, 739 [(שרה) (Chaldee, שְׁרֵא)].

263. Ibid, 739.

264. Ibid.

265. Ibid [*Daniel 2:22* (*the light dwelleth with him*)].

266. Rud. Kittel, ed., *Biblia Hebraica,* 1257. (שְׁרֵא) [Daniel (דניאל) 2:22].

267. Strong, *Strong's Exhaustive Concordance of the Bible,* 160 [Number 8271 (שְׁרֵא) *–free, unravel, reside, dwell*].

268. Note: The bells that "good" should ring are the same final words of the traditional translation of Genesis 1:21, ". . . and God saw that it was good."

269. Genesis 1:22 (KJV).

270. Strong, *Strong's Exhaustive Concordance of the Bible,* 20 [Number 776 (אֶרֶץ) *–to be firm; the earth*]. Note: Dr. Strong transliterates this word as "*eh'-rets*". In the ancient Hebrew of this work, words are transliterated phonetically. Its phonemes are: *ah*, *reh*, and *tz*—AReTz.

271. Note: "A ReTzaH" would be written as "א רצה"; where [א] means "I" and "רצה" would be Strong's Number 7521 (רצה), meaning "accomplish".

272. Strong, *Strong's Exhaustive Concordance of the Bible,* 146 [Number 7521 (רצה) *–to be pleased with:—acceptable, accomplish, approve, consent with, delight (self), favorable, like, take pleasure*].

273. Genesis 1:24 (KJV).

274. Ibid.

275. Rud. Kittel, ed., *Biblia Hebraica,* 2. (תּוֹצֵא) [Bereshit (בראשית) 1:24].

276. Strong, *Strong's Exhaustive Concordance of the Bible,* 67 [Number 3318 (יָצָא) *–to go (causative bring) out, in a great variety of applications, literal and figurative, direct and proximal*].

277. Rud. Kittel, ed., *Biblia Hebraica,* 2. (בְּהֵמָה) [Bereshit (בראשית) 1:24].

278. Strong, *Strong's Exhaustive Concordance of the Bible,* 23 [Number 929 (בְּהֵמָה) *–from an unused root (probably meaning to be mute); properly a dumb beast; especially any large quadruped or animal (often collective):—beast, cattle*].

279. Davidson, *The Analytical Hebrew and Chaldee Lexicon,* 13 [*Section V. Suffixes attached to the Prefix Prepositions* ל *and* ב *– Column (b)* ב *in*].

280. Strong, *Strong's Exhaustive Concordance of the Bible,* 42 [Number 1993 (חמה) *–a primary root to make a loud sound (like English "hum"); to rage, war, moan, or clamor*].

281. Ibid.

282. Ibid, 22 [Number 855 (את) *–coulter*]. Note: the use of the word, *coulter*, has its analog, or synonym, in the high-tech injecting pipette used in *intracytoplasmic sperm injection.*

283. Ibid, 73 [Number 3605 (כל) *–from* 3634 (כלל) *–to complete; (make) perfect*].

284. Ibid, 144 [Number 7431 (רֶמֶשׂ) *–from* 7430; *a reptile*].

285. Genesis 1:25 (KJV).

286. Rud. Kittel, ed., *Biblia Hebraica,* 2. (הָאֲדָמָה) [Bereshit (בראשית) 1:25]. Note: The middle three letters are (as Anglicized) A-D-M—Adam. The word, itself, is Strong's Number 127, means "*soil*". It is, per traditional translation mythology, derived from Number 119 (אָדַם or ADM, transliterated by Dr. Strong as "*aw-dam*") and means "*to show blood in the face, i.e. flush or turn red; ruddy.*" By very slight contrast, Number 120 (אָדָם or ADM, transliterated by Dr. Strong as "*aw-dawm*") has its meaning as "*from* 119*; ruddy, i.e., a human being (individual or the species, mankind, etc.*" By slight contrast, Number 121 (אָדָם or ADM, transliterated by Dr. Strong as "*aw-dawm*") has its meaning as "*from the same as* 120*; Adam, the name of the first man.*" Finally, also by very slight contrast, Number 122 (אָדֹם or ADM, transliterated by Dr. Strong as "*aw-dome*") has its meaning as "*from* 119*; rosy, red, ruddy.*" What these examples from an authoritative source demonstrate is that through the purposeful use of "vowel points" (the little marks underneath the letters of the Biblical Hebrew) a word may be linguistically engineered to be read as whatever the translators have decided it should. Thus, if one relies solely on what has been traditionally received and universally accepted, any retranslation of the biblical text would be pointless—as confinement to arcane and torturous rules of grammar and to dogmatic definitions of words will invariably "prove" traditional translation.

287. Ibid, 2 (הָאֲדָמָה) [Bereshit (בראשית) 1:25]. Note: the prefix, "the", is [ה].

288. Davidson, *The Analytical Hebrew and Chaldee Lexicon,* 8 (אֲדָמָה). Note: It is the first of five entries with the (unaccented) spelling of "אדמה".

289. Ibid. Note: Professor Davidson did not catalogue all the Hebrew letters which he identifies as denoting the "absolute state"; but such designations abound throughout his 784-page lexicon.

290. Rud. Kittel, ed., *Biblia Hebraica,* 2. (הָאֲדָמָה) [Bereshit (בראשית) 1:25]. Note: This present work assumes a variant reading of the word "הָאֲדָמָה"—where the first letter [ה] is the first prefix, "the"; the second letter [א] is the second prefix, "I"; the third and fourth letters [דם] constitute the root word "blood" [Strong's 1818]; and the fifth letter [ה] is a suffix denoting the "*absolute state*" of a word. In this instance, the "absolute state" of "the I-Blood" [that is, *the hybrid being*] is in having been genetically engineered.

291. Davidson, *The Analytical Hebrew and Chaldee Lexicon,* 8 (אֲדַמֶּה). Note: The entry is the fifth of five entries with the same unaccented spelling ("אדמה"). The root word is given as "דמה". Thus, the first letter [א] is assumed to be prefixed to the given root, "דמה".

292. Strong, *Strong's Exhaustive Concordance of the Bible,* 39 [Number 1818 (דָם) *–from* 1826; *compare* 119; *blood*]; [Number 1826 (דמם) *–to be dumb; by implication to be astonished*].

293. Genesis 1:26 (KJV).

294. Rud. Kittel, ed., *Biblia Hebraica,* 2. (נַעֲשֶׂה) [Bereshit (בראשית) 1:26].

295. Strong, *Strong's Exhaustive Concordance of the Bible,* 122 [Number 6213 (עָשָׂה) *–to do or to make, in the broadest sense and widest application:—accomplish, advance, appoint, become, etc*]. Note: The translated word, "accomplish", from the Hebrew word "עשה", appears at 1 Kings 5:9.

296. Ibid, 9 [Number 127 (אֲדָמָה) *–from* 119; *soil, country, earth, ground*].

297. Note: This present work puts forward a variant reading of the word "אָדָם)"— where the first letter [א] is the prefix, "I," and the second and third letters [דם] constitute the root word "blood" [Strong 1818]. The translated result is, "I-Blood" [that is, *the ancient hominid being hybridized by the reptilian biological entities*].

298. Genesis 1:26 (KJV).

299. Davidson, *The Analytical Hebrew and Chaldee Lexicon,* 9 [*Section I.—The Personal Pronoun*] (נוּ- ; our).

300. Strong, *Strong's Exhaustive Concordance of the Bible,* 131 [Number 6754 (צֶלֶם) *–to shade; a phantom; illusion, resemblance, image*].

301. Webster, Webster's Collegiate Dictionary.

302. Ibid, 497.

303. Rud. Kittel, ed., *Biblia Hebraica,* 2. (בְּצַלְמֵנוּ) [Bereshit (בראשית) 1:26].

304. Genesis 1:26 (KJV).

305. Rud. Kittel, ed., *Biblia Hebraica,* 2. (כִּדְמוּתֵנוּ) [Bereshit (בראשית) 1:26].

306. Davidson, *The Analytical Hebrew and Chaldee Lexicon,* 399 (Definition VIII).

307. Strong, *Strong's Exhaustive Concordance of the Bible,* 39 [Number 1818 (דָם)*–from* 1826; *blood*].

308. Note: The first of the two two-letter suffixes on the word "כִּדְמוּתֵנוּ" is "ות".

309. Davidson, *The Analytical Hebrew and Chaldee Lexicon,* 9 [*Section I.—The Personal Pronoun, Column A*] (נוּ- ; us).

310. Genesis 1:26 (KJV)

311. Rud. Kittel, ed., *Biblia Hebraica,* 2. (וְיִרְדּוּ) [Bereshit (בראשית) 1:26].

312. Davidson, *The Analytical Hebrew and Chaldee Lexicon,* 9 [*Section I.—The Personal Pronoun, Column A*] (וֹ- ; him).

313. Ibid, 9 [*Section I.—The Personal Pronoun, Column A*] (הם, ם- ; them).

314. Strong, *Strong's Exhaustive Concordance of the Bible,* 141 [Number 7287 (רָדָה)–*to tread down; subjugate; have dominion, rule over*].

315. Taylor, *The Alphabet: An Account of the Origin and Development of Letters.*

316. Brenton, *The Septuagint with Apocrypha: Greek and English.*

317. Genesis 1:30 (KJV).

318. "Vulgate," Vulgate.com, https://vulgate.org/, (accessed July 2020).

319. Rud. Kittel, ed., *Biblia Hebraica,* 2. (וּלְכָל) [Bereshit (בראשית) 1:30].

320. Strong, *Strong's Exhaustive Concordance of the Bible,* 73 [Number 3605 (כל)–*whole, all, any, every*].

321. Ibid, 73 [Number 3634 (כלל)–*to complete:—(make) perfect*].

322. Rud. Kittel, ed., *Biblia Hebraica,* 2. (חַיַּת) [Bereshit (בראשית) 1:30].

323. Strong, *Strong's Exhaustive Concordance of the Bible,* 50 [Number 2416 (חַי) –*from* 2421; *alive, hence raw (flesh), fresh, strong, life or living things (whether literally or figuratively, (wild) beast, company, congregation, living creature, living thing, maintenance, multitude, be old, quick, raw, running, springing, troop*]; [Number 2421 (חָיָה) –*to live (whether literally or figuratively); to revive*].

324. Ibid, 50 [Number 2416 (חַי) –*from* 2421; *alive*].

325. Brenton, *The Septuagint with Apocrypha: Greek and English,* 2 (θηρίοις) [Genesis (ΓΕΝΕΣΙΣ) 1:30].

326. Strong, *Strong's Exhaustive Concordance of the Bible* (*supplemental section,* "A concise dictionary of the words in the Greek/New Testament"), [Number 2342 (θηρίον thĕriōn) –*a dangerous animal:—(venomous, (wild) beast*], 47.

327. Rud. Kittel, ed., *Biblia Hebraica,* 2. (רוֹמֶשׂ) [Bereshit (בראשית) 1:30]. Note: There is a letter [וֹ] inserted into the word "רוֹמֶשׂ". The presence of that *modifier letter* changes the word from "reptile" to "[R]eptilian."

328. Strong, *Strong's Exhaustive Concordance of the Bible,* 144 [Number 7431 (רֶמֶשׂ) –*a reptile*].

329. Ibid, 116 [Number 5923–*a yoke*].

330. Strong, *Strong's Exhaustive Concordance of the Bible,* 22 [Number 834 (אֲשֶׁר) –*a primary relative pronoun of every gender and number*].

331. Ibid, 160 [Number 8271 (שְׁרֵא) *–free, unravel, reside, dwell*].
332. Rud. Kittel, ed., *Biblia Hebraica,* 2. (בוֹ) [Bereshit (בראשית) 1:30].
333. Brenton, *The Septuagint with Apocrypha: Greek and English,* 2 (*side-column translation*) [Genesis (ΓΕΝΕΣΙΣ) 1:30].
334. Rud. Kittel, ed., *Biblia Hebraica,* 2. (נֶפֶשׁ) [Bereshit (בראשית) 1:30].
335. Strong, *Strong's Exhaustive Concordance of the Bible* (*supplemental section,* "A concise dictionary of the words in the Greek/New Testament"), 106 [Number 5590 (φυχη psuchē)—*breath*].
336. Rud. Kittel, ed., *Biblia Hebraica,* 2. (חַיָּה) [Bereshit (בראשית) 1:30].
337. Brenton, *The Septuagint with Apocrypha: Greek and English,* 2 (ζωης) [Genesis (ΓΕΝΕΣΙΣ) 1:30].
338. Strong, *Strong's Exhaustive Concordance of the Bible* (*supplemental section,* "A concise dictionary of the words in the Greek/New Testament"), 45 [Number 2222 (ζωή zōē) *–life*].
339. Genesis 2:3 (KJV).
340. Rud. Kittel, ed., *Biblia Hebraica,* 2. [Bereshit (בראשית) 2:3].
341. Davidson, *The Analytical Hebrew and Chaldee Lexicon,* 113 [בָּרָא *–to create, form, make.* Niph.—I. *to be created.* II. *to be born.* Pi.—I. *to cut, cut down.* II. *to form, fashion.* Hiph. *to feed, fatten*].
342. Strong, *Strong's Exhaustive Concordance of the Bible,* 29 [Number 1245 (בָּרָא) *–to create, to cut down (a wood), select feed (as a formative process):—choose, create (creator), cut down, dispatch, do, make (fat)*].
343. Genesis 2:3 (KJV).
344. Rud. Kittel, ed., *Biblia Hebraica,* 2. (לַעֲשׂוֹת) [Bereshit (בראשית) 2:3].
345. Davidson, *The Analytical Hebrew and Chaldee Lexicon,* 399, Definition VIII.
346. Note: The root word of "לַעֲשׂוֹת" is "עָשָׂה". The word, "עָשׂ" is (most likely) the same word but with its final letter [ה] omitted by the text's author or by a later editor.
347. Strong, *Strong's Exhaustive Concordance of the Bible,* 122 [Number 6213 (עָשָׂה) *–to do or make, in the broadest sense and widest application*]. Note, Strong's H6213 appears 2,638 times in the King James Version—and it *is* used in the broadest sense and widest application.

Chapter 5

348. Zecharia Stichin, *The Lost Realms* (Santa Fe, NM: Bear & Company, Inc., 1990) 253.

349. Ibid, 254.

350. Ibid.

351. C.J. Ball, D. Litt, "Shumer and Shem: Some Philological Coincidences and Sequences" (London: From the Proceedings of the British Academy, Vol. VII, January 1, 1916).

352. "Enuma Elish," Sacred Texts, https://www.sacred-text.com/ane/enuma.htm, (accessed July 2020).

353. "The Seven Tablets of Creation," Sacred Texts, https://www.sacred-text.com/ane/stc/index.htm, (accessed July 2020).

354. Strong, *Strong's Exhaustive Concordance of the Bible,* 112 [Number 5674 (עָבַר). Note: It is very revealing that after Dr. Strong's disclaimers about the word's definition, the opening definition of the word is, "to cover (in copulation)". He offers a laundry-list of definitions used in the KJV translation, including the word, "other" [Number 5676 (עֵבֶר)].

355. Timothy Good, *Earth: An Alien Enterprise: The Shocking Truth Behind the Greatest Cover-Up in Human History* (New York: Pegasus Books, 2013) 94, 157-158.

356. Note: My internet search engine brought up dozens and dozens of photographic images in response to, "images statuary reptilians throughout world".

357. Daniel 1:4 (KJV).

358. "Enuma Elish", Sacred Texts. Note: The seventh line from the end of the First Table refers to "the name over all of them the Anunnaki."

359. Brenton, *The Septuagint with Apocrypha: Greek and English,* ii.

360. Ibid, Preface.

361. Ibid, 1 [Θεός].

362. Ibid, ii.

363. "The Theogony of Hesiod", Sacred Texts, http://www.sacred-texts.com/cla/hesiod/theogony.htm, (accessed July 2020).

364. "Enuma Elish", Sacred Texts.

365. Freedman and Mathews, *The Paleo-Hebrew Leviticus Scroll.*

366. Taylor, *The Alphabet: An Account of the Origin and Development of Letters.*

367. Ada Yardeni, *The Book of Hebrew Script—History, Palaeography, Script styles, Calligraphy & Design* (New Castle, Del.: Oak Knoll Press, 1997) 41.

368. Brenton, *The Septuagint with Apocrypha: Greek and English,* iii.

369. Daniel 7:12; Luke 6:31 (KJV).

370. Note: Perform your own internet search. My internet search engine brought up quite a few shocking articles and photographic images in response to, "images Queen Elizabeth depicted as Reptilian".

371. Good, *Earth: An Alien Enterprise: The Shocking Truth Behind the Greatest Cover-Up in Human History,* 406-407.

Chapter 6

372. Ibid, 155.

373. Green, *The Interlinear Bible—Hebrew-Greek-English,* 4 volume edition.

374. Rud. Kittel, ed., *Biblia Hebraica,* 1, 2. [Bereshit (בראשית) 1:1-31; 2:1-2:3].

375. Potts, *The Latest and Best Bible Translation—Yours! An Introduction to Easy Step-by-Step Translating What the Bible Really Says,* 8-23; 170-186.

376. Rud. Kittel, ed., *Biblia Hebraica,* 1, 2.

377. Potts, *The Latest and Best Bible Translation—Yours! An Introduction to Easy Step-by-Step Translating What the Bible Really Says*, 8-23; 170-186.

378. Freedman and Mathews, *The Paleo-Hebrew Leviticus Scroll.*

379. Rud. Kittel, ed., *Biblia Hebraica,* 1, 2.

380. Yardeni, *The Book of Hebrew Script—History, Palaeography, Script styles, Calligraphy & Design,* 41.

381. Rud. Kittel, ed., *Biblia Hebraica,* 1, 2.

382. "What is CRISPR-Cas9", https://www.yourgenome.org/facts/what-is-crispr-cas9, (accessed July 2020).

383. "CRISPR-Cpf1", Medical Life Science News, https://www.news-medical.net/life-sciences/CRISPR-Cpf1.aspx, (accessed July 2020).

384. Strong, *Strong's Exhaustive Concordance of the Bible,* 22 [Number 855].

Chapter 7

385. Brenton, *The Septuagint with Apocrypha: Greek and English*, ii.

386. Strong, *Strong's Exhaustive Concordance of the Bible,* 14 [Number 430 (אֱלֹהִים)].

387. "Parallel German and English Bible in PDF Format", https://christianity.stackexchange.com/questions/68006/parallel-german-martin-luther-1534-and-english-in-pdf-format [*Am Anfang schuf Gott Himmel und Erde*], (accessed July 2020).

388. Good, op. cit., p. 155. Additionally, species of extraterrestrial beings (E.T.'s) are referenced in the "Majestic-12 Group Special Operations Manual No. 1-01 (SOM-01)"—photocopies of which have been put online. https://www.specialoperationsmanual.com/the-manual/ (accessed December 2020).

389. Strong, *Strong's Exhaustive Concordance of the Bible,* 29 [Number 1254 (בָּרָא)].

390. Ibid, 22 [Number 855 (אֵת) *–coulter*].

391. Strong, *Strong's Exhaustive Concordance of the Bible,* 156 [Number 8064 (שָׁמַיִם) *–dual of an unused singular,* שָׁמֶה*; from an unused root meaning to be lofty:—air, heaven, heavens.*

392. Ibid, 154 [Number 8047 (שַׁמָּה) *–from* H8074; *ruin*].

393. Ibid, 154 [Number 8074 (שָׁמֵם) *–to stun, i.e. to devastate:—make amazed, be astonished, be an astonishment*].

394. Ibid, 20 [Number 776 (אֶרֶץ)*–from an unused root probably meaning to be firm; the earth:—earth, field, ground, land, nations, wilderness, world*].

395. Ibid, 146 [Number 7521 (רָצָה) *–to be pleased with:—accept, acceptable, accomplish, set affection*].

396. Ibid, 42 [Number 1961 (הָיָה) *–to exist, i.e. be or become*].

397. Ibid, 162 [Number 8414 (תֹּהוּ) *–to lie waste, desolation, i.e. a desert, a worthless thing:—without form, nothing, vain*].

398. Ibid, 42 [Number 1961 (הָיָה) *–to exist, i.e. be or become*].

399. Ibid, 23 [Number 922 (בֹּהוּ) *–from an unused root; to be empty*].

400. Ibid, 58 [Number 2822 (חֹשֶׁךְ)].

401. Ibid, 58 [Number 2820 (חָשַׁךְ)]. Note: The reader familiar with Biblical Hebrew will immediately notice the difference between the spellings, *in Biblical Hebrew,* between "חֹשֶׁךְ" and "חָשַׁךְ". Because the original texts were written in ancient Hebrew script (see Endnote 380) the word under study is spelled but one way, "𐤇𐤔𐤊".

402. Ibid, 116 [Number 5923 (עֹל) *–a yoke (as imposed on the neck), literally or figuratively*].

403. Ibid, 126 [Number 6440 (פָּנִים) *–plural (but always as singular) of an unused*

root [פָּנָה]; *the face (as the part that turns); used in a great variety of applications literally and figuratively:—countenance, endure, favor, heaviness, himself, more than, mouth, person, presence, prospect, state, straight, till, time past, times past*].

404. Ibid, 126 [Number 6440 (פָּנִים) *–plural (but always as singular) of an unused root* [פָּנָה]. Note: used here in the singular, as "פָּנָה" with a dropped 𐤄 (*hāy* | ה); and the meaning, "presence".

405. Ibid, 162 [Number 8415 (תְּהוֹם) *–an abyss (as a surging mass of water), especially the deep*].

406. Ibid, 42 [Number 1961 (הָיָה) *–to exist, i.e. be or become*].

407. Ibid, 62 [Number 3068 (יְהוָה) *–from* H1961; *(the) self-Existent or Eternal; Jeho-vah, Jewish national name of God:—Jehovah, the Lord*].

408. Ibid, 142 [Number 7307 (רוּחַ) *–wind, by resemblance, breath; by resemblance, spirit*].

409. Davidson, *The Analytical Hebrew and Chaldee Lexicon,* 678 [(רוּחַ) *–IV. mind, spirit, disposition*].

410. Rud. Kittel, ed., *Biblia Hebraica,* 1262. (אֱלָהִין) [Daniel (דניאל) 3:25].

411. Strong, *Strong's Exhaustive Concordance of the Bible,* 143 [Number 7363 (רָחַף) *–to brood, by implication to be relaxed:—flutter, move, shake*].

412. Davar, Davar4 Scripture Study (Biblia Hebraica – *search* "מְרַחֶפֶת"). [One result: Gen. 1:2].

413. Ibid (Biblia Hebraica – *search* "רחף"). No results.

414. Strong, *Strong's Exhaustive Concordance of the Bible,* 116 [Number 5923 (עֹל) *–a yoke (as imposed on the neck), literally or figuratively*].

415. Ibid, 117 [Number 5953 (עָלַל) *–to effect thoroughly*].

416. Davidson, *The Analytical Hebrew and Chaldee Lexicon,* 601 [(עָלַל) *–to repeat an action, to do habitually or effectually*].

417. Rud. Kittel, ed., *Biblia Hebraica,* 1. (הַמָּיִם) [Bereshit (בראשית) 1:2].

418. Strong, *Strong's Exhaustive Concordance of the Bible,* 86 [Number 4325 (מַיִם) *– noun; water; figuratively juice; by euphemism urine, semen:—piss, wasting, water*].

419. Davidson, *The Analytical Hebrew and Chaldee Lexicon,* 156 [(· ה) *–the Hebrew article*].

420. Rud. Kittel, ed., *Biblia Hebraica,* 1. (יְהִי) [Bereshit (בראשית) 1:3].

421. Note: The are multiple examples of the prefix form of the first person singular subject pronoun, *he, she,* or *it* in the biblical text itself. A good example is the famous phrase, "and it was so." The word for "and it was" is "וַיְהִי." The first letter [וַ] is the first prefix, "and." The second letter [יְ] is the word's second prefix, "it".

422. Strong, *Strong's Exhaustive Concordance of the Bible,* 42 [Number 1961 (הָיָה) *–to exist, i.e. be or become*].

423. Ibid, 11 [Number 216 (אוֹר) *–from* H215; *illumination or (concretely) luminary (in every sense including lightening, happiness, etc.:—bright, clear, daylight, lightening, morning, sun*].

424. Note: The contracted modification of "אוֹר" is to treat this word as having the root word, "יָרָה". Strong's H3384 (to lay, throw, or cast), with a "ו" substituting for the letter "י", which acts to modify the root word—in this instance from "cast" to "place". As is quite common in Hebrew, the final letter, "ה", is dropped from the word in the text.

425. Ibid, 42 [Number 1961 (הָיָה) *–to exist, i.e. be or become*].

426. Note: In the word under study (וַיְהִי) the first prefix is "ו", the second prefix is "י", and the verb is "הִי" (from הָיָה).

427. Note: Refer to Endnotes 423 and 424 above.

428. Strong, *Strong's Exhaustive Concordance of the Bible,* 140 [Number 7200 (רָאָה) *–to see, literally or figuratively (in numerous applications) direct and implied, transitive, intransitive or causative)*].

429. Ibid, 68 [Number 3372 (יָרֵא) *–to fear; morally to revere; causative to frighten*].

430. The term, "ălăh·ēm", consists of a root word, "ălăh", and a suffix, "·ēm", which makes the word plural. That is why the word could be treated as "alah-beings".

431. Note: Refer to Endnote 424.

432. Strong, *Strong's Exhaustive Concordance of the Bible,* 72 [Number 3588 (כִּי) *–a primary particle indicating causal relationships of all kinds, antecedent or consequent*].

433. Brenton, *The Septuagint with Apocrypha: Greek and English,* 1 (οτι) [Genesis (ΓΕΝΕΣΙΣ) 1:4].

434. Strong, *Strong's Exhaustive Concordance of the Bible* (*supplemental section,* "A concise dictionary of the words in the Greek/New Testament"), 70 [Number 3754 (οτι hŏtĭ) *–that, because, as concerning that, though*].

435. Ibid, 59 [Number 2896 (טוֹב) *–good (as an adjective) in the widest sense:—better, precious, merry, fair, bountiful, pleasant*].

436. Ibid, 23 [Number 914 (בָּדַל) *–in various senses literally or figuratively:—separate, distinguish*].

437. Ibid, 14 [Number 430].

438. Strong, *Strong's Exhaustive Concordance of the Bible,* 24 [Number 995 (בִּין) *–to separate mentally (or distinguish)*].

439. Note: Refer to Endnotes 423 and 424.

440. Strong, *Strong's Exhaustive Concordance of the Bible,* 58 [Number 2821 (חָשַׁךְ) *–to be dark (as withholding light*].

441. Ibid, 58 [Number 2820 (חָשַׂךְ) *–to restrain or (reflexively) refrain*].

442. Note: Because the Masoretic vowel pointings were developed well over a thousand years (or thousands of years) after the appearance of the ancient Hebrew alphabetic texts, this translation treats "חָשַׁךְ" and "חָשַׂךְ" as being the same spelling—as the ancient Hebrew spelling is "𐤇𐤔𐤊"; and does not differentiate between the letter "*shin* [שׁ]" and the artificial letter, "*sin* [שׂ]". The ancient /s/ sound has its own letter, "samek" [𐤎], as does the "samek" [ס] of Biblical Hebrew.

443. Strong, *Strong's Exhaustive Concordance of the Bible,* 138 [Number 7121 (קָרָא) *–used in a wide variety of applications:—to call out, call for, call forth, call upon*].

444. Ibid, 138 [Number 7122 (קָרָא) *–to encounter, whether accidentally or in a hostile manner*]. Note: the Biblical Hebrew spellings of these two words represented by H7121 and H7122 are identical.

445. Note: Refer to Endnote 388.

446. Davidson, *The Analytical Hebrew and Chaldee Lexicon,* 399 (Definition VIII).

447. Strong, *Strong's Exhaustive Concordance of the Bible*, 11 [Number 216 (אוֹר) *–from* H215; *illumination or (concretely) luminary (in every sense including lightening, happiness, etc.:—bright, clear, daylight, lightening, morning, sun*].

448. Davar, Davar4 Scripture Study (King James Version Bible – *search Strong's* 3117).

449. Strong, *Strong's Exhaustive Concordance of the Bible,* 63 [Number 3117 (יוֹם)].

450. Davidson, *The Analytical Hebrew and Chaldee Lexicon,* 35 [*Table of Paradigms*]. Note the for example of the *yăd* (י) as a prefixed pronoun, "it"; 233 [for a full explanation about the "conjunctive vav"]; and 9 [*Table of Paradigms*] *Section I.–The Personal Pronoun, Table A* (*they–them–their*).

451. Note: Refer to Endnotes 440, 441, and 442.

452. Rud. Kittel, ed., *Biblia Hebraica,* 1. (קָרָא) [Bereshit (בראשית) 1:5].

453. Davidson, *The Analytical Hebrew and Chaldee Lexicon,* 426 [לָיְלָה *–noun masc. sing. with paragoric* ה]. Note: “paragoric” means *silent* and *inconsequential.*

454. Ibid, 233.

455. Strong, *Strong's Exhaustive Concordance of the Bible,* 120 [Number 6153 (עֶרֶב) *–dusk, even, evening*].

456. Ibid, 120 [Number 6150 (עָרֵב) *–rather identical with* H6148 *through the idea of covering with a texture*].

457. Ibid [Number 6148 (עָרַב) *–to braid, i.e. intermix*].

458. Ibid [Number 6154 (עֵרֶב) *–from* H6148; *the web (or transverse threads of a cloth); also a mixture (or mongrel race)*].

459. Davidson, *The Analytical Hebrew and Chaldee Lexicon,* 612 [*I.* עָרַב –Right column: *Hithp.II. to have intercourse, be familiar with anyone*].

460. Strong, *Strong's Exhaustive Concordance of the Bible,* 29 [Number 1242 (בֹּקֶר) *–dawn (as the break of day); generally morning*].

461. Ibid [Number 1239 (בָּקַר) *–to plough; or (generally) to break forth:—search, seek out*].

462. Leviticus 27:33 (KJV).

463. Rud. Kittel, ed., *Biblia Hebraica,* 1. (“בֹּקֶר יוֹם אֶחָד...”) [Bereshit (בראשית) *excerpted from* 1:5].

464. Brenton, *The Septuagint with Apocrypha: Greek and English,* (εγένετο) 1 [Genesis (ΓΕΝΕΣΙΣ) 1:4].

465. Note: Refer to Endnote 388.

466. Rud. Kittel, ed., *Biblia Hebraica,* 1. (רָקִיעַ) [Bereshit (בראשית) 1:6].

467. Green, *The Interlinear Bible—Hebrew-Greek-English,* 1 (Genesis 1:6).

468. Job 37:18 (KJV).

469. Note: The word in Biblical Hebrew is “רָקִיעַ”. The letter “י” was inserted into the root word (רָקַע) by the original writer.

470. Rud. Kittel, ed., *Biblia Hebraica,* 1. (בְּתוֹךְ) [Bereshit (בראשית) 1:6].

471. Davar, Davar4 Scripture Study (King James Version Bible – *search H8432*).

472. Davidson, *The Analytical Hebrew and Chaldee Lexicon,* 56 (ב – Left column).

473. Strong, *Strong's Exhaustive Concordance of the Bible*, 86 [Number 4325 (מַיִם)

– *noun; water; figuratively juice; by euphemism urine, semen:—piss, wasting, water*].

474. Rud. Kittel, ed., *Biblia Hebraica,* 1. (מַבְדִּיל) [Bereshit (בראשית) 1:6].

475. Note: Refer to Endnote 388.

476. 1 Samuel 13:20, 21 (KJV).

477. Rud. Kittel, ed., *Biblia Hebraica,* 1. (הָרָקִיעַ) [Bereshit (בראשית) 1:7].

478. Strong, *Strong's Exhaustive Concordance of the Bible,* 146 [Number 7549 (רָקִיעַ) *–an expanse, i.e. the firmament*]; [Number 7554 (רָקַע) *–to pound, to expand, to overlay, make broad, spread abroad, spread over, spread out, stretch*].

479. Job 37:18 (KJV)

480. Strong, *Strong's Exhaustive Concordance of the Bible,* 86 [Number 4325 (מַיִם) – *noun; water; figuratively juice; by euphemism urine, semen:—piss, wasting, water*].

481. Ibid, 160 [Number 8281 (שׁרה) *–to free:—direct*].

482. Rud. Kittel, ed., *Biblia Hebraica,* 1267. (וּמְשָׁרֵא) [Daniel (דניאל) 5:12].

483. Ibid, 1 (מִתַּחַת) [Bereshit (בראשית) 1:7].

484. Strong, *Strong's Exhaustive Concordance of the Bible,* 164 [Number 8480 (תַּחַת) *–the same as* H8478*; Tachath, the name of a place in the Desert*].

485. Note: Refer to Endnote 480.

486. Note: Refer to Endnotes 481 and 482.

487. Rud. Kittel, ed., *Biblia Hebraica,* 1. (לָרָקִיעַ) [Bereshit (בראשית) 1:7].

488. Note: Refer to Endnote 388 and 430.

489. Davar, Davar4 Scripture Study (King James Bible *search* H8074 (שָׁמֵם) –appears 94 times in 87 verses. Examples are: "astonished" in Leviticus 26:32 and 1 Kings 9:8. The same root appears as "amazed" at Ezekiel 32:10].

490. Note: Refer to Endnote 488.

491. Rud. Kittel, ed., *Biblia Hebraica,* 1. [Bereshit (בראשית) 1:9].

492. Davidson, *The Analytical Hebrew and Chaldee Lexicon,* 656 (קוה) [*Left column – middle*] *II. Arab. to twist, wind, bind*]. Note: An appropriate and applicable scriptural citation is 1 Kings 10:28, where there is a reference to a "linen yard" (מקוה). The concept is of a bolt of fabric bound around itself. The operative verb is *to bind.* While Davidson offers other definitions, *to bind,* is what is in context in this verse. Nevertheless, the definitions (or concepts),

of *gather* or *collected together* could also be used here; although in a looser sense than the concept of *bind*. Ultimately, it is the selected sperm cell that the injecting pipette is to *bind* inside the selected egg cell. The concept of "I-Place" has already been covered. The injecting pipette *places* the sperm cell inside the egg cell.

493. Vulgate," Vulgate.com.

494. Brenton, *The Septuagint with Apocrypha: Greek and English.*

495. "Wycliffe", Bible Study Tools, https://biblestudytools.com/wyc/, (accessed July 2020).

496. Ibid.

497. Brenton, *The Septuagint with Apocrypha: Greek and English,* i.

498. Ibid, 1 (συναχθητω) [Genesis (ΓΕΝΕΣΙΣ) 1:9].

499. Strong [Greek], op cit., 92 [Number 4862 (συν – sŭn *as "soon") –denoting union; with or together*].

500. "Vulgate", Encyclopedia Britannica, http://www.britannica.com/topic/Vulgate, (accessed July 2020).

501. "Saint Jerome," Encyclopedia Britannica, http://www.britannica.com/biography/Saint-Jerome, (accessed July 2020).

502. "Genesis, Chapter 1", Vulgate.org, https://vulgate.org/ot/genesis_1.htm, (accessed July 2020).

503. https://biblestudytools.com/wyc/, (accessed July 2020).

504. "Genesis 1", Bible Study Tools, https://biblestudytools.com/wyc/genesis/1.html, (accessed July 2020).

505. Strong, *Strong's Exhaustive Concordance of the Bible,* 86 [Number 4325 (מַיִם)].

506. Ibid, 164 [Number 8480 (תַּחַת) *–the same as* H8478*; Tachath, the name of a place in the Desert*]. Note: that name-place appears six times in the Hebrew Bible—as an oasis in the desert—from which the word "fertility" is derived. An *oasis* is *fertile*.

507. Note: Refer to Endnote 489.

508. Davar, Davar4 Scripture Study (King James Bible *search* H413 –appears 38 times in 37 verses.

509. Ibid, (King James Bible *search* H3001 –appears 78 times in 67 verses.

510. Note: Refer to Endnotes 388 and 430.

511. "Spermatazoon," https://medical-dictionary.thefreedictionary.com/spermatozoon, (accessed July 2020).
512. Note: Refer to Endnote 510.
513. Note: Refer to Endnote 510.
514. Strong, *Strong's Exhaustive Concordance of the Bible,* 86 [Number 4325 (מַיִם)].
515. Davidson, *The Analytical Hebrew and Chaldee Lexicon,* 9 [*Table of Paradigms*] *Section I.—The Personal Pronoun, Nominal Suffix, Column A* (נוּ- ; our).
516. Note: Refer to Endnotes 481 and 482.
517. Davidson, *The Analytical Hebrew and Chaldee Lexicon,* 601 (עלל) [*Left column*].
518. Note: Refer to Endnotes 510.
519. Strong, *Strong's Exhaustive Concordance of the Bible,* 154 [Number 7969 (שָׁלוֹשׁ)].
520. Ibid, 155 [Number 8027 (שָׁלַשׁ) *–perhaps originally to intensify, i.e. treble; but apparently only used as denominated from* H7969, *to be (causative make) triplicate*].
521. Davar, Davar4 Scripture Study (Biblia Hebraica – *search* "שליש"). [One result: Psalm 80:6]. Note: in the King James Version Bible the verse is 80:5.
522. Psalm 80:5 (KJV)–*and givest them tears to drink in great measure* (שָׁלִישׁ)]. Note: It is curious that the editors of the Davar software assign Strong's Number 7991 to the KJV wording "in great measure"; as does J.P. Green, Sr., editor of *The Interlinear Bible.* His translation of the word, שָׁלִישׁ, is "a third time". It is also curious that Dr. James Strong assigns the word, שָׁלִישׁ, its own number (7991) even though that word appears only once in the entire Hebrew Bible. Clearly, however, the KJV wording, "in great measure" is in the context of Dr. Strong's observation, in 8027, of "*perhaps originally to intensify*". Of further curiosity, Benjamin Davidson does not define שָׁלִישׁ [Davidson, *The Analytical Hebrew and Chaldee Lexicon,* 719], but simply refers the curious to his main entry on the root, שָׁלַשׁ [*Ibid,* 722] where he makes no mention at all of the concept of *to intensify.*
523. Francis Brown (with the cooperation of S.R. Driver and Charles A. Briggs), *The Brown-Driver-Briggs Hebrew and English Lexicon: With an Appendix Containing the Biblical Aramaic,* (Peabody, Mass.: Hendrickson Publishers, Inc., 1996). Note: In their two-inch thick lexicon, Doctors Brown, Driver, and Briggs at least mention [1025] at the outset of their treatment of the root word, שׁלשׁ, that the meaning is "unknown".

524. Strong, *Strong's Exhaustive Concordance of the Bible,* 80 [Number 3974 (מָאוֹר) *–from* H215*; a luminous body or luminary, i.e. (abstractly) light (as an element:—bright, light*].

525. Davidson, *The Analytical Hebrew and Chaldee Lexicon,* 463 (מְאוֹר) [*Left column – two entries with two separate root words cited, "*ארר*" and "*אור*"*].

526. Strong, *Strong's Exhaustive Concordance of the Bible,* 21 [Number 779 (ארר) *–to execrate:—bitterly curse.* Note: Per Webster's Collegiate Dictionary (1946), meaning "*to implicate evil upon"*.

527. Davar, Davar4 Scripture Study (Biblia Hebraica *search* "מארת" matched with King James Version Bible – *two results*: Genesis 1:14 and Proverbs 3:33.

528. Proverbs 3:33 (KJV). *The curse of the Lord is in the house of the wicked.*

529. Davidson, *The Analytical Hebrew and Chaldee Lexicon,* 156 [ה *Left column – middle: the Hebrew article*].

530. Strong, *Strong's Exhaustive Concordance of the Bible,* 42 [Number 1961 (הָיָה) *–to exist, i.e. to be or become*].

531. Ibid, 62 [Number 3068 (יְהוָה) *– (the) Self-Existent* or *Eternal—Jehovah*].

532. Davidson, *The Analytical Hebrew and Chaldee Lexicon,* 426 [לַיְלָה *–noun masc. sing. with paragoric* ה]. Note: "paragoric" means *silent* and *inconsequential.*

533. Strong, *Strong's Exhaustive Concordance of the Bible,* 11 [Number 226 (אוֹת) *–from* H225; *(in the sense of appearing); a signal (literally or figuratively)*].

534. Ibid, 86 [Number 4325 (מַיִם) *– noun; water; figuratively juice; by euphemism urine, semen:—piss, wasting, water*].

535. Ibid, 157 [Number 8138 (שָׁנָה) *– to fold; i.e. duplicate (literally or figuratively)*].

536. "RNA Splicing," https://dnalc.cshl.edu/resources/3d/rna-splicing.html, (accessed October 2020).

537. Note: The Hebrew suffix, "ēm", commonly pluralizes common nouns.

538. Davidson, *The Analytical Hebrew and Chaldee Lexicon,* 70 [*Table of Paradigms*] *Section XXXVIII—Ninth Declension of the Masculines (Table O) Remarks 1. The original termination* י *– for which* ה*– is substituted. It is often restored; and affects the inflexion of the word.*

539. Davar, Davar4 Scripture Study (King James Version Bible *search* H6996. It appears 101 times in 100 verses).

540. Strong, *Strong's Exhaustive Concordance of the Bible,* 135 [Number 6962 (ק

(ט ו) *–to cut off*].

541. Davar, Davar4 Scripture Study (King James Version Bible *search* H6962. It appears seven times in seven verses).

542. "Andrology: Sperm Morphology", Fertility Centers of New England, https://www.fertilitycenter.com/fertility_cares_blog/andrology-blog-part-iv-sperm-morphology/, (accessed July 2020).

543. Ibid.

544. Note: Refer to Endnote 537.

545. Strong, *Strong's Exhaustive Concordance of the Bible,* 146 [Number 7521 (רָצָה) *–to accomplish*].

546. Note: Refer to Endnote 544.

547. Ibid.

548. Davidson, *The Analytical Hebrew and Chaldee Lexicon,* 766 (עלל) [*Left column*].

549. Davar, Davar4 Scripture Study (King James Version Bible *search* H5314. It appears three times in three verses): Exodus 23:12 [*the stranger may be refreshed*]; Exodus 31:17 [*he rested and was refreshed*]; 2 Samuel 16:14 [*and refreshed themselves there*].

550. Davidson, *The Analytical Hebrew and Chaldee Lexicon,* 739 (שָׁרָה) [*Right column* (*middle*)].

551. Daniel 2:22 (KJV). *Light dwelleth with him.*

552. Strong, *Strong's Exhaustive Concordance of the Bible,* 74 [Number 3671 (כָּנָף) *–an edge or extremity; specifically (of a bird or army) a wing)*].

553. Ibid, 74 [Number 3670 (כָּנַף) *–to project laterally, i.e. probably (reflexively) to withdraw:—be removed*].

554. Note: Refer to Endnote 544.

555. Davidson, *The Analytical Hebrew and Chaldee Lexicon,* 684 (רכך) [*Left column* (*middle*)].

556. Note: Refer to Endnote 544.

557. Davar, Davar4 Scripture Study (King James Version Bible *search* H559. It appears 5,308 times in 4,338 verses).

558. Brown-Driver-Briggs, 570, No. 3.

559. Strong, *Strong's Exhaustive Concordance of the Bible,* 29 [Number 1242 (בֹּקֶר) *–from* H1239; *dawn; (as the break of day); generally morning*]; [Num-

ber 1239 (בָּקַר) *–to plough, or generally, to break forth:—(make) inquiry, (make) search, seek out*].

560. Exodus 13:18 (KJV). *The children of Israel went up harnessed out of the land of Egypt*). Note: the word translated in the KJV as "harnessed" is "וַחֲמֻשִׁים" in the Biblia Hebraica.

561. Davidson, *The Analytical Hebrew and Chaldee Lexicon,* 399 [ל *may displace the article* ה*; towards, to, unto, at, on, in, within, every, belonging to, beneath, underneath, concerning, according to, after, if, as though, like, till that, so that, when. Frequently pleonastic with the verb*]. Note: The word, "pleonastic" means the use of more words than are necessary to express an idea.

562. Ibid, 56 (ב) [*Left column – in, within, among, at, near, by, on, before, to, unto, upon, against, for, on account of, because of, with, by, through, when,* (rarely *into*)].

563. Ibid, 685 (רֶמֶשׂ) [*Right column* (*middle*)]. Note: This translation does not differentiate between "שׁ" and "שׂ". Per the "shibboleth" test of Judges 12:6, this translation differentiates only between the phonemes /sh/ and /s/ as in the letters *shin* and *samek.*

564. Ibid, 233 (ו) [*Right column – and, also, but, yet, otherwise, for, since, because, that, it came to pass that, to the end that, through, then, even, which*].

565. Ibid, 399.

566. Ibid.

567. Ibid, 233.

568. Strong, *Strong's Exhaustive Concordance of the Bible,* 39 [Number 1818 (דָּם) *–from* H1826; *blood.*]

569. Davar, Davar4 Scripture Study (Biblia Hebraica *search* "נקב." No results found.)

570. Ibid (Biblia Hebraica *search* "שחח".)

571. Davidson, *The Analytical Hebrew and Chaldee Lexicon,* 683–684 (רך –683 [*Right column (top)*] *from root* רכך –684 [*Left column* (*middle*)].

572. Strong, *Strong's Exhaustive Concordance of the Bible,* 143 [Number 7397 (רֵכָה) *and* H7401 (רָכַךְ)].

573. Davar, Davar4 Scripture Study (King James Version Bible *search* H7401. It appears eight times in eight verses. Find "tender" at 2 Kings 22:19 and 2 Chron. 34:27. Find "soft" at Job 23:16; and "softer" at Psalms 55:21.)

574. Davidson, *The Analytical Hebrew and Chaldee Lexicon,* 192 (חָמָה) [*Left column (top)*]. Note for purists: The word "חָמָה" appears at that place in Davidson's

Lexicon; but that word will not be found in the *Biblia Hebraica*. What will appear in *BH* some 220 times in 208 verses is the word "הֵמָּה". That word is the entry following "הָמָה" on that same page. Professor Davidson states that the terminal ה is "paragoric"—that is, it is silent and and of no consequence. Its root is given as "הם", which will be found on 190 [*Right column (bottom)*], and defined as "they". The fly in the ointment is that neither the words "they" or "them" are in context for what the word "לֹהם" is expressing in actual translation.

575. Good, *Earth: An Alien Enterprise: The Shocking Truth Behind the Greatest Cover-Up in Human History,* 321.

576. Davar, Davar4 Scripture Study (Biblia Hebraica *search* "עוף". That word appears 27 times.)

577. Green, *The Interlinear Bible—Hebrew-Greek-English,* Vol. 2, 1330 (Job 5:7). Note: The word "עוף" is given there as "flying". It is translated as "*fly*" in "the sparks fly" in the King James Version of Job 5:7.

578. Davar, Davar4 Scripture Study (Biblia Hebraica *search* "הנה". That word appears 518 times in 495 verses.)

579. Ibid, (King James Version *search* H2007, H2008, and H2009.)

580. Strong, *Strong's Exhaustive Concordance of the Bible,* 22 [Number 859 (אַתָּה)].

581. Ibid, 73 [Number 3642 (כָּמַהּ)].

582. Green, *The Interlinear Bible—Hebrew-Greek-English,* Vol. 3, 1443 (Psalms 63:1).

583. Strong, *Strong's Exhaustive Concordance of the Bible,* 47 [Number 2232 (זָרַע) and 2233 (זֶרַע)].

584. Ibid, 126 [Number 6437 (פָּנָה) *–see* 6440 (פָּנִים) *–face...presence*].

585. Davidson, *The Analytical Hebrew and Chaldee Lexicon,* 609 (עֶצָּה) [*Right column (bottom)*].

586. Strong, *Strong's Exhaustive Concordance of the Bible,* 119 [Number 6087 (עצב)].

587. Davidson, *The Analytical Hebrew and Chaldee Lexicon,* 113 (בָּרָא) [*Left column (middle)*].

588. Strong, *Strong's Exhaustive Concordance of the Bible,* 127 [Number 6509 (פָּרָה)].

589. Ibid, 47 [Number 2232 (זָרַע) and 2233 (זֶרַע)].

590. Green, *The Interlinear Bible—Hebrew-Greek-English,* Vol. 3, 1443 (Psalms 63:1).

591. Davidson, *The Analytical Hebrew and Chaldee Lexicon,* 70 (בּוֹא) [*Begins in*

left column (bottom)].

592. Green, *The Interlinear Bible—Hebrew-Greek-English,* Vol. 1, 4 [(יֶרֶק) at Genesis 1:30].

593. Davar, Davar4 Scripture Study (King James Version *search* H6213. It appears 2,638 times in 2,286 verses. Find "prepared" at Exodus 12:39 (עָשׂוּ)).

594. Strong, *Strong's Exhaustive Concordance of the Bible,* 79 [Number 3996 (מֵאָה)].

595. Ibid, 10 [Number 181 (אוּד)]. Note: This Hebrew word appears only once in the Hebrew Bible—at Zechariah 3:2 in the context of "brand," that is, a *fire-brand* plucked out of the fire. What is the function of the firebrand here? It is to mix the coals (or wood) together with the blazing embers.

596. Ibid, 161 [Number 8336 (שֵׁשׁ)].

597. Davar, Davar4 Scripture Study (King James Version Bible *search* H8336. It appears 42 times in 37 verses).

598. Davidson, *The Analytical Hebrew and Chaldee Lexicon,* 12 [*Table of Paradigms*] *Section III.–Suffixes to the Noun in the Singular.*

599. Strong, Strong, *Strong's Exhaustive Concordance of the Bible,* 129 [Number 6632 (צָב)].

600. "Human DNA Was Designed by Aliens", Physics and Astronomy Zone, https://www.physics-astronomy.org/2018/01/humans-dna-was-designed-by-aliens.html, (accessed July 2020).

601. "Scientists Find Alien Code 'Embedded' in Human DNA", Ancient Code, https://www.ancient-code.com/scientists-find-alien-code-embedded-in-human-dna-evidence-of-ancient-alien-engineers/, (accessed July 2020).

602. "19 Pieces of Non-Human DNA Found in Human Genome", IFL Science, https://www.iflscience.com/health-and-medicine/ancient-viruses-are-hiding-within-your-dna/, (accessed July 2020).

603. "Shock Claim: Human DNA 'Was Designed by Aliens,' Say Scientists", Express, http://www.express.co.uk/news/science/777627/alien-dna-message-human, (accessed July 2020).

604. Davidson, *The Analytical Hebrew and Chaldee Lexicon,* 56 (ב) [*Left column – in, within, among, at, near, by, on, before, to, unto, upon, against, for, on account of, because of, with, by, through, when,* (rarely *into*)].

605. Ibid, 35 [for an example of the *yăd* (י) as a prefixed pronoun, "it"].

606. Ibid, 9 [*Table of Paradigms*] *Section I.–The Personal Pronoun, Table A* (*they–*

them–their).

607. Strong, *Strong's Exhaustive Concordance of the Bible,* 148 [Numbers 7646 through Number 7652].

608. Ibid, 148 [(שָׁבַע) *–to be complete*]. Note: Yes, in that definition Dr. Strong adds that Number 7650 is "used only as a denominative from 7651." In his definition for 7651 we learn his operational definition of "complete." It is "*seven (as the sacred full one).*" Given the actual context in which the Hebrew words appear, it appears that the word "שָׁבַע" [rather, O9W] is not about any seven—sacred or not. It is about "completion".

609. Davidson, *The Analytical Hebrew and Chaldee Lexicon,* 59 [*Table of Paradigms*] *Table D. Declension of Masculine Nouns.*

610. Strong, *Strong's Exhaustive Concordance of the Bible*, 76 [(כָּתַת)]. Note: This root word appears only once in the Hebrew Bible—at 2 Chronicles 34:7 as "כִּתַּת" (*"had beaten"*). There, in the KJV, "had beaten" is in the context of, "And he had broken down the altars and the groves, and had beaten the graven images into powder, and cut down all the idols throughout the land of Israel, he returned to Jerusalem."

611. Ibid, 147 [(שָׁבָב) *–to break up:—broken in pieces*]. Note: This root word itself does not appear in the Hebrew Bible. It appears only as the plural word, "שְׁבָבִים". The place it appears is Hosea 8:6 in the context of, "*shall be broken in pieces.*"

612. Ibid, 135 [(קָדֵשׁ) *–to be clean (ceremonially or morally)*].

613. Davar, Davar4 Scripture Study (King James Version Bible *search* H6942. It appears 173 times in 153 verses).

614. Davidson, *The Analytical Hebrew and Chaldee Lexicon,* 70 (בּוֹא) [*Begins in left column (bottom)*].

615. Note: See Endnote 610.

After having read this book, you have the true workings of ancient documentation of extraterrestrial Reptilian encounters with our own primate ancestors in our remote past. If you would, please share how you are affected by this revelation.

react@albertepottsauthor.com

www.ingramcontent.com/pod-product-compliance
Lightning Source LLC
Chambersburg PA
CBHW072144100526
44589CB00015B/2073
* 9 7 8 1 7 3 5 9 1 6 8 1 1 *

The well-known story of the seven days of creation is not religious parable. It is historical documentation of our genetically engineered fabrication by technologically advanced ancient aliens.

Ancient linguist Albert E. Potts reveals these shocking hidden truths with translations and examinations of each ancient Hebrew word of the Bible's Genesis 1. Unlock the secret of the space-age Remesh and their extraterrestrial project that created our human ancestors, inscribed in the ancient Hebrew language.

Discover:

- A history of encounters with the Remesh on Earth.
- An explanation of our ancestors' fabrication through a word-for-word translation of the Genesis 1 scripture of the ancient Hebrew Bible.
- Detailed descriptions of alien hybrid creation through advanced DNA technologies.
- A simplification of the sounds in the ancient Hebrew alphabet, and simplification of the actual translation.
- Responses to objections to this radical approach.

Unearth a new understanding of our past and awaken a revolutionary perspective for our future as the descendants of the original hybrids of alien "gods." Read *Genetic Genesis* today!

ALBERT E. POTTS is an author and ancient linguist with over 12 years of private study in the ancient and modern Hebrew language. Captivated with the power of ancient Hebrew to communicate historical information about humankind, he developed a 2000-page searchable database of all roots, prefixes, suffixes, and inserted letters of Genesis 1–11 of the Hebrew scriptural text. Captivated with the power of ancient Hebrew to communicate historical information about humankind, he has already originally translated the first 11 chapters of Genesis. His previous titles include *The Latest and Best Bible Translation—Yours!*, *Our Parent Alphabet*, and *Anatomy in Our Alphabet—Letters in Your Moutha*

Albert was educated in the Liberal Arts at the University of Tennessee, Knoxville, and in Nursing Science at University of Texas Health Science Center, San Antonio. He previously worked as a professional registered nurse for over 30 years and spent many years in the armed forces.

A devoted father, grandfather, husband, and dog owner, Albert currently resides in San Antonio, Texas. Learn more at albertepotts.com.

ISBN 978-1-7359168-1-1
US$14.95
51495>
9 781735 916811

www.ingramcontent.com/pod-product-compliance
Lightning Source LLC
Chambersburg PA
CBHW072142100526
44589CB00015B/2042
* 9 7 8 1 7 8 5 3 3 8 1 6 8 *